THE 31

SELF-STRONGHOLDS

A project of TRT Ministries

The 31 Self-Strongholds

The 31 Self-Strongholds
ISBN-0997170409
Copyright© 2016 by Tommy R. Twitty
Tommy R. Twitty Ministries
P.O. Box 613
Chesnee, SC 29323

The 31 Self-Strongholds

Table of Contents

Introduction

<u>The 31 Self-Strongholds</u>

You need to have the right mindset to win once you decide that losing is not an option.

It is the purpose of this book to help you get your kingdom back. So stop looking for an enemy, a devil or something great that is causing you to dethrone God and instead realize that it is the 31 self-enemies revealed in this book that have caused you to do so. They look harmless and as if they won't hurt us but in fact they are causing us harm and have the potential to kill us because we have become addicted to them.

Joshua 12 exposes the 31 kings who represent 31 different kingdoms that they were destined to conquer that are parallel to the strongholds and self-enemies we must conquer. But in order to do so we must understand the mindset of a conqueror and the power of the mind. To be a conqueror you have to be aggressive and step out of your comfort zone. You have to forget about what is around and surrounds you and then you have to be bodacious enough to take it by force. Breaking strongholds to become victorious consists of knowing what to do before you're told to do it.

As you journey through this book you will see that the 31 kings Joshua had to take down, each had a unique stronghold but each one knew who Joshua and the Israelites were before they got to them. Joshua became a conqueror because he discovered that he had to change the way he was thinking to change the way he lived. Just as you will have to discover to deal with the kings and the strongholds in your life. They too will know who you are as you change the way you think. As you read this book you will learn how to dethrone every king that is in front of you. You will learn that having a strategy is a vital part of the process and the only way to conquer these kings called self-enemies is through the mind of the Spirit which is why after reading this book you will have the mind of a conqueror.

Chapter 1

The Empire Strikes Back

(Taking Down the Kings of Stronghold)

This chapter is entitled the Empire Strikes Back because this book will help you to take down the dark lords in your mind. The reference to "*Star Wars*" is to expose the secret of this particular film and that is those of the "Empire" have decided to fight back and take over what Darth Vader has taken from them, only to find out that at the end of this film Luke Skywalker was fighting his father. We say that to say, it's hard to fight your own bloodline or to fight what is within yourself. It's just as hard to fight your own shadow and once you allow yourself to know what you are fighting against then you can develop a strategy to win. This strategy will help you to successfully break strongholds, but you must also have the mindset of a conqueror.

Every being has three parts to who they are. Everyone has a body, a soul and a spirit and each has its own mind. When preparing for battle against strongholds, it is necessary for you to know which mind is working and thinking for you and being willing to confront the things of your mind. You have to know how to empower your mind and have a mindset or a set mind to win according to God's instructions.

Ephesians six and twelve says we wrestle not against flesh and blood, but against (1) principalities, (2) powers, (3) rulers of the darkness of this world, and (4) spiritual wickedness in high places. So which king are you facing, the king of principalities and its strongholds, the king of powers and their strongholds, the strongholds of the king of wickedness in high places or the king of rulers of the darkness and the strongholds and the spirits they bring? What force has Satan assigned to attack you this time? Do you have a strategy to face these kings? Will you be able to defeat these kings by yourself? Will you be able to defeat these kings with your own finances or will need friends to help you defeat these demonic forces? Do you have a strategy to fight each territory of strongholds? How will you ever be able to take down demonic forces?

Regardless of which king it is, answering these questions and defeating them will require more than just knowing scriptures and binding what you don't know. Stop trying to guess what kind of spirit or stronghold that you are fighting because this one may just be the result of a discussion of the flesh. Everything is not a demon or a devil but you need to know that in spite of which stronghold, king or devil that has assigned itself to you, it cannot be conquered by your feelings. You must also know that every new battle, every new territory causes you to have to fight a new king so fighting as if it was an old battle and just declaring that it is the Devil cannot be an option if you intend to win.

At this stage in life you must be assured that this is God; know that where you are is where He wants you to be because He has sent you. The enemy senses, is drawn to and attacks instability because he is afraid that you will believe what God says you are and God says you are more than a conqueror. Although you may not know how God is going to do it, you do know that He's going to do it because what's coming against you is not greater than He that is in you. If you incur setbacks, just know that they are opportunities to make a liar out of the devil. The more he comes at you the more familiar you become with his tactics so what once caused you to have anxiety attacks and breakdowns will no longer have power over you. When these strongholds no longer have power over you, you will discover that there is someone inside of you that will keep telling you that you can go forward because the more trials and tribulations you go through the stronger you become. You will soon realize that you have the mind of a conqueror and although you do not deserve everything God has and will bless you with; He did make you a promise.

So it was with Joshua, he understood that in order for Israel to gain the promises of God, they would need a strategy to take down every king, but more importantly this strategy would have to include seeking and following God's instructions and knowing that because every king was different God's plan for victory would be different and designed specifically for each so that only He would get the glory.

Joshua's conquest did not truly begin until Ai. They really were not able to accomplish anything until they understood what they needed to know to conquer on their journey. In order for them to advance on their kingdom assignment they would have to be obedient which in turn caused them to have the mindset of a conqueror. You can't bring down a kingdom until you bring down the king which entails knowing who you're fighting and having a strategy to do so. This knowledge was the start of a kingdom crusade and as a result of having the mindset of a conqueror the assignment manifested into possessing promise instead of just talking about it. Know that with every kingdom you decide to take down there are principalities made up of kings that are not godly. Reference to principalities comes from Revelation chapter 11, the 15th verse and does not refer to physical beings, but the four ranks of power identified in Ephesians 6:12. Until you dethrone the four ranks of power which are principalities, powers, rulers of the darkness of this world, and spiritual wickedness in high places as well as realize that people are not your enemy, you won't be able to bring these principalities down.

It is the purpose of this book to help you get your kingdom back. So stop looking for an enemy, a devil or something great that is causing you to dethrone God because it is these 31 self-enemies that have caused you to dethrone God. These things look harmless and as if they won't hurt us when in fact they are killing us. It is these things we have become addicted too and are causing us harm. In order to understand Joshua 12, which exposes the 31 kings; who represent 31 different kingdoms and strongholds, we must understand the power of the mind when we operate with the mindset of a conqueror.

> **Joshua 12:1 GW**
> *"These are the kings of the land east of the Jordan River that the people of Israel defeated. Israel also took possession of their lands from the Arnon Valley to Mount Hermon, and all the eastern plains."*

You cannot have possession if you do not bring down the king and you cannot bring down the king unless you understand the kingdom. In Luke 17, the Pharisees are demanding Jesus to tell them when the Kingdom of God will come.

> **Luke 17: 20 - 21**
> *"Now when He was asked by the Pharisees when the kingdom of God would come, He answered them and said, "The kingdom of God does not come with observation; [21] nor will they say, 'See here!' or 'See there!'[d] For indeed, the kingdom of God is within you."*

Jesus explained to the Pharisees that the Kingdom of God is not something that you look for but that the Kingdom of God is in us, therefore; if the kingdom of God is within us then there must be a king that lives within us. There cannot be a kingdom without a king and until you understand the King of the dominion that is within you then you cannot take down kingdoms. You will never be able to defeat the kingdom that is coming against you until you discover the King that is within you. The Apostle Paul says in Romans chapter 14, that the kingdom of God is peace, joy and righteousness and when you understand what the kingdom of God is in you will stop comparing it to things that are not of God. When you truly understand that a sovereign

King lives inside of you, you'll have peace, joy and righteousness in the Holy Spirit.

If you want to take possession you have to know your authority and be willing to take a chance even when you don't know what the outcome will look like. It can't matter to you what people may think of you, you must understand that you are not just talking territorial possession but you are taking over territories. If you want to be blessed and take what's yours with your authority you have to take them by force. If you are authorized to take it, then stop just claiming it and take it by force. In order to defeat and take the kingdoms of Satan by force we must understand warfare.

Warfare does not start outside of who we are, but warfare starts in our minds. If you can defeat the warfare of your minds you can take down kingdoms. Satan uses warfare of the mind to set up his kingdom within our minds and if he sets up warfare in our mind he takes over the kingdom that is within us. We have to quit allowing Satan to have a throne room in our mind which causes us to dethrone God. In Joshua 12, the Bible tells us that there were 31 kings that Joshua and the Israelites dethroned.

For the Israelites, the differences were at Jericho they attacked by day and at Ai they attacked at night. At Jericho they circled the walls of the city for seven days but at Ai they had chosen men to get behind the city and wait until it was time. At Ai there was no blast or sound, as there was with the walls of Jericho because Joshua defeated this king with a sword. You have to know when to use the trumpet and when to use the sword for battles. God gave them instructions for Jericho; Joshua ensured they followed the instructions and God performed a miracle. Joshua used his advisor's plan at Ai so they had to rely on their strength and what they thought was a strategic plan for victory. God gave them the king of Jericho, the king of Ai would not come down the same.

The 31 Self-Strongholds

Joshua eight comes shortly after chapter six's victory at Jericho. Ai had defeated the Israelites and sent them running out of town because the Israelites had assumed that they were a small town and it wouldn't take much to defeat them. Joshua, not knowing there was sin in the camp, took the advice of his advisor and sent 3,000 men to Ai. In preparing for battle you have to consider all of the ramifications, but when it came to Ai, Joshua didn't. You have to consider what is in your camp, what is in your heart and what is powering your mind.

Once Joshua dealt with the sin in the camp, the Lord says in Joshua chapter eight beginning at verse one (NLT), "Do not be afraid or discouraged. Take all your fighting men and attack Ai, for I have given you the king of Ai, his people, his town and his land. You will destroy them as you destroyed Jericho and its king. But this time you may keep the plunder and the livestock for yourselves."

To help you determine the powers that are fighting you, in your mind, we have taken 31 self-strongholds that Satan uses to set up kingdoms within all of our minds, but if you use the power of your mind as a conqueror, you can take down these kingdoms and once again have joy, peace and righteousness in the Holy Spirit.

Satan's kingdoms are built by setting up territorial strongholds, by deceiving the mind, and planting thoughts of argument and confusion to blind one's vision and purpose in life. Satan sets up these territorial strongholds that cause territorial bondage and they lead you to fighting those you say you love. Satan knows that if we don't hurry up and extinguish the thoughts that he is planting he can continue to take over our mind. But God exposes these kingdoms, by exposing the lie that is within us. Satan wants to keep us from knowing the truth, the knowledge of God, he knows that if we gain the knowledge of God he is defenseless and if he can't get the kingdom of our mind he can't have our promise.

2 Corinthians 10:4-6AMP

"The weapons of our warfare are not physical [weapons of flesh and blood]. Our weapons are divinely powerful for the destruction of fortresses. ⁵ We are destroying sophisticated arguments and every exalted and proud thing that sets itself up against the [true] knowledge of God, and we are taking every thought and purpose captive to the obedience of Christ, ⁶ being ready to punish every act of disobedience, when your own obedience [as a church] is complete."

You can only expose a lie or thoughts that create warfare if you lead every thought away captive to the obedience of Christ. You have to give every lie of Satan to Jesus and if you don't you'll become disobedient, insecure and incomplete.

1 Corinthians 10:11-13 MSG

"These are all warning markers—DANGER!—in our history books, written down so that we don't repeat their mistakes. Our positions in the story are parallel—they at the beginning, we at the end—and we are just as capable of messing it up as they were. Don't be so naive and self-confident. You're not exempt. You could fall flat on your face as easily as anyone else. Forget about self-confidence; it's useless. Cultivate God-confidence. ¹³ No test or temptation that comes your way is beyond the course of what others have had to face. All you need to remember is that God will never let you down; he'll never let you be pushed past your limit; he'll always be there to help you come through it."

1 Corinthians 10:11-13 ERV

"The things that happened to those people are examples. They were written to be warnings for us. We live in the time that all those past histories were pointing to. ¹² So anyone who thinks

they are standing strong should be careful that they don't
fall. 13 The only temptations that you have are the same
temptations that all people have. But you can trust God. He will
not let you be tempted more than you can bear. But when you
are tempted, God will also give you a way to escape that
temptation. Then you will be able to endure it."

When the enemy plants a thought and you conceive it; you have sinned. The Bible tells us that when God recognized the thought of Satan to do wrong, He kicked him out of heaven. Don't ever think that you can't be tempted. God won't temp you with evil, but the book of James says that we are lead away by our own lusts. 1 Peter 5:8 ERV, paraphrased says, that we ought to be mindful of the Devil our enemy because he goes around like a roaring lion looking for someone to attack, but Satan's authority is limited and given only by the permission of God, he understands that he does not have the power to make man do anything. God gave man free will but if you give Satan power to make a decision for you he'll use it. Satan can make a suggestion, but we have the power to veto it and until you vote him out he will be president or king, but in this season we want him out and we are overturning who has been in charge.

Satan uses deception to cause man to see what is not seen. He seeks how he can cause a divide by causing man or woman to see what is not there to see. If he can get you to perceive it or to see it, he can get you to conceive it. Once you have conceived a thought of Satan's he starts speaking to you and causing you to hear what is not really being spoken. Satan understands that he has to distort your power of perception so it can be turned into his power of deception. If he can get you to stop seeing things the way that God showed them to you, he can take your perception.

First, Satan wants to take your vision causing you to stop seeing it the way that God gave it to you and show you what he wants you to see. If you become distracted while the enemy is showing you his vision, he will start speaking to you so he can cause you to hear what you are not hearing, yet you will think that God is speaking to you. So now if Satan is showing you vision and you have allowed him to speak to you, harmlessly you think God is still speaking because Satan has never shown himself as the devil. He wants you to think that you are still Luke Skywalker and Darth Vader is the enemy. Once he convinces you to see what is not really there and to hear what is not really being spoken then he can get you to believe what is not really there and what you call faith is not really there, but Satan is telling you that you are God over it while he's the shot caller.

The enemy now takes the power of deception to create self-affliction. In Genesis 3, Satan gets Eve to see, hear and believe what was not really there. She is drawn by her own perceptions and it causes her to fall because she thought that the fruit would give her wisdom and power. If at any time in life you feel the need to be more than you are, you are falling. In Matthew 4, we read of a time that Satan tried to deceive Jesus in the wilderness with temptation and his influence, called deception. He wanted to get Jesus to commit self-affliction to Himself.

> **Matt. 4:8b-9 NLT**
> *"all the kingdoms of the world and their glory. [9] "I will give it all to you," he said, "if you will kneel down and worship me."*

So what does Satan want? He wants us to worship him. Satan does not have the power to make men or women do anything, he only has the power to cause them to change their perception, which will lead them to hearing what is not God and then believing what is not God. Satan uses these 31 strongholds to keep from the fulfillment of our promise and our destiny but he can only use these strongholds if we buy into them. In this chapter we introduce you to and teach you how he uses five of these strongholds.

Satan uses the stronghold called self-will and causes you to get caught up in your own will but in order for Satan to do what he wants to do he needs your permission or your self-will. He wants you to question why others are doing things and to self appoint yourself to do something. Self-appointing causes you to become caught up, stubborn, wanting your own agenda, your own desires, hard headed, selfish, self-centered and to become out of control. You'll know that Satan has taken over your will when you have lost your fight and you have lost conviction. You'll know that you have lost your own self will when you no longer care.

Satan also uses the stronghold called self - indulgence. Self-indulgent means seeking only the gratification of self in any of its forms such as self-out of control because one's own appetite, desires, urges, lack of self-control, lack of will power, struggling from withdrawals from one's habits and addictions. Self-indulgence means to become passive, over tolerant, and sympathetic by catering to something or someone unnecessarily, causing someone to become too dependent on you helping and doing for them when they are able to do for themselves.

Satan uses the stronghold called self-seeking. Self-seeking means to love yourself more than your purpose and assignment ordained by God for you to fulfill. A self-seeking person would rather fulfill their own desires than to fulfill the call or purpose that God has placed on their life. (Reference Ch. 8)

> **1 CORINTHIANS 13:4-5 ERV**
> *"Love is patient and kind. Love is not jealous, it does not brag, and it is not proud.*
> *5 Love is not rude, it is not SELFISH, and it cannot be made angry easily. Love does not remember wrongs done against it."*

Satan uses the stronghold called self-complacency which results in the spirit of pride that takes delight in your own qualities and rest with the satisfaction found within yourself. A person that is complacent is at the point in life when they are settling for being average or mediocre and the spirit of laziness comes over you and you don't choose to try to get it off.

Satan uses the stronghold called self-glorifying which means always seeking the praise of others rather than its own. People who struggle with this stronghold are always looking for the spotlight to shine on them and always needing extra attention because they're always bringing extra drama.

> **ISAIAH 14:12-13 NKJV**
> *"How you are fallen from heaven,*
> *O Lucifer, son of the morning! How you are cut down to the ground, You who weakened the nations!*
> *[13] For you have said in your heart: 'I will ascend into heaven, I will exalt my throne above the stars of God; I will also sit on the mount of the congregation on the farthest sides of the north;"*

Satan was Self – Glorified according to

> **Ezekiel 28:14-17**
> *"You were one of the chosen Cherubs who spread your wings over my throne. I put you on the holy mountain of God. You walked among the jewels that sparkled like fire. [15] You were good and honest when I created you, but then you became evil. "Your business brought you many riches. But they also put cruelty inside you, and you sinned. So I treated you like something unclean and threw you off the mountain of God. You were one of the chosen Cherubs who spread your wings over my throne. But I forced you to leave the jewels that sparkled like fire. [17] Your beauty made you proud. Your glory ruined your wisdom. So I threw you down to the ground, and now other*

kings stare at you. You defiled your sanctuaries. By the multitude of your iniquities, By the iniquity of your trading; Therefore I brought fire from your midst; It devoured you, And I turned you to ashes upon the earth. In the sight of all who saw you."

Satan's goal is to get us to do what he did which is to get us out of God's presence and will by worshiping ourselves. These five strongholds was the cause of Satan's fall and they still have the same power and potential to destroy our relationship with God if we are not persuaded to be victorious by having the mind of a conqueror. Let's look at the other strongholds that we must also be delivered and guard our minds from as we take down the kings of strongholds.

Chapter 2

The Stronghold of Self-Confidence
(Man in the Mirror)

I Corinthians 13:10 AMP
[10] But when that which is complete and perfect comes, that which is incomplete and partial will pass away.

James 1:22-25 ERV
[22] Do what God's teaching says; don't just listen and do nothing. When you only sit and listen, you are fooling yourselves. [23] Hearing God's teaching and doing nothing is like looking at your face in the mirror [24] and doing nothing about what you saw. You go away and immediately forget how bad you looked. [25] But when you look into God's perfect law that sets people free, pay attention to it. If you do what it says, you will have God's blessing. Never just listen to his teaching and forget what you heard.

The stronghold of self-confidence begins with the "Man in the Mirror", the person that you are and see when you look in the mirror because mirrors don't lie. The purpose of a mirror is to be a symbol of physical or spiritual reflection. It is the mirror's job to reveal who we are in the flesh as well as in the spirit. We use mirrors everyday to reflect our physical images but we also use them in our vehicles to alert us of potential dangers and the things that are behind us. We place mirrors at corners of buildings and hallways to see what is around the corner or what may be coming. In bathrooms, bedrooms and other rooms or locations mirrors are used to see our physical selves in different places or to stand in front of them every day to see what's out of place or to prepare ourselves for each day.

The 31 Self-Strongholds

We usually don't look at ourselves truly until we are alone but until you know yourself you won't know what it is God wants you to see because you keep using the mirror to dress up the image of you. We only look at ourselves to make sure that we have everything on the outside together, but a rear-view mirror should provide a greater observation of the potential dangers around you and in you. So, do you have that kind of view in your mirror? What do you see when you look in the mirror? Are you looking at you or your image?

Spiritually the mirror provides a dim or blurred version of reality, as in a riddle or an enigma, but when perfection comes we shall see in reality and face to face who we are. The Greek word for image is enigma. Enigma means a person or thing that is mysterious or puzzling. Someone or something that is difficult to understand or explain. It also means someone's reflection, appearance or reflection that is changing constantly. For now we imperfectly see, but we shall know and understand more fully and clearly, in the same manner for which God has known and seen us. *(Reference 1 Corinthians 13:8-10)*

Our spiritual mirrors truthfully reflect the consequences of our actions. Faith always brings conviction and truth. When you are convicted by truth the truth hurts because truth accepts faith and when you accept truth it will set you free from the bondage of sin and strongholds. After Jacob stopped wrestling with himself he could see God. In Judges 7:4-6, God tells Gideon that he has too many people following him. He instructs Gideon to take them down to the water so He can show him those who will use their tongue to lap the water like a dog as opposed to those that will kneel down to lick and look into the water (mirror) to see their own reflection (image). Those that will be looking in the reflection of the water, as though it were a mirror, are caught up in their own self-reflection rather than watching like a dog who is not caught up in seeing himself; rather, he is caught up in looking and protecting someone else. God told Gideon to send those that did not lap the water, back. He wanted Gideon to get them out of his life because people that are caught up in themselves only care about how they look and they will never care about how someone else looks. These kinds of people will get you killed entering into a war.

Our spiritual mirrors reflect back to our eternal surroundings, the people, places and events that are currently apart of the life that we have created. A mirrors purpose is designed to cast a reflection but in order for a mirror to cast reflections it requires light. We have the light of the moon and the sun with the moon being the lesser light and the sun being the greater light so the moon gets its light from the sun. It has no light of its own.

Light is symbolic for illumination and enlightenment and these in turn represent awareness and wisdom. Therefore, in order for us to honestly evaluate ourselves and the world that we have created around us; we must view our current reflection with an enlightened mind. Keep in mind the mirror can only reflect what is truly before it. Whatever we view in our personal and our spiritual mirrors is our current truth. What we see is not only our personal truths and reputation but also the truth of the world which we have created around ourselves.

In the beginning God formed and created man and He did so in two processes. The first process was to form man in His image and the second was to form man in His likeness. Genesis 1:27AMP "So God created man in His own image, in the image and likeness of God He created him; male and female He created them." Genesis 2:7 ERV states, "Then the Lord God took dust from the ground and made a man. He breathed the breath of life into the man's nose and the man became a living thing." It was only then that man became something but if God ever takes Himself out of man, he'll become nothing again.

In the mirror we see our image, not our likeness. We think that we see self but it is only our image. In the 1st process God created man in His image, or in the negative, man's image is his reflection in the mirror, his enigma, or his negative and what man sees is incomplete. This process is similar to that of a camera that has film and a flash. When the picture is taken the flash causes the shutter to reach out capture the image/negative that was in the lens and to place it on the film. The image that is on the film is called the negative. The photographer takes the negative film into the green room or dark room and develops the film until it becomes positive or is the likeness of the image that was taken which begins the second process.

In the **2nd** process God made man in His likeness, which is positive, complete, mature and finished. He formed man out of the dust of the ground which is the negative or image and then He breathed into the negative from His dark room, until man became the likeness or the positive reflection of God which is what God is doing in our lives. He is developing us from our negative image that is incomplete into our positive image which is complete and a likeness of Him. God is trying to break the stronghold over our life called SELF, which is our worst enemy. He's placing the MIRROR in front of us for a self-examination. So He can deliver us from immaturity to maturity, from incomplete to complete, from beginning to end, from start to finish and from negative to positive. If you look deeply in the mirror and see yourself as you really are without camouflage, make-up, pretending or faking it to make it.

In Genesis 1:26-27, we see where God created male and female, but he first made man from the dust of the ground. In the second process God created the same man that He had just made by breathing life into man until he became a living being. He formed man in His own image and He made man in His likeness. Why did man have to go through two processes? The same man that He had just made was not alive. He had a body but he did not have a spirit. He could see himself but he couldn't see God. God never touched man with Himself in the same place. The man that God formed is not the same man that God created because they were in two different places. Although Eden was prepared when God formed man, man was not formed in Eden. Man was formed in the world but God had to wait until man was ready so that He could plant man in the place that He had prepared which was Eden. It was not until man became complete that He could use man and plant him in the place that He had prepared. Man will never be what he should be until he stops trying to fix himself and allow God to transport him out of the body and into the spirit.

The word *made* comes from the Hebrew word ASAH which means to form out of something that is already there. *Created* comes from the word BARA, which means to form something out of nothing. What God is saying in Genesis 1:26-27 is "I will create man out of nothing and at the same time I will make him into something. God's plan for our lives is to take us from ASHA to BARA, from nothing which is where we came from to the something that we are becoming. We're moving from a place called nowhere to a place called somewhere and from a no-body to somebody.

SELF EXAMINATION: Ask yourself the following questions.

1. Why do you look in the mirror?
2. How do you perceive yourself right now?
3. As you look in the mirror, do you like what's looking back at you?
4. As you look in the mirror, what's wrong with what you see?
5. What's in place or out of place?
6. If you can change anything right now with how you see yourself, what would you change?

Self-confidence becomes a stronghold when a person becomes overconfident, high-minded, and arrogant as a result of relying upon their own wisdom, strength and righteousness. The Apostle Paul wrote in Philippians 3:3-4 NIV, "For it is we who are the circumcision, we who serve God by His Spirit, who boast in Christ Jesus, and who put no confidence in the flesh – though I myself have reasons for such confidence. If someone else thinks they have reasons to put confidence in the flesh, I have more:" Paul at this time was immature and arrogant but he was humbled through life as he went through three transitions. First of all, he was Paul who had declared he was greater than all of the other Apostles. Secondly, he was Paul who was the least of all the Apostles and finally was Paul who declared that he was the least of all the saints.

When we look at Peter we see that he was distracted by self-confidence. Peter relied more on his flesh than the Spirit and mind of Christ. In Luke 22:34 and Matthew 26:34, Jesus told Peter that he would deny him three times before the rooster crows but Peter's confidence in his flesh causes him to deny the words of Christ and to declare that he would not deny Him. His over confidence not only made him think he was having faith and confidence in God but also resulted in him denying Christ. His faith and confidence was not in God but in his flesh.

Another example of over confidence occurs when God is speaking to us and we reject the voice and Word of God because we're living a life of denial and we have begun to trust in the flesh more than we do God. Peter's self-confidence caused him to be over confident because of his stronghold of self-denial but notice how Jesus breaks the stronghold over Peter's life. Jesus calls to him and He says to Peter in Luke 22:31-32; "Simon, Simon, Satan has a desire to sift you like wheat but I have prayed for you that your faith may not fail and when you are converted or turned back strengthen your brothers." What Jesus was saying was that by praying over Peter's life He saw into Peter's future where Satan began to litigate to God over the life, seasons and future of Peter's destiny, Jesus went into prayer and interceded in the future not into Peter's past nor his present but his future.

Jesus litigated for Peter's future until He changed the outcome of his future. He did this by breaking the plans, tactics and strategies that Satan had planned for Peter. Jesus had prophesied to Peter telling him several things: Satan desires to destroy you but I have interceded in prayer that your faith will take on the mindset of a conqueror and that you Peter, when you're converted and have overcome your self-denial, you Peter, will begin to discover your moment of "Eureka!" and break the stronghold of over confidence and self-denial. Jesus's prayer for Peter was not only that he would come out but that once he was converted; he would go back with new empowerment and favor and strengthen his brothers.

Chapter 3

The Stronghold of Self-Consciousness

(Mirrors Don't Lie)

James 1:22-24 AMP
²² Do what God's teaching says; don't just listen and do nothing. When you only sit and listen, you are fooling yourselves. ²³ Hearing God's teaching and doing nothing is like looking at your face in the mirror ²⁴ and doing nothing about what you saw. You go away and immediately forget how bad you looked. ²⁵ But when you look into God's perfect law that sets people free, pay attention to it. If you do what it says, you will have God's blessing. Never just listen to his teaching and forget what you heard.

Have you ever asked yourself what is it about you that you don't like? Have you ever betrayed yourself? Do you think that what you see in the mirror is the truth? Do you sometimes feel ashamed? When God reveals your nakedness, or exposes you to Himself, do you allow the shame to make you feel like you are unwanted by God. William Shakespeare's, *Hamlet*, is quoted for saying "to thine own self be true and it must follow, as the night the day, thou canst not then be false to any man." He is saying that if you cannot be true to yourself you won't be true to anyone else. In this instance if you have been exposed or if in your nakedness you need to admit that there is a problem, to thine own self be true. If you can own up to your shortcomings, you will be free to yourself and nothing or no man can shackle or hinder you because the truth will continue to set you free day and night.

In order for us to be free from the strongholds that we are dealing with we must be true and honest with ourselves, confront and come face to face with the person in the mirror. We must begin to spiritually examine who and what it is we see in the mirror. We must determine how long we are going to look at what it is that we have already been exposed to in the struggles and throughout the issues of our life.

In order to become naked and not ashamed we must do "self" inventory. This inventory or assessment is similar to going to the doctor, when he/she asks you what's wrong with you. Where does it hurt? How long have you been feeling like this? What is the level of your pain on a scale of 1-10? The reason that the doctors ask these questions is because everything does not show up on the x-ray and before the doctor can help you to eliminate the problem and the pain you have got to be honest. If you don't think there is anything wrong or think that you can hide it, you're in denial that something is wrong with you. Denying the hurt will cause you to be depressed as well as suppress the hurt that is going on inside of you.

If you will not be honest and truthful about the strongholds of your afflictions you will never get help, you will always carry, live in and be fearful of what is hurting you. How bad do you want to be free? God will never fix your situation until you admit what it is that you are struggling with and or what it is that is hurting you.

Are you binding and loosening the strongman or is the strongman binding and loosening you? You have got to get self out of the way. God can't help your positive until you get out of the way with your negative. God is like an M.R.I., He can see what's going on in your negative image and make it positive if you are honest within yourself. If you don't deal with the hurt then you will go to a worst state, the place of fearing what it is that is hurting you. To thine own self be true.

You have got to deal with the hurt, the pain and the fear because fear can paralyze you and cause you to be afraid of going forward. Until you can overcome self-denial and begin to do self-inventory, you will never be free, delivered, healed, and blessed. You will not have the mindset of a conqueror nor will you possess all of the promises that God has made you and most of all, His desire and purpose that you be 100% free.

The stronghold of self-consciousness is personal. Satan uses this stronghold to cause individuals to only think of themselves. Everything that a self-conscious person says or does is typically about them. A self-conscious person can be having a conversation with a person that is in need of help but instead of hearing the other individual they always make the conversation about them because these individuals are self-centered and self-focused.

The symptoms and signs of someone that is struggling with the stronghold of self-consciousness

Individuals that struggle with being insecure and having low self-esteem will do any and everything to gain unnecessary attention. These people are self-centered. They are selfish when it comes to sharing success because they tolerate people, they don't celebrate people. Often times these individuals are in a backslidden condition or they have already become a backslider and are living a life of self-denial.

Luke 15:25-32 talks about the Prodigal son and many times when this scripture is discussed, it is easier to identify with the younger son who has backslid into the world, comes to repentance, is renewed and got up from his backslidden tendencies. He returns to his father's house, he is restored and has a renewed covenant with his father. Frequently in this parable we overlook the older brother or the older son that didn't go back into the world but stayed at home like many do in the church.

Many people are like the elder son who does everything according to what they are suppose to but is still in a backslidden condition and struggles with the symptoms of this stronghold. Like the older brother you didn't go back out clubbing. You stayed in the house called "The Church" but because of self-denial, you struggle with the stronghold of self-consciousness. You are a backslider or are backsliding right in the house/church.

You come to church every Sunday, Bible Study or Empowerment night, you pay your tithes and offering, serving on multi-ministries and you're faithful to the ministry but because of insecurity, low self-esteem and needing unnecessary attention; you refuse to share success, to be a team player and you become territorial. You're in self-denial that you are insecure because you think that you are too strong to be insecure. Insecure people can't complement other people, and they don't know how to celebrate other people because of their insecurities. You're just like the older brother who refuses to celebrate another brother or sister that has been restored back into fellowship, covenant and into their position.

Side Note: Why people don't celebrate others?

There are two reasons for the inability to celebrate others, the first being a level of fear. When people feel like you are progressing or elevating, it makes those that are stagnated who have no plans of progressing feel like you are going to leave them and now they want you to stay where they are because they feel that if you go up you will forget about them. You have to overcome this spirit of fear. The second reason is they feel like you will gain more attention then they will. These are people that are used to seeing you in the shadow and now they can't handle God moving you to a place above them. These same people you can't shut them up or sit them down when something good is happening for them but they can't wait to sit you down when you're being celebrated.

We all have the potential to become self-conscious because of low self-esteem and self denial. While the younger brother who had backslid, repented, renewed covenant and was being celebrated the older brother remained insecure, unstable, and territorial. The older brother needed all of the father's attention, he refused to share success, or to show up for his brother's celebration. He stayed out in the field by assigning himself his own assignment as an excuse not to celebrate with his brother. The Bible says in verse 28, the older son was angry and wouldn't go to the celebration and his father had to go out and beg his older son to come and be a part of his younger brother's celebration.

Too many times this very thing is happening in church when we should be celebrating that the one who was backslidden and fallen back into their old lifestyle has been delivered by God, restored and elevated into a new place in life that has begun to bless them spiritually, physically and financially, anger prevails. Rather than celebrating our brothers and sisters, those who struggle with the stronghold of self-consciousness only tolerate them and become angry and jealous enough to try to sabotage the time of celebration.

Chapter 4

The Stronghold of Self-Importance

(Mirrors Don't Lie)

Satan uses the stronghold of self-importance to make a person very offensive (aggressive), insecure, unstable and fragile. They think and believe that everything is always about them. If whatever is going on and whatever may be happening is not about them they don't want anything to do with it because they always have to be the center of attention. The individuals struggling with this stronghold believe they know more about everything than anybody. They are good as long as things are going good, but when bad stuff happens they look like a totally different person. Romans 12:3ERV says "God has given me a special gift and that is why I have something to say to each one of you. Don't think that you are better than you really are. You must see yourself (look at yourself in the mirror) just as you are. Decide what you are by the faith God has given each of us."

Genesis 3:4-5 ERV says, "But the snake said to the woman, "You will not die. God knows that if you eat the fruit from that tree you will learn about good and evil, and then you will be like God!" Satan's emphasis on Eve learning about good and evil indicates that she did not know what good and evil was. Some things that you want to know you are not ready for. After learning of the tree Eve began to desire to be like a God because she wanted more than what God had for her. Satan had deceived Eve into believing that she was more important than she really was. We should never forget where we came from because when you do, you forget who you are and you try to be more than you are. Satan's deception was not just to make Eve think his lies and deception sounded like the truth but that his lies also looked like the truth.

The term deception or deceiving simply means making a lie to look like the truth. In Genesis 3: 6 AMP it says, "when the woman saw that the tree was good, suitable, and pleasant for food, and it was delightful to look at, and a tree to be desired; in order to make one wise. She took of its fruit and ate." The term deception also means to be misled, a fraudulent misrepresentation as a counterfeit. The word fraudulent comes from the word fraud which is an illegal and false representation caused by robbing someone of their personal gain by the act of deception by pretending to be someone you're not or into thinking that you can do something you can't by being fake and disguising yourself as an imposter.

So how did Eve see that the tree was good? In the beginning she resisted but she later gave in to the deception. She saw that the tree was to be desired and she began to lust for the evil, the gain. She desired the evil and believed that it was God all because she wanted and needed to be more important than she was.

Once Eve was deceived by the lie she began to be misled. Satan led her to another place and because she wanted to be more important she left her place although everything that she needed was in her place. Eve was getting what she wanted unaware that she was about to lose what she had. After being misled by Satan he committed a fraudulent act against Eve.

As a counterfeit he misrepresented the tree to Eve and made her believe that this tree was the best tree of all the trees that God had which was far from the truth. Romans 12:3AMP says, "For by the grace (unmerited favor of God) given to me I warn everyone among you not to estimate and think of himself more highly than he ought [not to have an exaggerated opinion of his own importance], but rate his ability with sober judgment, each according to the degree of faith apportioned by God to him."

Chapter 5

The Stronghold of Self-Depreciation

(Mirrors Don't Lie)

James 1:21-23 Amplified version says this, "So get rid of all uncleanness and the rampant outgrowth of wickedness and in a humble [gentle, modest] spirit receive and welcome the Word which implanted and rooted [in your hearts] contains the power to save your souls. But be doers of the Word [obey the message] and not merely listeners [into deception by reasoning contrary to the truth]. For if anyone only listens to the Word without obeying it and being a doer of it, he is like a man who looks carefully at his [own] natural face in a mirror;" The stronghold of self-depreciation is used by Satan to bring about a struggle for the people of God in the area of self-worth. Self-depreciation means to be undervalued, underestimated, belittled by someone or to be diminished in valued over a period of time. Satan uses this stronghold to make one feel that their life, service or contribution doesn't really mean anything. He takes these feelings of uselessness and uses them on individuals in three processes, schemes and or attacks.

The first process is to suppress which means to be under, to subdue, to become dormant which is similar to falling into a deep sleep almost like coming under anesthesia that causes you to avoid feeling or experiencing the pain that is really hurting you. Suppression also means to become silent or quiet, to shut down and to fall into a silent frustration. It is Satan's plan to first suppress how we feel about what has offended us.

The second process, scheme or attack is to depress, which is the act of pushing or pulling us down. The signs and symptoms of depression are fatigue, exhaustion, sleep disorders (not enough or too much sleep), tiredness, eating disorders (eating too much or not eating enough), feelings of emptiness, anxiousness (from anxiety attacks or panicking), aching, sadness, lack of joy, difficulty in thinking, a loss of concentration and meditation (the inability to stay focused - always distracted).

The final process, scheme or attack is to oppress or to cause oppression. To oppress means to be persecuted, abused (physically, mentally and spiritually), to be broken, tormented and discouraged, to be in bondage, debt, or to be lost. After Satan uses suppression to cause us to suppress what we're feeling in our soulish being and to cause us to be in self-denial from silent frustration and attacking our spirit, the enemy causes us to be depressed. He does so by attacking our emotional and physical being causing dysfunction and disorders and by attacking our confidence to the point of utterly destroying our spirit, body and soul. Finally, he brings oppression to cause one to become broken, tormented and afflicted. The spirit of oppression ultimately causes you to be in Satan's debt like the children of Israel were indebted in Egypt.

Exodus 1:11-12 NLT states "So the Egyptians made the Israelites their slaves. They appointed brutal slave drivers over them hoping to wear them down with crushing labor forcing them to build the cities of Pithom and Rameses as supply centers for the king. The more the Egyptians oppressed them the more the Israelites multiplied and spread causing the Egyptians to become more alarmed."

Satan's ultimate plan with the stronghold of self-depreciation is to attack the saints, the believer, and all the people of God by making them fall under the stronghold of self-depreciation through the three processes. The first process is suppressing you into silent frustration. Secondly, to depress you and to cause you to act outside your character and thirdly, to oppress you by bringing you into this bondage called self-depreciation where he binds your spirit through torment and affliction so that you will cut off all of your communication with God.

In Ruth 1:19-21AMP Satan uses the stronghold of self-depreciation against Naomi. The Bible says, "So they both went on until they came to Bethlehem. And when they arrived in Bethlehem, the whole town was stirred about them, and said Is this Naomi? And she said to them, call me not Naomi [Pleasant]; call me Mara [Bitter], for the Almighty has dealt very bitterly with me. I went out full, but the Lord has brought me home again empty. Why call me Naomi, since the Lord has testified against me, and the Almighty has afflicted me?"

Naomi had gone through 10 years of missing her season and finally she comes back to Bethlehem to begin her new season but the enemy had formed a stronghold of self-depreciation that made her feel undervalued and depreciated. She begins to change her name from Naomi which means delightful, pleasant and happy to Mara which is to be broken, bitter, hurt and empty. This stronghold of self-depreciation almost caused her to miss one of the greatest seasons of her life but thanks be to God for someone like Ruth that understood how to minister into and intercede for her life to keep her from missing her greatest season ever!

If Ruth had not stayed connected to Naomi while she was being attacked by this stronghold, which caused her to lose her identity, purpose, focus and assignment; she would have missed another season. During this attack Naomi lost her identity, her call and when you lose your call you lose your purpose. The spirit of self-depreciation caused her to devalue others and to move from them because the enemy knows you will need them in your life. In this state of mind, the enemy causes you to get to the place of almost doing a lot of things but thank God that He changed your mind. He sent someone that did not and would not give up on you to keep you from missing your greatest season.

In Ruth 1:16 ERV, the Bible says, "But Ruth said, don't force me to leave you! Don't force me to go back to my own people. Let me go with you. Wherever you go, I will go. Wherever you sleep, I will sleep. Your people will be my people. Your God will be my God." When you are under attack and struggling with this stronghold and forcing the right people out of your life it causes you to attract the wrong people into your life. Naomi was forcing Ruth out of her life because she was drunk with bitterness, hurt, pain, feeling and believing that her life was over and that everything and everyone that had ever mattered to her had been taken from her but thanks be to God she still had Ruth who stayed in her life. She became Naomi's designated driver in the time of her drunkenness. Who is your designated driver?

I Samuel 1:5-8 ERV states, "Elkanah always gave an equal share of the food to Hannah. He did this because he loved her very much, even though the Lord had not let Hannah have any children. Peninnah always upset Hannah and made her feel bad because the Lord had not made her able to have children. Every year when their family went to the Lord's house at Shiloh this happened. Peninnah would upset Hannah so much that she would begin to cry and would not eat anything. One year after this happened, her husband Elkanah said to her, "Hannah, why are you crying? Why won't you eat? Why are you sad? You have me. Isn't that better than having even ten sons?"

Hannah had become frustrated because she could not get pass the distraction of her enemy. She entertained her enemy for 7 years. Her self-depreciation caused her relationship to depreciate. Once again Satan used the stronghold of self-depreciation to cause Hannah to keep missing season after season. The enemy used the spirit and the stronghold of self-depreciation through Peninnah to provoke Hannah into believing she was not appreciated and that she was undervalued. It wasn't until she rose up and went back into the House of God to worship through her emptying and pouring out, that stronghold of self-depreciation was broken over her life.

The spirit of self-depreciation causes unnatural attacks and begins bringing additional problems and struggles that causes an individual to begin experiencing an overwhelmingly high level of stress and deep-dark depression. It causes you to find yourself crying constantly on and off during the day. The main attack of this spirit of depression is to get you to act out of flesh and to become distracted from the call and assignment on your life. It makes you feel like a complete failure unable to do anything right, but the ultimate goal is to try to get you to quit, and to walk away from God and all those that sincerely love you by tormenting your soul and confusing your mind, binding your spirit and destroying your relationships so the enemy can have your life. Peninnah wanted Hannah's life and thought she could get it by convincing Hannah through this stronghold of self depreciation that she was worthless, unwanted and unloved but when Hannah cried out of her soul in worship it destroyed the stronghold of self-depreciation.

Elijah also struggled with the stronghold of self-depreciation, 1 Kings 19:2-4 NLT says, "So Jezebel sent this message to Elijah: May the gods strike me and even kill me if by this time tomorrow I have not killed you just as you killed them." Elijah was afraid and fled for his life so he went to Beersheba, a town in Judah and he left his servant there. He then went on alone into the wilderness, traveling all day until he sat down under a broom tree and prayed that he might die. "I have had enough,

Lord," he said. "Take my life, for I am no better than my ancestors who have already died."

I Kings 19:9-10 NLT tells us that "There he came to a cave, where he spent the night. But the Lord said to him, "what are you doing here, Elijah?" Elijah replied, "I have zealously served the Lord God Almighty. But the people of Israel have broken their covenant with you, torn down your altars, and killed every one of your prophets. I am the only one left and now they are trying to kill me too."

According to verse 10 he was afraid for his life and believed that he was the only one left trying to live and do right. Elijah's struggle with the stronghold of self-depreciation is evident in the fact that he began to isolate himself in a place of seclusion or solitary confinement by hiding in a cave. He was in denial even when God confronted him in verse nine and asked him, "What are you doing here, Elijah?" God was confronting Elijah about his feelings of self-deprecation and his struggle with fear. The stronghold had caused the "Man of God", Elijah, to fall under the three processes of self-depreciation (suppression, depression and oppression). Elijah was now in denial and still trying to be spiritual with God rather than being truthful. He was suppressing his feelings of fear, depressed, struggling and burned out. Elijah was oppressed and suicidal (he was contemplating his own death). His spirit was tormented but he had just finished celebrating the greatest victory of his life.

Elijah had just completed his last assignment and stood before King Ahab in 1 Kings 17 and declared that it wouldn't rain until he says so. It had been three years of famine and after three years of famine Elijah called the people of God and the false prophets of Baal to meet him on Mount Carmel. He said to the people of God, how long you will be confused about making a decision to serve God or Baal. Elijah got victory that day by praying to God and fire came down from Heaven. He killed 850 false prophets and shortly after that Elijah got another victory by praying unto God and releasing rain from Heaven after a three year drought and famine. Just when rain was released and Elijah completed his assignment and celebrated the victory of God; the enemy begins to attack him with the spirit and stronghold of self-depreciation.

I Kings 19:2 tell us that Jezebel sent a message to Elijah that she was going to kill him. After God gives us victory for fulfilling our assignment we shouldn't get so caught up in trying to emotionally celebrate the victory but keep in mind that the enemy understands that now he has to start his new attack to try to kill us. We must understand the new assignment!! Similarly, the Bible says that after 400 years the children of Israel escaped Pharaoh and his army, crossed over the Red Sea and watched Pharaoh and his armies drown in the Red Sea. The Israelites begin to pull out their tambourines, to sing and to dance and while celebrating their victory the Bible says the next day they went back to murmuring and complaining because they begin to be attacked by the bitterness of self-depreciation. Jesus' stronghold of self-depreciation is seen in:

Matthew 26: 38-44 NKJV

[38] *"Then He said to them, "My soul is EXCEEDINGLY SORROWFUL, EVEN TO DEATH. Stay here and watch with Me."*

[39] *He went a little farther and fell on His face, and prayed, saying, "O My Father, if it is possible, let this cup pass from Me; NEVERTHELESS, not as I will, but as You will."*

[40] *Then He came to the disciples and found them sleeping, and said to Peter, "What! Could you not watch with Me one hour?*

[41] *Watch and pray, LEST YOU ENTER INTO TEMPTATION. The spirit indeed is willing, but the flesh is weak."*

[42] *Again, a second time, He went away and prayed, saying, "O My Father, if this cup cannot pass away from Me unless I drink it, Your will be done."*

[43] *And He came and found them asleep again, for their eyes were HEAVY.*

[44] *So He left them, went away again, and prayed the third time, saying the same words."*

In order to overcome the stronghold of self-depreciation, we like Jesus must first and foremost always have what is called a "Nevertheless!" Nevertheless simply means "in spite of" or "whatever". When the enemy tries to attack your life physically, mentally or spiritually, you have got to have an "in spite of" praise. In spite of conditions, in spite of your circumstances, in spite of your problems, in spite of your heart and in spite of your pain, you have to declare that I'm going to trust God, stay faithful and be true to my assignment, my call and my purpose.

Secondly, you have to have a "Whatever" declaration. The Bible says the three Hebrew boys were threatened by King Nebuchadnezzar that if they did not bow down and worship the false god they would be thrown into the fiery furnace. The three Hebrew boys told the King it makes no difference whatever you think you can do to us. It makes no difference what you think you can say to us. It makes no difference whatever you think you can do to hurt us or whatever you think you can do to threaten us because the God whom we serve is able to deliver us from whatever you have in store for us!

Chapter 6

The Stronghold of Self-Vindication
(Taking the Law into Your Own Hands)

Deuteronomy 32:35 EXB

"I will punish those who do wrong [vengeance is mine;]; I will repay them. Soon their foot will slip, because their day of trouble [disaster] is near, and their punishment [doom] will come quickly."

Satan uses the stronghold called self-vindication to cause us to take vengeance and retaliation into our own hands when vengeance belongs to God. He uses the stronghold of self-vindication to plant deception in the mind of individuals and he convinces them to stand up for their own rights and to avenge themselves whether they're wrong or right. We see in the Word of God many examples of believers who vindicated themselves and took revenge on their enemy without God's consent causing God to cut off their "Covenant of Agreement" as well as their promises because the Law of Retaliation had been broken. Anyone who breaks this Spiritual Law is also a covenant breaker.

A covenant breaker is one that takes the problem out of God's hand and put it into their hands. Satan forms this stronghold of self-vindication to cause us to take things our enemy has done to us and retaliate causing us to default on our promissory agreement which results in the promises of God going into foreclosure.

The word vindicate means to be cleared from any accusations, to uphold or to be justified from any agreement, to assert, to maintain, to defend, to claim for one's self or another. In Roman Civil Law vindication was used to claim or regain possession, to claim the title of property through legal procedure or to assert one's right to possession. Vindication is a Latin word that means to lay legal claims to property, to free someone from servitude by claiming himself or herself as a free man or woman. It also means to exonerate, to be cleared from doubt, to protect and avenge.

The stronghold of self-vindication is used by the enemy to get us to vindicate ourselves by attacking, assaulting, or doing something bad to someone who has hurt us or treated us badly to get revenge against someone by retaliating. It will also cause us to get back at someone or to take vengeance into our own hands.

To retaliate means to hit back, strike back, even the Score, get revenge, give as good as you get, to get back at, or give tit for tat. Some of you are fighting God thinking that you are fighting your enemy, stop retaliating and trust that God has your back and your front.

The Symptoms, Signs and Side Effects of Self-Vindication

Self-vindication and retaliation affects us emotionally, causes spiritual trauma and has a number of other symptoms and side effects. Do you easily become violent, fearful, angry, irritable, or have mood swings, self-blame, feelings of sadness, guilt, shame, hopeless, anxiety or confusion, difficulty concentrating, in denial or disbelief, withdraw from others and or feel disconnected or numb. Other symptoms and signs include insomnia or nightmares, easily startled, a racing heartbeat, aches and pains, fatigue, easily aggravated and muscle tensions. These physical and emotional symptoms will cause an individual to have trouble functioning at home, work and or in a variety of other areas. Chronic fatigue that traumatizes a person to live a life of fear and to make them feel that they are the victim and being victimized by someone all the time is a side effect of the self-vindication stronghold. "Stop playing the victim." King Saul suffered and struggled with the stronghold of self-vindication; called The Saul Syndrome.

In 1 Samuel 18:5-11 ERV, "David went to fight wherever Saul sent him. He was very successful so Saul put him in charge of the soldiers which pleased everyone, even Saul's officers. David went out to fight against the Philistines and on the way home after the battles the women in every town in Israel would come out to meet him. They sang and danced for joy as they played their tambourines and lyres right in front of Saul! The women sang, "Saul has killed his thousands but David has killed his tens of thousands." Their song upset Saul and he became very angry. Saul thought, "The women give David credit for killing tens of thousands of the enemy, and they give me credit for only thousands. A little more of this and they will give him the kingdom itself!" So from that time on Saul watched David very closely. The next day an evil spirit from God took control of Saul and he went wild in his house. David played the harp to calm him as he usually did but Saul with a spear in his hand thought, "I'll pin David to the wall." Saul threw the spear twice, but David jumped out of the way both times.

The Saul Syndrome

The Saul Syndrome began because he felt careless, insecure and was out of fellowship which caused and created emotional and spiritual trauma for Saul called self-vindication. The first syndrome of Saul is a need for constant attention. The second syndrome of Saul is a sense of entitlement and the third syndrome of Saul is the lack of empathy. A person with a lack of empathy is simply one that lacks concern and emotion for what someone else is feeling concerning their hurt and pain but they always want someone to feel their hurt and pain. The fourth syndrome of Saul is being envious or jealous of others and always believing that others are envious or jealous of you. The fifth syndrome of Saul begins with being arrogant, having a bad attitude and lacking integrity and discipline. The sixth syndrome of Saul is seen in someone who is so driven to accomplish success they will kill or destroy another's reputation or life to have it.

Satan knows if we become vengeful we will end up like Cain who was angry and retaliated against his brother Abel and killed him or like Esau was against Jacob who for 20 years hunted his brother to kill him because he couldn't let go of his brother Jacob's betraying and hustling him out of his birthright and inheritance. Also, the brothers of Joseph became jealous, envious and retaliated against Joseph and conspired to kill him because he was a dreamer. King Saul became insecure and jealous of David and retaliated and plotted to kill David simply because the people were giving more praise and honor to David. Some people will retaliate or vindicate to bring you down or destroy your life because they can't handle the favor and the anointing God has on you.

The 31 Self-Strongholds

The stronghold called self-vindication is a weapon used by the enemy to cause you to lose your focus by becoming distracted from your assignment and become angry and bitter at life, the people who hurt you, the people who want to hurt you, and at how the people have hurt you. These feelings cause you to begin to self-vindicate and retaliate and like Cain you lose self-control. Losing control of your anger and hurt causes you to kill your brother and sister. You may not kill your brothers and sisters like Cain killed his brother Abel by stabbing him with a knife but many through retaliation or vindication backstab with their tongue of words, lies, and deception that brings devastation or destruction.

Although Joseph's brothers separated him from his father's house and family for over 20 years, sold him as a slave causing him to become a prisoner of Pharaoh and serving a life sentence on death row, Joseph didn't allow what his brothers did to him to cause him to retaliate or vindicate himself

GENESIS 50:19-20 EXB

19 Then Joseph said to them, "Don't be afraid. Can I do what only God can do [Am I in the place of God]? 20 You meant TO HURT [TO HARM; OR EVIL AGAINST] ME, but God turned your evil into [meant it for] good to save the lives of many people, which is being done."

Joseph didn't allow the STRONGHOLD OF SELF – VINDICATION to create bondage for his life but rather he turned it over to God. What his brothers and the devil meant for evil to harm, hurt, kill and destroy him, God meant it for his good.

ROMANS 12:19 GW

19 Don't take revenge, dear friends. Instead, let God's anger take care of it. After all, Scripture says, "I alone have the right to take revenge. I will pay back, says the Lord."

Satan knows if we turn it over to God not only will God revenge and take vengeance out on our enemy but if we trust God, in return God will

40

give us restitution and pay us back for the trouble and harm we have experienced through our tribulation, persecution, shame, hurt and suffering.

The word restitution is defined as the act of returning something that was lost or stolen to its owner, or payment that is given to someone that has suffered damage, trouble, hurt, pain, etc.

DEUTERONOMY 32:35-36 AMP

[35] *"Vengeance is Mine, and recompense, in the time when their foot shall slide; for the day of their disaster is at hand and their doom comes speedily. [36] For the Lord will revoke sentence for His people and relent for His servants' sake when He sees that their power is gone and none remains, whether bond or free."*

PSALMS 17:2-3 AMP

[2] *"Let my sentence of vindication come from You! May Your eyes behold the things that are just and upright. [3] You have proved my heart; You have visited me in the night; You have tried me and find nothing [no evil purpose in me]; I have purposed that my mouth shall not transgress."*

PSALMS 43:1-2 AMP

[1] *"Judge and vindicate me, O God; plead and defend my cause against an ungodly nation. O deliver me from the deceitful and unjust man! [2] For You are the God of my strength [MY STRONGHOLD—in Whom I take refuge]; why have You cast me off? Why go I mourning because of the oppression of the enemy?"*

PSALMS 138:8 NIV

[8] *"The Lord will VINDICATE me; your love, Lord, endures forever— do not abandon the works of your hands."*

ISAIAH 54:17 AMP

[17] *"But no weapon that is formed against you shall prosper, and every tongue that shall rise against you in judgment you shall show to be in the wrong. This [peace, righteousness, security, triumph over opposition] is the heritage of the servants of the Lord [those in whom the ideal Servant of the Lord is reproduced]; this is the righteousness or the VINDICATION which they obtain from Me [this is that which I impart to them as their justification], says the Lord."*

EXODUS 3:19-22 MSG

[19-22] *"I know that the king of Egypt won't let you go unless forced to, so I'll intervene and hit Egypt where it hurts—oh, my miracles will send them reeling!—after which they'll be glad to send you off. I'll see to it that this people get a hearty send-off by the Egyptians—when you leave, you won't leave EMPTY-HANDED! Each woman will ask her neighbor and any guests in her house for objects of silver and gold, for jewelry and extra clothes; you'll put them on your sons and daughters. Oh, you'll clean the Egyptians out!"*

2 CHRONICLES 20:15-17 AMP

"He said Hearken all Judah, you inhabitants of Jerusalem, and you King Jehoshaphat. The Lord says this to you: Be not afraid or dismayed at this great multitude; FOR THE BATTLE IS NOT YOURS, BUT GOD'S. [16] *Tomorrow go down to them. Behold, they will come up by the Ascent of Ziz, and you will find them at the end of the ravine before the Wilderness of Jeruel.* [17] *YOU SHALL NOT NEED TO FIGHT IN THIS BATTLE; take your positions, standstill, and see the deliverance of the Lord [Who is] with you, O Judah and Jerusalem. Fear not nor be dismayed. Tomorrow go out against them, for the Lord is with you."*

2 CHRONICLES 20:22-26 AMP

[22] *"And when they began to sing and to praise, the Lord set ambushments against the men of Ammon, Moab, and Mount Seir who had come against Judah, and they were [SELF-] slaughtered;* [23] *For [suspecting betrayal] the men of Ammon and Moab rose against those of Mount Seir, utterly destroying them. And when they had made an end of the men of Seir, they all helped to destroy one another.* [24] *And when Judah came to the watchtower of the wilderness, they looked at the multitude, and behold, they were dead bodies fallen to the earth, and none had escaped!* [25] *When Jehoshaphat and his people came to take the spoil, they found among them much cattle, goods, garments, and precious things which they took for themselves, more than they could carry away, so much they were three days in gathering the spoil.* [26] *On the fourth day they assembled in the Valley of Beracah. There they blessed the Lord. So the name of the place is still called the Valley of Beracah [blessing]."*

Chapter 7

The Stronghold of Self-Feelings

(Mirrors Don't Lie)

Romans 8:1 HCSB
"Therefore, no condemnation now exists for those in Christ Jesus,"
Condemnation means to self-impose blame.

The stronghold of self-feelings involves self-awareness which deals with one's struggles with their self. These feelings cause an individual to be self-centered, unaccountable and unable to be trusted to make rational decisions. Symptoms of this stronghold are low self-esteem, self-pity, and an inability to forgive yourself. People that struggle with self-feeling suffer from mental and spiritual low self-esteem because they not only have a problem forgiving themselves but they also struggle with God's forgiveness as well as other peoples' forgiveness and this hinders them from having successful relationships. They live in fear of decisions because of their emotions and are always second guessing themselves. Their lack of confidence as a saint and a believer prevents them from overcoming their pass failures and mistakes and being healed from their brokenness so they become unstable, inconsistent in their decisions and have a lack of spiritual confidence and self-confidence.

The stronghold of self-feelings is birthed by the spirit of rejection derived from the fear of abandonment. The spirit of rejection causes those that are under the influence of this stronghold to build walls or defense mechanisms so they can protect themselves from being hurt again. Have you built up self defense mechanisms against those in your family? If so, you are weakening your defenses against the enemy. Whenever those that struggle with the spirit of rejection find themselves in a serious relationship their defense mechanisms or walls go up for protection and form its own firewalls to fight off anything or anyone from getting to close to them. The spirit of rejection releases anger, hatred and bitterness and causes one to retaliate because of the injustice of their pain. Also this spirit and stronghold is the reason for a person's greatest fear which is being alone and thinking everyone who matters to them will eventually leave. They begin to find fault in their relationships and deliberately create unnecessary arguments and controversy to guard them because they are afraid of having their heart broken again from any kind of developing relationship. They always look to push the eject button before they allow themselves to become too involved.

Rejection is defined as abandonment or to abandon, forsake entirely, renounce, to throw away or to cast off by self-condemnation and the feeling of guilt. The root of the stronghold of self-feelings comes from of rejection. Past hurt and the pain of being rejected impacted them in their childhood so now they struggle with relationships in adulthood. These relationship struggles causes those that are under the influence of self-feelings to feel like everyone that they have ever loved or cared for not only have rejected them, but have abandoned them by either pushing them away, breaking up with them, leaving them, dying on them, betraying them, forsaking them, or giving up on them.

Another symptom of self-feelings is progressive nervousness that can lead to a nervous disorder, depression, defensiveness, and paranoia. A sign these individuals will show is always being suspicious of others which leads to them experiencing different types of phobias (fears). The spirit of rejection causes individuals to become paranoid of people and things which then cause them to act irrational and have excessive fear of letting go of their past and being too afraid to face their future. This type of fear of the future paralyzes them, stopping them from making future decisions.

The side effects of the stronghold of self-feelings caused by the spirit of rejection are being insecure, judgmental, and an attraction to shallow relationships of all types. Those who struggle with this stronghold always blame themselves and others because of self-imposed guilt that causes one to find it hard to believe that they can be forgiven or to forgive themselves from their past failures and mistakes. This stronghold causes a person to struggle with self-destructive behaviors, imaginary guilt and to operate out of negativity by always being negative of the things they see or toward others because they can't get past their own guilt, failure and hurt.

The side effects of the spirit of rejection causes anger problems, a violent temper, mood swings, abusive behavior that can lead to arguments, fights and even murder, suicide or mental or spiritual breakdown, out of control screaming, yelling, cursing and tantrums. Remember the root of the stronghold of self-feelings is rejection so those that are in bondage to the spirit of rejection rebel when they hear (NO)!! NO you can't have this. NO, you can't do this. NO, you are not ready for this, now. NO, this is not what you should be doing. Throughout their life they've struggled because someone was always telling them NO. So now when they hear NO, they become angry, lose their temper, struggle with tendencies of delusional disorder, begin to act out of character and rebel against authority, even the authority of God!!

GENESIS 4:4-7 NCV
4 'Abel brought the best parts from some of the firstborn of his flock. The Lord ACCEPTED Abel and his gift,
5 but he did not ACCEPT Cain and his gift. So Cain BECAME VERY ANGRY and felt REJECTED.
6 The Lord asked Cain, "Why are you ANGRY? Why do you look so unhappy?
7 If you do things well, I will accept you, but if you do not do them well, sin is ready to attack you. Sin wants you, but you must rule over it."

In the above passage God is saying that I am not discriminating against you. I am not accepting your brother and rejecting you because I favored Abel over you. I am accepting him because he favored Me over his disobedience.

Many people want to know why spiritually, financially, and socially they lack or don't have and it's because they are not stable. God does not honor when you have and you do; but God honors when you don't have and you still do. God tests you when you are at your lowest. He does not test you when things are working for you but when things are not so good to ensure that you'll do right when you do have. When you're in the house of God, do you understand that God has shown you favor and prepared an assignment for you or are you thinking that God should be grateful that you're in the house?

God accepts you when you do something that costs you to do it, not Him. A person that struggles with rejection needs too much attention and you have to know that if God isn't saying anything to you, you must be alright. When God is talks to Cain, he talks to Cain about his attitude, his countenance, and his anger not about what he was giving. So He, God, favored Abel because Abel never put a price on his giving and he came with a right spirit. Able came to worship as a cheerful giver; therefore, God desired to bless him. If you want God to favor you then He should not have to tell you how to come to worship. God will redeem the time if He can trust you now with what He has given although it may seem like nothing to you. God wants to accept Cain, but Cain is rejecting obedience and order.

> **1 CHRONICLES 4:9-10 NKJV**
> *⁹"Now Jabez was more honorable than his brothers, and his mother called his name Jabez, saying, "Because I BORE HIM IN PAIN."*
> *¹⁰ And Jabez called on the God of Israel saying, "Oh, that YOU WOULD BLESS ME INDEED, and ENLARGE MY TERRITORY, that YOUR HAND WOULD BE WITH ME, and THAT YOU WOULD KEEP ME FROM EVIL, THAT I MAY NOT CAUSE PAIN!" So God granted him what he requested."*

The name Jabez means to be rejected and unaccepted, to cause pain and sorrow, birthed out of pain and sorrow, having contractions of unmeasurable pain and sorrow due to physical, mental and spiritual rejection. Jabez was rejected from the day he was born because of someone else's pain and sorrow. He struggled with the fear of rejection from childhood to adulthood and this caused him to be in bondage to the stronghold of self-feelings. He was called pain and sorrow and he now causes others pain and sorrow in a diversity of relationships. It was not until he overcame his stronghold of rejection that he was healed from his affliction to go forward and start over in new relationships. You can start over again!!!!

MIRROR PUNISHMENT

It wasn't until Jabez moved past mirror punishment (to always see one's self as a failure) that he stopped seeing himself as a failure and a man of pain and sorrow because of the spirit of rejection that he began to look in the mirror differently by doing a new self-examination. He overcame the stronghold of self-feelings from rejection that was birthed in his life. Mirror punishment only allowed Jabez to see himself in the mirror that reflected his past failure but when he overcame his stronghold of self-feelings/rejection Jabez quit seeing himself in the past and began to see his self in the future. He saw a reflection of someone that is more than a conqueror!!!

Jabez discovered from the day he was born he was rejected and unwanted by his mother because she named him Jabez. In biblical days it was the father who took the responsibility in naming their children but 1 Chronicles 4:9 distinctly says the mother named him Jabez. The father must be missing out of his son's life therefore causing his mother to also struggling with the stronghold of self-feelings from the spirit of rejection. She in turn takes her hurt, pain, grief and anger out on her son and exposed his entire childhood to unnecessary drama called rejection because she didn't find happiness in her relationship.

She exposed her son to unhappiness but now like Jabez it is time for you to overcome the stronghold of self-feelings caused by rejection that someone else exposed you to which has caused much of your life from childhood to adulthood to be dysfunctional and broken. But Jabez cried out to God as he looked in the mirror to analyze and an examine himself and asked God to not only forgive him but to give him the power of forgiveness that he would forgive himself and everyone that has hurt him from birth to adulthood.

The Power of Forgiveness

Once you have the power of forgiveness you will never be hurt again. You may be shaken but you won't be hurt nor will you take things personal. Jabez realized the power of forgiveness required 4 things: 1st – that God may forgive him, 2nd – that he may forgive himself because he felt like all his life that he would never be accepted but rather rejected, 3rd – that he forgives those that had hurt him and 4th – he asked for the power of forgiveness to forgive those that he hurt.

> **MATTHEW 6:14-15 AMP**
> *14 "For if you FORGIVE people their trespasses [their reckless and willful sins, leaving them, letting them go, and giving up resentment], your heavenly Father will also FORGIVE you.*
> *15 But if you do not FORGIVE others their trespasses [their reckless and willful sins, leaving them, letting them go, and giving up resentment], neither will your Father FORGIVE you your trespasses."*

Jabez asked God for 4 things:

1. He prayed for prosperity and expansion to enlarge his territory. (To be stretched)
2. He prayed for POWER AND STRENGTH that God's hand of blessing would be upon him.
3. He prayed for protection that God would keep him from evil and from going backwards.
4. He prayed for a painless life to free him from sorrow, stress and worry. Like Jabez, Jacob also held onto God until God blessed him indeed which gave him title and ownership.

Now is the time to break the cycle of rejection that causes the cycle of pain. Jabez first had to be healed from the pain before he could be blessed. You must be healed from pain caused by the stronghold of self-feeling that comes from the spirit of rejection. You can't be blessed until you're healed first!!! Jabez asked God to heal him from his hurt and pain through the power of forgiveness which gives victory over the pain of rejection.

GENESIS 35:16-18 AMP

16 "And they journeyed from Bethel and had but a little way to go to Ephrath [Bethlehem] when Rachel suffered the pangs of childbirth and had hard labor.

17 When she was in hard labor, the midwife said to her, Do not be afraid; you shall have this son also.

18 And as her soul was departing, for she died, she called his name Ben-oni [son of my sorrow]; but his father called him Benjamin [son of the right hand]."

GENESIS 32:25-28 ERV

25 "When the man saw that he could not defeat Jacob, he touched Jacob's leg and put it out of joint.

26 Then the man said to Jacob, "Let me go. The sun is coming up." But Jacob said, "I will not let you go. You must bless me."

27 And the man said to him, "What is your name?" And Jacob said, "My name is Jacob."

28 Then the man said, "Your name will not be Jacob. Your name will now be Israel. I give you this name because you have fought with God and with men, and you have won."

JOSHUA 5:8 WEB

8 "When they were done circumcising the whole nation, they stayed in their places in the camp until they were (healed)."

You cannot move forward in life, start new relationships and mature in life for God's promotion until you are healed. Once you are healed from this stronghold you overcome and claim victory to get you to your next place and season in your life!

Chapter 8

The Stronghold of Self-Seeking

(Mirrors Don't Lie)

James 3:14-17 NKJV

14 But if you have bitter envy and self-seeking in your hearts, do not boast and lie against the truth. 15 This wisdom does not descend from above, but *is* earthly, sensual, demonic. 16 For where envy and self-seeking *exist,* confusion and every evil thing *are* there. 17 But the wisdom that is from above is first pure, then peaceable, gentle, willing to yield, full of mercy and good fruits, without partiality and without hypocrisy.

If you have gotten to the place that God cannot tell you anything then you have gotten to a place that you know too much. James 3:14-17 NKJV says "But if you have bitter envy and self-seeking in your hearts, do not boast and lie against the truth. 15 This wisdom does not descend from above, but *is* earthly, sensual, demonic. 16 For where envy and self-seeking *exist,* confusion and every evil thing *are* there.17 But the wisdom that is from above is first pure, then peaceable, gentle, willing to yield, full of mercy and good fruits, without partiality and without hypocrisy."

When a person has bitter jealousy they become crazy. They begin to brag and lie about the truth and when someone begins to brag that much then there has to be something they are trying to hide.

The stronghold of self-seeking is used by Satan to cause one to only see things from one's own perception. It was through the stronghold of deception that Satan used on Eve to deceive her into becoming self-seeking and believing what she was doing was right and pleasing to God. The Bible says in Genesis 3:2-5 "that she (Eve) saw that it was good for food." The stronghold of self-seeking caused Eve to be in bondage by seeking her own selfish desires while trying to be more and to be someone she wasn't. Anytime this spirit or stronghold of self-seeking attaches itself to your life it causes you to lose your identity. Eve was selfish and she wanted more and was in bondage to this stronghold of self-seeking so who was she jealous of? Adam? No, she wanted power, more than what she thought Adam had. "Never want to be more than the One that gave you life"

The definition of self-seeking is to be self-serving, self-interested, to have selfish-ambition or the act or practice of selfishly-advancing one's own selfish end out of self-reasoning; seeking only to further one's own interest for getting ahead in life by using any means necessary. Self-seeking births jealousy, envy, spitefulness, gossip, slander, betrayal, judgmental tendencies, suspicions of others as well as criticism of others. Un-Christ-like competition, cruelty, and arrogance cause an individual to become a compulsive liar.

In order to understand the impact of self-seeking we must see how self-seeking impacts the information received through our body. Our body uses our 5 senses to receive information through what we call the 5 gatekeepers. The Eye Gate is the keeper or guard of our vision, the Ear Gate guards sound, the Touch Gate guards feelings, the Nose Gate guards smell and the Mouth Gate guards communication. We also need to understand the soul of a man embodies three parts: the mind, will and emotions. Because the soul has a mind, it has a will and therefore it operates out of its emotions. The emotions operate out of what it sees, hears, touches, smells and taste which are our five senses. Our five senses lead us according to our feelings but what would happen if we begin to lose our senses? What would happen if we begin to lose our ability to see and therefore we lose our vision? What would happen if we lost our ability to hear sound? What if we lost the ability to touch, to have an awareness of how things feel or what if we lost our ability to smell or taste? What if we couldn't taste the difference between bitter and sweet in our food?

Aristotle is credited with first classifying the five senses touch, smell, taste, hear and see all of which are called sensory perception. Our sensory perception causes the senses to navigate our daily lives but as we get older our five senses get worse. So in reality the five senses that we trust in lose their strength, power and credibility. The more you trust in the flesh which are your five senses in time you'll discover the more your five senses will fail you. This failure of senses is why you can't trust in the flesh but you must trust in God. As life progresses we discover your "seeing" which gives you vision diminishes as your eyes become bad so you will need glasses. Your "hearing" becomes dull as you get older and then you need a hearing aid. Your "touch" loses its sense of feeling, your nose loses its ability to smell fragrances and your "mouth" loses its voice and gift whether it's for singing or speaking.

How do we compensate in life when we discover we have lost all sense of direction because what we counted on and have believed in has easily deceived us through the deception of information that the body receives from our soul. Many have been in bondage for trusting the ungodly soul-ties called the stronghold of self-seeking. This stronghold allowed the soul, the mind, will and emotions to lead them astray. If your mind is in a state of confusion it causes your will to make bad decisions that will cause your emotions to become unstable in what you see, hear, touch, smell and taste. If and when this happens it causes you to lose your equilibrium as well as focus, vision, and your sense of direction.

The stronghold of self-seeking is formed through a deception of demonic attacks on your gateways. Your gateways are gates or portals that the enemy uses for entrance or exit to import or export bad information as well as lies and deceit to cause you to trust more in your five senses and flesh than the Spirit of our faith.

The Symptoms and Signs of the Stronghold called Self-Seeking as a result of trusting in the five Senses or Gates of the flesh.

The first symptom of this stronghold is unnatural sicknesses caused through demonic attacks against an individual's physical and mental state of being that indicates spiritual warfare. A sign of this attack is you find yourself at a stand- still and confused about decisions in a place called the crossroads of life. Being stuck at a place in life that causes you to be at a stand-still or crossroads becomes the place of confusion for making decisions. Psalms 40:2 ISB says "He lifted me out of the slimy pit, out of the mud and mire; he set my feet on a rock and gave me a firm place to stand."

The second symptom an individual struggles with is self-addiction such as pornography and it causes an individual to seek pleasure with their own sexual desires. Other addictive substances that individuals use to self-medicate are alcohol, illegal drugs and even prescription drugs. The prescription drugs were originally given to the individual by the doctor to numb the physical pain or to cope with mental stress, depression and oppression but now they are used to shut themselves off from the world and life.

The side effects a self-seeker may have are self-injurious behaviors such as over-medicating, isolating, black-out spells, forgetfulness, and being tempted by things that have never tempted them before as this stronghold attracts them to new heights of temptation. The antidotes and answers to be delivered healed and set free from this self-seeking stronghold is found in 2 Corinthians 5:7 NKJV, "For we walk by faith, not by sight."

The Greek meaning for sight is not by appearance, not by the evidence of what we see but by the evidence of what we believe which are the things not seen (the invisible world). The five senses of the flesh help you to see and trust in the visible world that's carnal and fleshly but faith helps you to see in the invisible world according to Hebrews 11:1 NKJV which says, "Now faith is the substance of things hoped for, the evidence of things not seen."

Faith senses verses five senses

The first faith sensors level is called confession, the spiritual mouth gate.

Romans 10:9 NKJV
"that if you confess with your mouth the Lord Jesus and believe in your heart that God has raised Him from the dead, you will be saved."

Psalms 34:8 NKJV *says "oh, taste (mouth gate) and see that the Lord is good; blessed is the man who trusts in Him!"*

The second faith sensors level is the spiritual hearing gate. The spiritual hearing gate gives us in-depth sensitivity to hear God with spiritual k-9 senses.

Romans 8:14 NKJV

"For as many as are led by the Spirit of God, these are sons of God"

Romans 10:17 NKJV

"So then faith comes by hearing and hearing by the word of God."

The third faith sensors level is the spiritual eye, the sight gate. Faith helps you to see with clarity. Faith gives you 20/20 vision to see the invisible world.

2 Corinthians 5:7 NKJV
"For we walk by faith, not by sight"

2 KINGS 6:16-17 NKJV
16 "So he answered, "Do not fear, for those who are with us are more than those who are with them." And Elisha (through faith saw an invisible world) prayed, and said, "Lord, I pray, open his eyes that he may see." Then the Lord opened the eyes of the young man, and he SAW. And behold, the mountain was full of horses and chariots of fire all around Elisha."

MARK 8:22-25 ERV
"Jesus and his followers came to Bethsaida. Some people brought a blind man to him and begged him to touch the man. 23 So Jesus held the blind man's hand and led him out of the village. Then he spit on the man's EYES. He laid his hands on him and asked, "Can you SEE now?"24 The man LOOKED up and said,

"Yes, I SEE people. They LOOK like trees walking around."
25 Again Jesus laid his hands on the man's eyes, and the man opened them wide. His eyes were healed, and he was able to SEE everything clearly."

The fourth faith sensors level is called smell (spiritual nose/smell gate). Faith causes us to sense or smell through what is called discernment to reach the throne room and the heart of God. Smelling is a sense of observation. The word sense in the Hebrew means Shabach which means to sense triumph and victory without seeing it.

Mark 10:46-51 talks about blind Bartimaeus. He was blind and couldn't see but he had faith that Jesus was coming through Jericho which means he couldn't see Jesus but he sensed Jesus through his faith sensors until his healing and deliverance was manifested. So he begins to shout with a voice of triumph because he claimed his victory through faith.

PSALMS 47:1 NKJV
"1 Oh, clap your hands, all you peoples! Shout to God with the voice of triumph!"

EPHESIANS 5:2 WEB
2 "Walk in love, even as Christ also loved you, and gave himself up for us, an offering and a sacrifice to God for a SWEET-SMELLING FRAGRANCE."

GENESIS 2:7 ERV
7 "Then the Lord God took dust from the ground and made a man. He breathed the breath of life into the man's NOSE, and the man became a living thing."

God placed faith in the man by trusting man with his own dominion and authority over the earth.

JOHN 12:3 ERV
3 "Mary brought in a pint of expensive perfume made of pure nard. She poured the perfume on Jesus' feet. Then she wiped his

feet with her hair. And the sweet SMELL from the perfume filled the whole house."

Her faith changed the atmosphere from a bad odor to the sweet smell of perfume. (Are you chosen to change the atmosphere?) The fifth level of faith sensors is called touch or spiritual touch gate.

> **LUKE 8:45-48 NKJV**
>
> *"And Jesus said, "Who touched Me?" When all denied it, Peter and those with him said, "Master, the multitudes throng and press You, and You say, "Who touched Me? But Jesus said, "Somebody touched Me, for I perceived power going out from Me." 47 Now when the woman saw that she was not hidden, she came trembling; and falling down before Him, she declared to Him in the presence of all the people the reason she had TOUCHED Him and how she was healed immediately. And He said to her, "Daughter, be of good cheer YOUR FAITH HAS MADE YOU WELL. Go in peace."*
>
> **MATTHEW 18:19 KJV**
>
> *"Again I say unto you, That if two of you shall agree on earth as TOUCHING anything that they shall ask, it shall be done for them of my Father which is in heaven."*

Breaking the demonic stronghold of self-seeking and all of its symptoms, signs and side effects.

MARK 5:25-28 MSG talks about "A woman who had suffered a condition of hemorrhaging for twelve years—a long succession of physicians had treated her, and treated her badly, taking all her money and leaving her worse off than before—had heard about Jesus. She slipped in from behind and TOUCHED his robe. She was thinking to herself, "If I can put a finger on his robe, I can get well.

The 31 Self-Strongholds

The woman with the issue of blood for 12 years struggled with the stronghold of self-seeking and was in bondage because she trusted in her five senses of the flesh. She trusted in man (doctor) (v. 26) and in her money because the Bible says, she spent all of her money and instead of getting better she grew worse.

According to verse 27, when she stopped trusting in her five senses and the flesh it says she heard about Jesus, and that He was passing through the city. After 12 years, this woman quit trusting in the flesh but used her faith to walk behind Jesus and touch Him. As she touched in faith she believed that if she touched the hem of His garment she would be:

1. Healed from 12 years of sickness that had attacked her body with pain and suffering.

2. Healed in relationships because of her sickness according to biblical Laws, this woman was ceremonially unclean so she couldn't be in a social relationship with a man.

3. Financially healed after this sickness. This sickness had caused her to lose financially, leaving her broke because she had spent all that she had on doctors and medicine. Now she could regain financial stability.

4. Restored to a place of worship. Biblical Law says anyone with this woman's condition of hemorrhaging could not take part in praise and worship within the temple.

So for 12 years this woman was in bondage to this stronghold of self-seeking and operated in the flesh of her five senses. After 12 years she overcame the symptoms, signs and side effects. She found the antidote and the answer called faith. She used her faith to step out while she was friendless, sick, single, broken and without any money and touched Jesus with the touch of faith by using her touch gate and this act of faith immediately changed her life.

HEBREWS 11:1 NKJV

"Now faith is the substance of things hoped for, the evidence of things not seen."

MATTHEW 18:19 KJV

"Again I say unto you, That if two of you shall agree on earth as touching anything that they shall ask, it shall be done for them of my Father which is in heaven."

Chapter 9

The Stronghold of Self-Examination

(Spiritual Check-up & Self Evaluation)

2 Corinthians 13:5-8 AMP (Also reference MSG version)
⁵ Test and evaluate yourselves to see whether you are in the faith and living your lives as [committed] believers. Examine yourselves [not me]! Or do you not recognize this about yourselves [by an ongoing experience] that Jesus Christ is in you—unless indeed you fail the test and are rejected as counterfeit? ⁶ But I hope you will acknowledge that we do not fail the test nor are we to be rejected. ⁷ But I pray to God that you may do nothing wrong. Not so that we [and our teaching] may appear to be approved, but that you may continue doing what is right, even though we [by comparison] may seem to have failed. ⁸ For we can do nothing against the truth, but only for the truth [and the gospel—the good news of salvation].

William Shakespeare is quoted and known for saying "to thine own self be true," don't default in this season or look for the fault of others. Examine yourself be sensitive to the Holy Spirit and make sure your calling doesn't lose purpose.

Satan uses the stronghold called self-examination to try to stop us from doing an inspection and an inventory on ourselves through deception. He causes us to judge someone else's life instead of doing an examination on ourselves and our own life. A self-examination consist of closely analyzing or evaluate your attitude, behavior, and life to determine where you are in this place, time and season of your life and to determine where God is calling you to in your new assignment. Doing a self-examination involves studying your own motives and to assess your thoughts and how they perceive someone else versus how they see themselves.

If you struggle with this stronghold you hide or conceal your own sin, guilt and wrong doing but judge others for their wrong doings. To be examined means to be tested or proven by doing a self-assessment and a self-evaluation but the stronghold of self-examination causes an individual to begin to find fault in everyone else when things go wrong rather than to see their own hidden fault, guilt or wrong doing. They are afraid to confront their own problems and make decisions because of so much self-doubt. They appear to always second guess themselves and everyone else when it's time to make choices and decisions that concern their future.

Matthew 7:1-5 ERV

1 "Don't judge others, and God will not judge you. 2 If you judge others, you will be judged the same way you judge them. God will treat you the same way you treat others.
3 "Why do you notice the small piece of dust that is in your friend's eye, but you don't notice the big piece of wood that is in your own? 4 Why do you say to your friend, 'Let me take that piece of dust out of your eye'? Look at yourself first! You still have that   big piece of wood in your own eye. 5 You are a hypocrite! First, take the wood out of your own eye. Then you will see clearly to get the dust out of your friend's eye."

Galatians 6:1-3 KJV
"Brethren, if a man be overtaken in a fault, ye which are spiritual, restore such a one in the spirit of meekness; considering thyself, lest though also be tempted. Bear ye one another's burdens, and so fulfill the law of Christ. For if a man thinks himself to be something when he is nothing he deceiveth himself."

The 31 Self-Strongholds

What this passage of scripture is saying is if a fellow man or woman has been taken over in a fault, the wrong has overtaken him or her and they cannot get themselves out of it or they have become prisoner to the fault and they are not only in fault but they have defaulted and they don't know how to get back to the promise, the spiritual mature should restore he or she back. They have broken the promissory agreement and the only way for them to come back into covenant is to be restored by a person of promise who is in covenant and who has the ability to restore them. Someone who is spiritual which in this text is someone that is mature must restore them to the covenant.

Once you have broken the promissory you are no longer in fault but default and you cannot restore yourself because you don't see what you have done. You have to own up to what it is that you have done. Examine yourself and ask someone that is spiritually mature who will hold you accountable in your wrong doing instead of someone else that is in fault. Those that are mature must understand that you are not going to judge them, tell them that they are going to hell or try to restore with the law but in the Spirit of meekness, humility, gentleness and grace.

Although you may believe you are mature be sure that you do not go and attempt to restore anyone because of your opinion of who you are but only go if you've been sent by God. You need to consider thyself and If you are not spiritually mature to handle what is happening don't go because that same spirit will come upon and overtake you.

The stronghold of self-examination causes an individual to begin developing low self-esteem and insecurities when they've once had high self-esteem and confidence. A person starts to have low self-esteem when they lose faith and begin to put their trust in their flesh or in man. When the stronghold of self-examination and self-doubt attacks your life it causes you to doubt everything you are and everything you are trying to be and do that is good and fulfilling. You now begin to question and doubt your identity, your call, your assignment in life and your relationships as well as your ministry. As this stronghold attacks you grow weary in well doing and in all the good things you do and have ever done making you doubtful of all your sacrifices, all of the time that you have ever sowed or all the times you've ever blessed anybody. This stronghold of self-doubt created from the stronghold of self-examination begins to make you feel like everybody is out to get you, take advantage and or take you for granted. It also causes you not to see your faults but find fault in everything and everybody else.

Paul wrote to the church of the Galatians because they began to come under the bondage of the stronghold called self-examination. They began to form self-doubt in their relationship with God, in their ministry, in the church and within themselves as questioned whether or not all the sacrifices they had made was all for nothing. All these thoughts came because they saw themselves as being more because of all that they had been given and had done for the Kingdom of God, the church, as well as God and others. The enemy crept into the church of Galatia and began sowing seeds of discord and taking advantage of the vulnerabilities and fragilities of the people of God because they felt as if their life was not progressing nor was it getting any better. The enemy's plan was and is to distract the people of God and cause them to miss another season just when God is ready to bless them all for their sacrifices. Keep in mind you will win if you don't quit.

In Galatians 3:1 AMP Paul says to the Galatians, "O you poor and silly and thoughtless and unreflecting and senseless Galatians! Who has fascinated or bewitched or casted a spell over you, unto whom - right before your very eyes - Jesus Christ (the Messiah) was openly and graphically set forth and portrayed as crucified?" Who's possessing your body or your thoughts? Have you said to yourself, "I don't even know who I am and or what I am supposed to be doing?" You look in the mirror you see nothing but if you examine the negative at least it will reflect what you need to work on and afterwards will begin to reflect the positive. Who has bewitched you to think that what you know is real because you witnessed it, is not who Jesus the Christ is? The church of Galatia had gotten caught up because they felt like all that they had done was in vain and it caused them to grow weary in well doing. If you're experiencing these symptoms you need to get up and tell God, I won't give up now.

Lamentations 3:40 EXB

"Let us examine [check] and see [investigate] what we have done [our ways] and then return to the Lord [repent]"

You are in this predicament because of what you have done. Check, examine and investigate what you have done and own it because you can't get better or repent until you own up to what you have done. Once you repent, you will turn away from what it is that you are doing and return.

Psalms 26:2 NLT

"Put me on trial, Lord, and cross examine me. Test my motives and my heart."

Allow God to put you on the stand. The Galatians were like Thomas in John 20:27 ERV. How could Thomas doubt when he had walked with Jesus, who had told him of all that would be?

The symptoms, signs and side effects of the stronghold called self-examination.

The stronghold of self-doubt causes an individual to see life in a negative way; they become self-destructive and unstable. They begin doubting who they are, what they are called to do and what they are becoming. Every time they see themselves advancing in life or something good begins to happen for them they begin to question themselves and the good that is happening for them. This stronghold of self-doubt has caused them to miss another season. Can you afford to lose another season caused by the stronghold of self-examination and the stronghold of self-doubt?

The stronghold of self-examination that forms from self-doubt has side effects such as mental illness which is a medical condition that disrupts a person's thinking, feeling, mood, ability to relate to others; and daily functions. This side effect causes self-pity, a victim mentality, and indecision. It forms ungodly soul – ties and causes an individual to become very argumentative as well as a "know it all." Another side effect of this stronghold is that it causes an individual to become resentful and to create distance between those that hold them accountable.

The signs of the side effects of this stronghold is a person that is very judgmental, negative, stubborn, establishes patterns of disobedience, become rebellious against authority and they refuse to be disciplined. The side effects of this stronghold makes an individual live in self-denial and self -defense (very defensive), be opinionated and very critical and still refuse to examine or to do an inventory on themselves because they believe they are always right and everyone else is always wrong.

The word doubt in the Greek means DIAKRINO which means to condemn, to cancel, to terminate, to discriminate, to separate, and to bring confusion. The legal business terminology for DIAKRINO is to put a lien on the property or something of value of yours because of your doubt.

> **Matthew 14:28-31 NKJV**
> *"And Peter answered Him and said, "Lord, if it is You, command me to come to You on the water." So He said, "Come," And when Peter had come down out of the boat, he walked on the water to go to Jesus. But when he saw that the wind was boisterous, he was afraid; and beginning to sink he cried out, saying, "Lord, save me!" And immediately Jesus stretched out His hand and caught him, and said to him, "O you of little faith, why did you doubt?"*

Jesus had commissioned His disciples to cross over to the other side of the sea because He had given them a new assignment. The Bible says while they were crossing over to the other side a storm came and began to not only shake the boat that they were on but it also shook their faith causing them to begin to doubt and to question the assignment which Jesus had just given them to fulfill. The scripture tells us they were all so afraid and doubtful that they became more focused on their storm than their assignment. The word also states that Jesus came walking on the water and when Peter saw Him, he asked for permission to walk on the water. Peter stepped out of the natural into the Supernatural by using his faith to believe God and he did the impossible. Luke 18:27 declares "What is impossible with man is possible with God."

This stronghold is one of only a few that is a spiritually demonic force that attacks believers while they are on the move. For example; the Galatians had sacrificed, done well and were ready to be blessed when they were attacked by this stronghold. By faith Peter successfully walked on the water but when he doubted he began to sink. The Bible says he saw the wind (storm) and began to sink. This simply means the storm (issues/concerns/doubt) began to form a stronghold of self-examination or self-doubt and immediately attacked the life of Peter and Jesus immediately stretched out His hand. If Jesus gives you permission to do anything you can do it, even when you're failing. Even when we are weak we are strong because in our weakness we are strong through Him. When we admit what we are weak at. It's only through self-examination that we can admit where we are weak and then Jesus can say to us, I got you.

Jesus had sent the disciples to the other side for a new assignment and anytime you get new blessings or ask for elevation you need to know what comes with it. You will need more faith the closer you get to Jesus when you are doing more and helping others, you always get hit. The storm doesn't come until you move. If you want things to go easy sit down and stop moving but if you want more God, you will get hit.

Self-doubt also called DIAKRINO crept (surprised, caught unaware) in and caused a stop payment on Peter's progress toward success. How? He gave it a ride. This spiritually demonic stronghold attached itself to you in a storm and you gave it a ride. You took it where it could not have ever gone on its own. You gave it a pass and have now transported spiritually demonic migrants to your life. You have allowed things to creep in unaware. You did not watch out for the creeping things, and the moment you operated in that stronghold of self-doubt, you canceled out your progress. Peter began to sink because he started to think of what he was doing, not what Jesus was doing.

The Hebrew word ANAKRINO means to examine, to investigate and to be given another chance and a new opportunity. ANAKRINO cancels DIAKRINO. ANAKRINO means you've been given another opportunity to re-take the test that you previously failed, hence you've been given a make-up test. God is saying to us in this season in spite of DIAKRINO, our doubt that caused us to lose faith, He is giving us another chance to succeed at what we previously failed. Breaking and overcoming the stronghold of self-examination that has caused us to doubt God, ourselves and everyone that has ever played a part in our lives or season and helped us to advance along the way, is the only way to this a new opportunity. It is now time to take advantage of the opportunity and learn from our failures because of DIAKRINO and not fail in ANAKRINO. Through this new opportunity that God has given you for a make-up test, you can be promoted to the next level, the next assignment, and in the place of your new purpose but this time you must complete, finish and become totally victorious. Never again can you doubt what God has said, called, assigned, anointed and or blessed you to do! In spite of previous failures and doubts, this time we are coming out as well as going in totally victorious! (ANAKRINO)

Chapter 10

The Stronghold of Self-Hate

(Don't Player Hate)

Ephesians 4:30 – 32 AMP (Also reference the GW translation)
30 And do not grieve the Holy Spirit of God [but seek to please Him], by whom you were sealed and marked [branded as God's own] for the day of redemption [the final deliverance from the consequences of sin]. 31 Let all bitterness and wrath and anger and clamor [perpetual animosity, resentment, strife, fault-finding] and slander be put away from you, along with every kind of malice [all spitefulness, verbal abuse, malevolence]. 32 Be kind and helpful to one another, tender-hearted [compassionate, understanding], forgiving one another [readily and freely], just as God in Christ also forgave [c]you.

Satan uses the stronghold called self-hate to cause a person to have extreme dislike or hatred for them self. The stronghold of self-hate targets a person who has been neglected, rejected, betrayed, given up for adoption or to someone else to take care of them as a child, and or that grew up in a hostile environment.

Someone who has suffered physically, mentally and spiritually because of an abusive relationship whose trust and love has been damaged from patterns or feelings of unworthiness. These feelings cause them to finds ways to hide their real feelings or emotions. This stronghold attacks a person after it studies their feelings, behaviors, habits and mindset. The repeated patterns and/or habits are behaviors that develop addictions and struggles which allow the enemy to take advantage of a person's vulnerability and fragilities. The stronghold causes an individual to become distracted by their pain, hurt and ultimately they will try to sabotage their own success. Self-hate afflicts and inflicts to cause an individual's downfall so you must stop being angry and mad at yourself and learn how to forgive yourself.

Self-hatred is synonymous with shame resulting from a strong dislike of yourself and your actions. It is a painful emotion resulting from a perceived or real awareness of your inability to suppress guilt. This stronghold creates three types of patterns; predictability, suppression and false feelings.

Predictability means to predict in advance or to foresee something, to anticipate one's actions by making the same decisions through the spirit of familiarity of your past. The enemy and his demonic forces keep records of your past and present decisions and studies your habits or patterns so periodically we need to switch up what we're doing and how we do it.

Suppression is to stop, bind and tie up, to keep something a secret or to hide something from yourself by concealing the truth. This pattern is a survival mechanism that causes one to suppress their true emotions. The stronghold's assignment is to birth self-hate by keeping your mind from knowing what your unconscious mind is thinking and feeling. The goal of this stronghold is to manipulate your mind and emotions causing the Holy Spirit to become vexed because you cannot hear truth. It is your unconscious mind that deals with your conviction(s) which help you to forgive and to apologize for your wrongness.

Self-hatred holds your thinking and ability to believe that all hope is gone causing your hope and trust in God to become a prisoner and hostage to its demonic force. Your anger, pain and self-hate is used by this stronghold to cause you to believe that you're unworthy and God will never forgive you. It convinces you that nothing good will ever happen for you because of what you have done and what has happened in your life. Now guilt and shame have destroyed your confidence in yourself, your trust in God and everyone that you've ever trusted.

The third type of pattern is false feelings. This pattern causes a person to develop false emotions by deceiving a person of their true feelings of hurt, brokenness, anger and rejection. This pattern overrides your feelings and emotions by creating false feelings through lies and deception. It keeps you from confronting the real issues of your struggle, hurt and pain. False feelings convince you that you are alright when in reality you are not. You put on a mask to disguise the exterior when really on the inside you're about to explode. You feel like you're losing it, falling apart and you're confused. This false feeling convinced you that it will go away or work itself out, but it doesn't. These feelings are similar to what Jacob felt and experienced until he wrestled with God.

The stronghold of self-hate targets youth at an early age through victimizations of child abuse, mental, verbal and sexual abuse such as molestation and statutory rape. Such abuse causes a child to grow up hating themselves with the spirit of self-hate and as they grow older and become an adult they struggle with three factors; shame, fear and control (S.F.C.). They were victims or victimized by some perpetrator, pedophile, family member, babysitter, neighbor, teacher, preacher or leader which caused self-hate to take control of their lives. Because they were violated by someone they trusted. As an adult the stronghold of self-hate has caused their life to detour from the path of their destiny. Now, this individual has grown up and become the same thing they hated because of shame, fear and control (S.F.C.).

The first factor is called shame and means to have a sense of being hopelessly flawed, unworthy, unclean or dirty. Shame leads a person to feel different and less valuable than other individuals. Shame is a painful feeling that is mixed with regret, self-hate and dishonor. It causes a person to begin to believe that they are a bad person and God must hate them. Their belief in the shame causes them to say these things to themselves such as, Is there something wrong with me? What have I done so wrong that God would allow this to happen to me? Why me? Why did this happen to me? They begin to feel like God and life are out to get them and that there's a curse on their life and they'll never catch a break. The factor, called shame, births guilt and causes you to feel like, what happened to you in your childhood, being violated was your fault. It causes you to grow up feeling shame and guilt because shame births guilt.

The second factor called fear torments you, causes you to begin hurting yourself, feeling like your life has ended and is over. Fear says to an individual, what would happen if someone finds out what has happened to you? Fear says to an individual, if someone does find out that you were raped, molested or abused they will not like you or not understand you because of the shame and guilt you feel from being violated. These factors have now caused you to live in fear and torment and instead of feeling like the victim, fear causes you to feel like it was your fault. So now you feel like you must keep everything that has ever gone wrong to yourself. You feel as if you can't trust anyone or tell anybody. The fear factor births the third factor called control and aborts life. Shame births guilt, guilt births fear, fear births control and control aborts life.

The third factor called control can be compared to birth control pills which can prevent pregnancies that produces life. It is similar to how control stops you from producing what God has promised you for your life. The ultimate plan of the stronghold called self-hate is to create shame, fear, and control. Birth control stops a person from producing a life of fulfillment, purpose, abundance, and a life of success by causing an individual to continue to live their past life of wrong decisions, mistakes, failures and what someone whom they trusted and loved has done to betray them. After being dropped, betrayed, cheated on, abused, sexually molested, raped and sexually assaulted their love has turned to hate. Now they not only hate the people that they once loved and trusted but they hate themselves as much if not more.

The stronghold of self-hate will control how you live, what you do, and what you think. It will also control the power to forgive and the ability to love again. If an individual refuses to be healed from brokenness because of the control factor it will cause them to feed on their hate towards everyone including themselves. You will become numb and you won't want to feel anything for anyone. Your mind set is not to let anyone ever hurt you again. The stronghold of self-hate is a spiritual attack and it causes a person to change their true identity and to begin living a false identity which causes a person to start being someone they were not destined to be.

2 Samuel 4:4 ERV
"Saul's son Jonathan had a son named Mephibosheth. He was five years old when the news came from Jezreel that Saul and Jonathan had been killed. The woman who cared for

Mephibosheth picked him up and ran away. But while running away, she dropped the boy, and he became crippled in both feet."

2 SAMUEL 9:8 GWT
"Mephibosheth bowed down again and answered, "Who am I that you would look at a DEAD DOG like me?" (SELF – HATE) Mephibosheth's name means to be SHAMED, crippled, or broken, to be exterminated and to be shattered.

Mephibosheth said everyone that I've ever trusted had either died on me, dropped me, betrayed me or left me. That's why my name is Mephibosheth and because my life is broken, crippled and now shattered I struggle with the stronghold of self-hate from which comes shame, fear and control.

He was dropped by someone he trusted when he was 5 years old. He was broken and cripple from childhood to adulthood which caused Mephibosheth to struggle with self-hate that changed his identity as well as destiny.

Mephibosheth was the son of Jonathan who was a prince. His grandfather Saul was a king which makes Mephibosheth part of a royal family, a king's descendent but because he was dropped it changed who he was and what he would become. The stronghold of self-hate made Mephibosheth feel unworthy, without value and unappreciated but thank God for re-founding favor because in 2 Samuel 9:8 King David asked, "is there anyone remaining or still alive that's a part of Jonathan and Saul's family?"

Side effects of the stronghold of self-hate

The side effects of this stronghold are anxiety, attacks, intimidation, mistrust, struggles with the failure syndrome, rejection, violence, anger, tantrums, abuse, sexual inadequacy, and superstition. A person dealing with this stronghold entertains demonic activities such as Ouija boards and astrology such as horoscopes and zodiac signs. The person that struggles with self-hate can also be a saved individual that has backslidden and began experiencing the loss of their gifts and the anointing of God that's upon their life. They begin pleasing themselves rather than pleasing God and lose focus on the assignment that was given to them by God. The side effects can cause you to lose focus of your calling and ministry. What you successfully did at one time you now begin to fail at. Judges 16:20 tells of Samson's struggle with the stronghold of self-hate which caused him to lose his gift, his anointing of strength and his vision. The Bible says that he went to shake himself as he had done many times before to use his gift and strength and discovered that God was not there. No gift, no anointing, no power and without vision we perish!

> **RUTH 1:20 GNT**
> *"Don't call me Naomi," she responded. "Instead, call me Mara, for the Almighty has made life very bitter for me."*

The Bible says there was a woman named Naomi that struggled with the stronghold of self-hate. She went 10 years, experiencing the worst times of her life. She had lost her husband, her two sons, her house, her property and her friends. But the worst thing she experienced in those 10 years was that she lost her relationship with God. She found herself in a 10 year cycle and her experience was if anything could go wrong it went wrong. The stronghold of self-hate caused Naomi to change her name to Mara, but Naomi's name means beautiful, pleasant, delight, happy and love. She changed her name to Mara which means bitter, hateful, broken, rejected and shame. So Naomi, a God-fearing woman who 10 years prior loved God, experienced 10 years of struggle, hurt, pain and bitterness that left her broken. She began to hate who she was so much so that she would change her name. Naomi was about to fulfill her 10 year cycle which represent her Chronos, which represents a circle or cycle of failure that she struggled with in time. But now, 10 years later, she is transcending from Chronos to Kairos which means as she was entering back into Bethlehem her 10 year cycle ended, but she could not enter back into Bethlehem with this stronghold of self-hate. She must come back, not as Mara, the bitter or hated, but as Naomi, beautiful and loved because if she enters in as Mara she'll be stuck in another cycled called Chronos. If she comes back as Naomi in the Kairos it will mean that she has broken her 10 year cycle.

Thank God for Ruth, her daughter-in-law who becomes the designated driver for this bitter, broken, hateful and hated woman. Ruth ministers deliverance, healing and renewed strength back into Naomi and this helps break the 10 year cycle. Naomi now comes back into her new season, breaks the cycle and get out of the Chronos. For 10 years she was stuck in time, her Chronos, but now she steps into her Kairos which manifested at the right time, God's time, the opportune time, the prophetic time, the redeeming time and her season.

Ephesians 5:15 WEB says "...redeeming the time, because the days are evil." This means God is redeeming the time that you have lost and you are accumulating compensation for the pain, suffering and lost, and He will pay you for every day you've suffered and lost.

Chapter 11

The Stronghold of Self-Afflictions

Job 36:8-14 AMP
"And if they are bound in bonds [of adversity],
And held by cords of affliction,
⁹Then He declares to them [the true character of] their deeds
And their transgressions, that they have acted arrogantly [with
presumption and notions of self-sufficiency].
¹⁰"He opens their ears to instruction and discipline,
And commands that they return from evil.
¹¹"If they hear and serve Him, They will end their days in
prosperity And their years in pleasantness and joy.
¹²"But if they do not hear and obey, they will die by the sword [of
God's destructive judgments] And they will die [in ignorance]
without [true] knowledge.
¹³"But the godless in heart store up anger [at the divine
discipline]; They do not cry [to Him] for help when He binds them
[with cords of affliction].
¹⁴"They die in youth, And their life ends among the [a]cult
prostitutes.

Satan by deception uses the stronghold called self-affliction to cause an individual to commit self-harm or self-injury. The stronghold of self-affliction comes from the word afflict which means to cause pain or suffering, to stir up trouble, to torment, the sense of being rejected or humiliated, to be harassed, to be knocked down, to be weakened, to be struck, to become crippled, dysfunctional or paralyzed; in one's thinking. They start off by spiritually injecting what is called a spiritual self-poison which is defined as intentionally injecting injury or afflicting an individual's spiritual mind by causing self-poisoning. Self-poison will cause a person to develop a broken, bitter and contaminated spirit.

After the enemy causes a person to self-poison themselves within their spirit, the first thing Satan does to cause self-harm is to attack an individual's spiritual capacity. Secondly, he starts harming their mental mind (soul) by causing the soul to open up and become attracted to ungodly soul-ties. Thirdly, he self-harms through self-injury to the physical being of a person. During this time you will discover they are letting their exterior or physical appearance go down.

For example, the way they take care of themselves or the way they dress. They quit taking care of their hair because they don't care how it looks. They quit taking care of their body. They stop keeping themselves clean and fresh and their hygiene produces a bad odor. They begin to neglect their house by not cleaning it and taking care of all the responsibilities that come with a house. Neglecting how they look, how they act, and how they live is why they begin to look at their life as a liability and no longer an asset.

The stronghold of self-affliction causes an individual to fall into a deep depression, a state of confusion and to begin giving up on life and everybody that they care about.

The stronghold of self-affliction or self-harm deteriorates a person's abilities to spiritually, mentally and physically cope with problems. This stronghold distracts you from your life and releases emotional pain that convinces you that causing self-injury, destroying everything and everybody that has ever hurt you or disliked you, getting more attention by throwing a tantrum and being completely out of control will make you feel better.

Actions of this nature cause you to have what are called a spiritual, mental and physical black-out in which you literally lose complete control. This demonic spirit of affliction takes over and begins to control what you say, what you do, and how you do it.

The symptoms, signs and side effects of Self-Affliction

The self-affliction symptoms, signs and side effects are borderline personality disorders which also includes suffering from depression, anxiety disorders, substance abuse, eating disorders, post – traumatic stress disorder as well as experiencing bouts of low self-esteem which causes emotional lapses, dizziness and also black – out spells with a loss of certain memories of what happened during the day. The stronghold of self-affliction causes individuals to become addicted to antidepressants, experience rages of violence which cause them to do things or contemplate doing something that will cause injury. Examples of these types of self-affliction are cutting themselves, beating their head against something, shattering glass or hitting a wall with their hand or fist and becoming uncontrollable, abusively hitting innocent, defenseless people all out of rage. They find themselves so out of control that they don't recognize the degree of harm or damage they have done until it's all over.

Self-harm is the most common affliction that we begin to witness. We see the development of this stronghold in adolescents and young adults usually first appearing between the ages of 12 - 24 years old because they have allowed a hidden rage to be so suppressed inside of them due to the things happening to them privately. There are many forms of abuse that will cause this affliction such as child abuse, bullying, neglect, rejection or seeing their parents being abused, cheated on, violated, a death that they couldn't move past or a sickness that may have lingered. These violations cause them to be on the verge of giving up on life and can occur within their homes, schools, churches, community, etc. Any form of abuse whether it be sexual or not will be the root cause of the stronghold of self-affliction that will control and dominate their lives.

3 Types of Afflictions:

1. PHYSICAL AFFLICTION - 2 CORINTHIANS 12:7 - A thorn in the flesh

2. MENTAL AFFLICTION - ROMANS 12:1 - Renewing of the mind

3. SPIRITUAL AFFLICTION - PROVERBS 6:16-19 - The 6 things the Lord hates and the 7th is an abomination to Him.

The 31 Self-Strongholds

PHYSICAL AFFLICTIONS

Physical afflictions deal with self-injury which means to intentionally cause direct injury to one's self by deliberately afflicting one's body with massive pain and hurt. It is when an individual becomes self – abusive because of a deep dark demonic influence whose primary goal is to cause that individual to either completely harm themselves through suicidal thoughts, a suicide attempt or to succeed in suicide.

The stronghold of self-affliction uses its demonic influence to cause an individual to also hurt somebody else by using abusive force to afflict and torment them physically through brutality, torture, and terror to the point of completely demolishing themselves or someone else to the point of eventually killing a person because of the stronghold of self-hate that has partnered with this stronghold of self-affliction.

2 CORINTHIANS 12:7-10 NKJV
[7] "And lest I should be exalted above measure by the abundance of the revelations, a thorn in the flesh was given to me, a messenger of Satan to buffet me, lest I be exalted above measure.
[8] Concerning this thing I pleaded with the Lord three times that it might depart from me.
[9] And He said to me, "My grace is sufficient for you, for My strength is made perfect in weakness." Therefore most gladly I will rather boast in my infirmities, that the power of Christ may rest upon me.
[10] Therefore I take pleasure in infirmities, in reproaches, in needs, in persecutions, in distresses, for Christ's sake. For when I am weak, then I am strong."

PSALMS 39:10 NKJV
[10] " Remove Your plague from me; I am consumed by the blow of Your hand."

PSALMS 69:29 NKJV

29 " But I am poor and sorrowful; Let Your salvation, O God, set me up on high."

MENTAL AFFLICTION

Mental affliction deals with the soul being seduced by ungodly attractions and ungodly soul–ties. Ungodly soul–ties are ungodly soul connections between two people who have been mentally, physically and spiritually intimate with each other or who have had an intense emotional or mental association or relationship. Such a connection is considered to be unhealthy and destructive and causes one's soul and mental being to be tied together in an ungodly attraction. The attraction produces spiritual perversion which means it is a corrupt, unnatural, abnormal, unhealthy, evil, wicked, bad and wrong connection.

A person begins to be attracted to ungodly soul–ties because of mental afflictions that produce the struggles of perverted tendencies such as masturbation which simply means the act of a person seducing themselves by looking at perverted magazines, watching porn videos, chatting and watching the internet for enticement and or anything that can lure you out and expose your soul and begins to entertain your soul with exotic entertainment.

1 THESSALONIANS 4:3-5 AMP

3 "For this is the will of God, that you should be consecrated (separated and set apart for pure and holy living): that you should abstain and shrink from all sexual vice,
4 That each one of you should know how to possess (control, manage) his own body in consecration (purity, separated from things profane) and honor,
5 Not [to be used] in the passion of lust like the heathen, who are ignorant of the true God and have no knowledge of His will,"

GALATIANS 5:16 AMP

16 "But I say, walk and live [habitually] in the [Holy] Spirit [responsive to and controlled and guided by the Spirit]; then you will certainly not gratify the cravings and desires of the flesh (of human nature without God)."

GENESIS 38:8-10 AMP
8 " Then Judah told Onan, Marry your brother's widow; live with her and raise offspring for your brother.
9 But Onan knew that the family would not be his, so when he cohabited with his brother's widow, he prevented conception, lest he should raise up a child for his brother.
10 And the thing which he did displeased the Lord; therefore He slew him also."

ROMANS 12:2 NKJV
2 "And do not be conformed to this world, but be transformed by the renewing of your mind, that you may prove what is that good and acceptable and perfect will of God."

2 TIMOTHY 1:7 NKJV
7 "For God has not given us a spirit of fear, but of power and of love and of a sound mind."

PSALMS 25:17 NKJV
17 "The troubles of my heart have enlarged; Bring me out of my distresses!"

JEREMIAH 17:14 NKJV
14 "Heal me, O Lord, and I shall be healed; Save me, and I shall be saved For You are my praise."

SPIRITUAL AFFLICTIONS

Spiritual affliction causes a broken heart to become a contaminated spirit.

2 CORINTHIANS 3:6 NIV
*[6] "He has made us competent as ministers of a new covenant—
not of the letter but of the Spirit; for the letter kills, but the Spirit
gives life."*

The word affliction means to afflict, to suffer ill, tormented, to suffer hardships, to be troubled and to undergo misery. The Greek word for afflict is Ka-Koo which means to vex-afflict or render harm.

PROVERBS 6:16-19 AMP
*[16] "These six things the Lord hates, indeed, seven are an
abomination to Him:
[17] A proud look [the spirit that makes one overestimate himself
and underestimate others], a lying tongue, and hands that shed
innocent blood,
[18] A heart that manufactures wicked thoughts and plans, feet
that are swift in running to evil,
[19] A false witness who breathes out lies [even under oath], and
he who sows discord among his brethren.*

ROMANS 10:1- 4 ERV (SPIRITUAL AFFLICTION)
*[1] "Brothers and sisters, what I want most is for all the people of
Israel to be saved. That is my prayer to God.
[2] I can say this about them: They really try hard to follow God,
but they don't know the right way.
[3] They did not know the way that God makes people right with
him. And they tried to make themselves right in their own way.
So they did not accept God's way of making people right.
[4] Christ ended the law so that everyone who believes in him is
made right with God."*

Eve was deceived because of her spiritual afflictions. Spiritual affliction is evident when someone thinks they're hearing and seeing God when in reality they're being deceived by the devil and misguided by the stronghold. Because they believe that the voice of the serpent is God speaking. Eve also believed that when she saw the fruit that was forbidden to eat, she saw that it was good, the Bible says.

Satan's ultimate strategy is to blind you by taking away your spiritual vision and to lead you out of the Will of God in order to destroy the intimacy and relationship that you have shared with your Heavenly Father. The destruction of that relationship and by being out of God's will ultimately causes you to lose everything God has ever given you and promised you.

PSALMS 34:19 NKJV
19 "Many are the AFFLICTIONS of the righteous, But the Lord delivers him out of them all."

PSALMS 119:71 KJV
71 "It is good for me that I have been AFFLICTED; that I might learn thy statutes."

2 CORINTHIANS 4:17-18 NKJV
17 "For our LIGHT AFFLICTION, which is but for a moment, is working for us a far more exceeding and eternal weight of glory, 18 while we do not look at the things which are seen, but at the things which are not seen. For the things which are seen are temporary, but the things which are not seen are eternal."

MARK 5:1-10 ERV
1 "Jesus and his followers went across the lake to the area where the Gerasene people lived. When Jesus got out of the boat, a man came to him from the caves where the dead are buried. This man had an evil spirit living inside him. 3 He lived in the burial caves. No one could keep him tied up, even with chains. 4 Many times people had put chains on his hands and feet, but he broke the chains. No one was strong enough to control him. 5 Day and night he stayed around the burial caves and on the hills. He would scream and cut himself with rocks. 6 While Jesus was still far away, the man saw him. He ran to Jesus and bowed down before him. 7-8 As Jesus was saying, "You evil spirit, come out of this man," the man shouted loudly, "What

do you want with me, Jesus, Son of the Most High God? I beg you in God's name not to punish me!"
⁹ Then Jesus asked the man, "What is your name?" The man answered, "My name is Legion, because there are many spirits inside me."
¹⁰ The spirits inside the man begged Jesus again and again not to send them out of that area."

The Gospel of Mark talks about the man at the tomb that was bound by the stronghold of self-affliction and self-harm. He kept harming and cutting himself and every time someone tried to tie him up or bind him with shackles or handcuffs, he would break the chains. Because no man could tame him or control him; neither could anyone in his environment or circle help him, he continued to commit self-affliction, self-harm and self-injury.

Too many times, the people that think they are helping us only end up hurting us because they don't know what it takes to help us. The Bible says the way these people tried to help this man was by controlling, taming or by binding him. The man didn't need binding, handcuffs or to be tied up. The man needed to be loosed and freed but the people that were trying to help him tried to bind him rather than free him. Thanks be to God that the man's help, deliverance and freedom was coming from the other side but it had just been held up in a major spiritual storm on the other side of the sea.

Jesus and his disciples had an assignment to bring deliverance and breakthrough to this man and all those who would receive it by freeing them from this stronghold called self-affliction, from this demonic force of Satan's principalities that had been causing these people to not only live in fear but to be tormented. The Bible says immediately when Jesus and the disciples stepped off the boat that this demonic stronghold called Legion who caused self-affliction, self-harm and self-injury, recognized its time had run out! This stronghold was ruling in the "Chronos" but it's time had expired. This man would no longer experience the enemies' strongholds of self-affliction because it was his "Kairos" moment, his opportunity for deliverance!

2 CORINTHIANS 4:17 NKJV
[17] "For our LIGHT AFFLICTION, which is but for a MOMENT, WORKING FOR US A FAR MORE EXCEEDING AND ETERNAL WEIGHT OF GLORY;"

2 CORINTHIANS 4:17 HCSB
[17] "For our MOMENTARY LIGHT AFFLICTION is producing for us an absolutely incomparable eternal weight of glory."

The Bible says after Jesus delivered the man from the stronghold of self-affliction that the man was sitting clothed and in his right mind. When you are free from living a life of self-affliction or self-harm you gain swagger, confidence, joy, peace, love, praise and your worship back!!! "Let's get back to Eden and live on top of the world!!!"

Chapter 12

The Stronghold of Self-Motives

(Unmask Yourself)

Satan uses the stronghold called self-motives on individuals to only care about themselves. Their only concern is with one's self interest, primarily to benefit themselves, their own welfare, and to become self-serving not caring about anyone else but themselves.

> **PHILIPPIANS 1:17 NLT**
> [17] *"Those others do not have pure MOTIVES as they preach about Christ. They preach with SELFISH ambition, not sincerely, intending to make my chains more painful to me."*

> **JAMES 4:3 NLT**
> [3] *"And even when you ask, you don't get it because your MOTIVES are all wrong—you want only what will give you pleasure."*

Individuals that struggle with the stronghold of self-motives also struggle with hypocrisy making them a hypocrite. A hypocrite is person that pretends to be someone they are not in disguise and wearing a mask. This stronghold of self-motives comes in many disguises always masking itself along with parading by self-serving, and justifying their actions like being a modern day Robin hood.

The symptoms, signs and side effects of this stronghold called self-motives causes an individual to become a kleptomaniac, a thief, a robber, and a liar by pretending what they're doing and their actions are helping the poor and the needy. When in reality they're self-serving while wearing a mask and playing the part of a hypocrite.

It's time to stop being a hypocrite, unmask, stop hiding behind the disguises and stop pretending to be someone you're not. You have worn the mask and disguises long enough while struggling with this stronghold called self-motives. Will the real you come forth and reveal what's behind the mask?

People who have self-motives gravitate towards people with negative self-views. They find themselves desiring self-verification, validation, and love because they're very competitive. They love surrounding themselves and hanging out with people that are disorganized, broken, unstable, have low self-esteem and are insecure. People that struggle with self-motives need to feel that they're the smartest, the most gifted and the most important one in their circle. They become intimidated or threaten by people that they feel are smarter than them, more gifted than them, more anointed than them and have more than them and they begin to sow seeds of discord in the ears and in the life of people that are weak and fragile to poison and to persuade them to stay away from people that they are intimidated by.

A person who operates out of the self-motives stronghold usually operates out of counterfeit thinking and by becoming an imposter, procrastinator, imitator, perpetrator, fraud, and a hypocrite.

Mark 11:12 - 13 KJV

12 "And on the morrow, when they were come from Bethany, he was hungry:
13 And seeing a fig tree afar off having leaves, he came, if haply he might find anything thereon: and when he came to it, he found nothing but leaves; for the time of figs was not yet.
14 And Jesus answered and said unto it, No man eat fruit of thee hereafter forever. And his disciples heard it.

The Bible says Jesus was hungry and begins to go toward the fig tree to eat. The reason Jesus cursed the fig tree was that it appeared to have fruit and didn't so the fig tree can be compared to an imposter, a fake and with a hidden agenda. Jesus cursed it, exposed it for what it was. Jesus unmasked it and cursed it at its root system. Usually a tree begins to dry up from its leaves then branches and then outside but Jesus cursed this fig tree at its root system first. The Bible says the next day when Jesus and His disciples showed back up at the fig tree it was dried up from its root because Jesus exposed the fig tree for appearing to have something it didn't.

Genesis 3:1-7 talks about Eve struggling with the stronghold of self-motive because she was deceived by Satan to self-serve. He caused her to believe that she was entitled and privileged to eat off any tree in the garden because God had left her and her husband, Adam, in charge of not only the Garden of Eden but the whole earth and gave them dominion and authority to manage and rule everything in the earth. Satan convinced Eve that because she had worked hard and sacrificed everything for God she should be able to eat anywhere in the garden she wanted too. Satan deceived and convinced the woman to eat from the tree of knowledge of good and evil out of self-motive by self-serving. She disobeyed God and was evicted and banned from promise for life.

Self-motive starts off being innocent, harmless, as a result of ambitions, goals and desiring more in life. It causes you to in the beginning to have a passion for what you do and a heart and burden to do it. You freely volunteer to do; to help people, to help families, to help friends, to help church and ministry as well as communities, etc. but over time you begin to feel the need to self-serve yourself out of entitlement. Now you feel like you've given, sacrificed, and because you don't see a return on what you have done you to take what's not yours and begin to steal, lie, and to do things that are fraudulent, and convince yourself at the same time that you're deserving of what you have taken. You have convinced yourself because of all the time you put in and all the sacrifices you have made by volunteering your time, gifts, and support that now you can self-serve by taking whatever you think you deserve or want.

When you allow self-motives to bind you by self-serving it births the Spirit of Greed. You become selfish and as you think about all of your sacrifices, all the things you've been through and all of your suffering for the sake of life and ministry. Allowing the Spirit of Greed to take over through self-motives will cause you to self-serve and give you the mindset that you deserving and entitled.

The 31 Self-Strongholds

2 KINGS 5:19-27 TLB

¹⁹ "All right," Elisha said. So Naaman started home again.
²⁰ But Gehazi, Elisha's servant, said to himself, "My master shouldn't have let this fellow get away without taking his gifts. I will chase after him and get something from him."
²¹ So Gehazi caught up with him. When Naaman saw him coming, he jumped down from his chariot and ran to meet him. "Is everything all right?" he asked.
²² "Yes," he said, "but my master has sent me to tell you that two young prophets from the hills of Ephraim have just arrived, and he would like $2,000 in silver and two suits to give to them."
²³ "Take $4,000," Naaman insisted. He gave him two expensive robes, tied up the money in two bags, and gave them to two of his servants to carry back with Gehazi.
²⁴ But when they arrived at the hill where Elisha lived, Gehazi took the bags from the servants and sent the men back. Then he hid the money in his house.
²⁵ When he went in to his master, Elisha asked him, "Where have you been, Gehazi?" "I haven't been anywhere," he replied.
²⁶ But Elisha asked him, "Don't you realize that I was there in thought when Naaman stepped down from his chariot to meet you? Is this the time to receive money and clothing and olive farms and vineyards and sheep and oxen and servants?
²⁷ Because you have done this, Naaman's leprosy shall be upon you and upon your children and your children's children forever." And Gehazi walked from the room a leper, his skin as white as snow."

Here we find an assistant who serves the "Man of God" called Elisha. In the beginning he served faithfully with no hidden agenda. But over a period of time he begins to allow the stronghold of self-motives to birth the Spirit of Greed to blind his passion, purpose and assignment of how to serve in the ministry of Elisha. Gehazi had come to the place that this stronghold of self-motive along with the Spirit of Greed had caused him to no longer consider it an honor and a privilege to serve beside the Man of God faithfully. He no longer looked at it as an honor to be mentored by his Spiritual Life Coach but he took on self-motives as if the Man of God and ministry owed him something in return.

According to 2 KINGS 5:21-23, Gehazi looked for an opportunity to compensate himself for his service and sacrifices over the years for him being a part of Elisha's ministry by manipulating Naaman into giving him money for his healing. For year he was faithful to Elisha's ministry and saw it was an honor and a privilege to be taught, mentored and empowered as he followed the Man of God. The Spirit of Greed caused him to begin to see it as a job and no longer as a ministry so now he felt like he should be paid for everything he did. Gehazi no longer followed the ministry for how he could build it but for what he could get out of it.

THE STRONGHOLD OF SELF – MOTIVES SYMPTOMS, SIGNS AND SIDE EFFECTS

Naaman struggled with the Spirit of Pride and the disease called leprosy that was incurable at that time. Naaman is pictured as someone with authority, a leader but he is leading and struggling with the Spirit of Pride. Gehazi is a servant of God that struggled with the Spirit of Greed. He started off serving God faithfully for nothing and volunteered his service for the Kingdom but over a period of time the stronghold of self-motives and the Spirit of Greed crept in. Naaman was healed and delivered from his pride by going down in the Jordan 7 times out of obedience and was converted but Gehazi never got delivered from his stronghold of self-motives and the Spirit of Greed. So now the pride and the sin that was on Naaman is now on Gehazi.

2 KINGS 5:25-27 MSG
25 "He returned and stood before his master. Elisha said, "So what have you been up to, Gehazi?" "Nothing much," he said.
26-27 Elisha said, "Didn't you know I was with you in spirit when that man stepped down from his chariot to greet you? Tell me, is this a time to look after yourself, lining your pockets with gifts? Naaman's skin disease will now infect you and your family, with no relief in sight." Gehazi walked away, his skin flaky and white like snow."

THE STRONGHOLD OF SELF – MOTIVES 7 DEADLY SINS

The 1st is called PRIDE.
The 2nd is called ENVY.
The 3rd is called GLUTTONY.
The 4th is called LUST.
The 5th is called ANGER.
The 6th is called GREED.
The 7th is called LAZINESS.

THE 7 DEADLY SINS OF MAN!

1. PRIDE is the excessive belief in one's own abilities.

2. ENVY is the desire for other's status, life, abilities or situations.

3. GLUTTONY is the desire to consume more than that which one requires; means to eat more than you can digest.
4. LUST is the craving for the pleasure of the body.

5. ANGER is manifest and vindicated revenge.

6. GREED means to covet what's not yours that belong to someone else. Greed also means never enough. It also means taking what's not yours. There is a saying concerning Greed. "He who loves money never has money enough."

7. LAZINESS means the act of being to slow or trifling at doing something.

> **MATTHEW 19:27-30 GW**
> [27] *"Then Peter replied to him, "Look, we've given up everything to follow you. What will we get out of it?"*
> [28] *Jesus said to them, "I can guarantee this truth: When the Son of Man sits on his glorious throne in the world to come, you, my followers, will also sit on twelve thrones, judging the twelve tribes of Israel.*

[29] And everyone who gave up homes, brothers or sisters, father, mother, children, or fields because of my name will receive a hundred times more and will inherit eternal life.
[30] However, many who are first will be last, and many who are last will be first."

The spirit of self-motives tried to assign itself to Peter and the other 11 disciples after following Jesus' Ministry for 3 years. The Bible says Peter and the other disciples said to Jesus we have given up everything to follow you and to be a part of your ministry. Now, what are we going to get out of this or what are we going to get from this? The disciples begin to struggle with the stronghold of self-motives and the Spirit of Greed. They no longer appreciated the privilege and honor to follow Jesus' ministry or the blessing and privilege of being mentored, empowered and anointed by Jesus. They began to struggle with self-motives which convinced them to think about what's in it for me, what will I get out of this. I'm tired of serving for nothing, who's going to pay me to do this and I don't get paid for doing this. They begin to make what they had the passion and love to do, a job; and no longer a ministry. They started following Jesus' Ministry for the right reason but now they were following it for the wrong reason, self-motives, because they began to focus only on their sacrifices, the time they had invested, the business they gave up, the life they gave up, the friends they gave up, the family they gave up and the money they gave up to follow Jesus' Ministry.

Peter begins to tell Jesus in Matthew 19:27, we have given up everything to follow you but what will we get out of this? Jesus answered, if any man has given up his life; sacrificed, suffered, and sowed into the Kingdom for My sake, he will not only be compensated in this life but he shall also be compensated eternally in the life to come. Jesus asked Peter, do you not believe that you shall receive 100 times more for the sacrifice, suffering, the time, and the commitment that you've given up for the Kingdom as well as ministry? (MARK 10:30)

2 PETER 3:9 GW

[9] *"The Lord isn't slow to do what he promised, as some people think. Rather, he is patient for your sake. He doesn't want to destroy anyone but wants all people to have an opportunity to turn to him and change the way they think and act."*

Chapter 13

The Stronghold of Selfish-Desires

(Help, I'm in Lust with Me (Myself))

James 1: 13-15 GWT
[13] When someone is tempted, he shouldn't say that God is tempting him. God can't be tempted by evil, and God doesn't tempt anyone. [14] Everyone is tempted by his own desires as they lure him away and trap him. [15] Then desire becomes pregnant and gives birth to sin. When sin grows up, it gives birth to death.

Satan uses the spirit of covetousness to cause the stronghold selfish desires.

GALATIANS 5:17-21 CEB
[17] "A person's SELFISH DESIRES are set against the Spirit, and the Spirit is set against one's SELFISH DESIRES. They are opposed to each other, so you shouldn't do whatever you want to do.
[18] But if you are being led by the Spirit, you aren't under the Law.
[19] The actions that are produced by SELFISH MOTIVES are obvious, since they include sexual immorality, moral corruption, doing whatever feels good,
[20] idolatry, drug use and casting spells, hate, fighting, obsession, losing your temper, competitive opposition, conflict, SELFISHNESS, group rivalry,
[21] jealousy, drunkenness, partying, and other things like that. I warn you as I have already warned you, that those who do these kinds of things won't inherit God's kingdom."

PROVERBS 18:1 NIV
[1] "An unfriendly person pursues SELFISH ends
and against all sound judgment starts quarrels."

When one operates from selfish-desires they bring much suffering, pain, hurt and betrayal to whoever they're in relationship with. The Bible says it was Judas' selfish-desires that caused him to betray Jesus. Selfish-desires is another name for the lust of the flesh.

1 JOHN 2:16-17 AMP

16 For all that is in the world—the lust and sensual craving of the flesh and the lust and longing of the eyes and the boastful pride of life [pretentious confidence in one's resources or in the stability of earthly things]—these do not come from the Father, but are from the world. 17 The world is passing away, and with it its lusts [the shameful pursuits and ungodly longings]; but the one who does the will of God and carries out His purposes lives forever.

The devil uses three Weapons to destroy mankind;

1. The lust of the flesh. The woman saw the tree was good for food.
2. The lust of the eye. It was pleasing to her eyes.
3. The pride of life. She saw that the tree was desired to make one wise.

GENESIS 3:6 NLV
6 "The woman saw that the tree was good for food, and pleasing to the eyes, and could fill the desire of making one wise. So she took of its fruit and ate and she also gave some to her husband, and he ate."

Satan did the same thing to Jesus in Luke chapter 4. The devil tempted *Jesus with...*

1. The lust of the flesh - Turned bread into stone. (Luke 4:3)
2. The lust of the eye - Showed Jesus the whole world. (Luke 4:5)
3. The pride of life - Satan told Jesus to throw Himself down from the mountain. (Luke 4:9)

Selfishness means seeking one's own advantage, pleasure, or well-being without regards for anyone else. Selfish people desire to succeed at the expense of others.

THE SYMPTOMS, SIGNS AND SIDE EFFECTS OF SELFISH – DESIRES.

The symptoms of selfish-desires ae revealed when an individual begins to find themselves being self-absorbed, self-centered, self-infatuated, self-interested, self-involved, self-loving, self-obsessed, self-seeking, and self-serving.

The side effects of selfish-desires cause extraordinary lust, greed, and hatred to the point that the emotions of an individual begins to dominate one's soul. The side effects cause an individual to become attracted and to have unnatural soul-ties and causes spiritual blindness that creates ungodly pride that leads to destruction. Selfish-desires poison the heart, corrupt and confuse the mind, it binds people and causes them to take on a journey filled with evil actions.

THERE ARE 6 SELFISH CHARACTERISTICS THAT CAN DESTROY A RELATIONSHIP.

1. A SELFISH PERSON ALWAYS CREATES THEIR OWN CONDITIONS ON HOW THE RELATIONSHIP SHOULD GO.
2. A SELFISH PERSON ALWAYS BIRTH LIES AND MANIPULATION.

3. A SELFISH PERSON WILL ALWAYS LEAD TO HURT.

4. A SELFISH PERSON WILL ALWAYS BLOCK THE BUILDING OF TRUST.

5. A SELFISH PERSON IS ALWAYS ROOTED IN THE PAIN OF INSECURITY.

6. A SELFISH PERSON MAKES IT IMPOSSIBLE TO HAVE A REAL RELATIONSHIP WITH.

A SELFISH PERSON ALWAYS CREATES THEIR CONDITIONS FOR HOW THE RELATIONSHIP SHOULD GO.

Whenever there are unnecessary conditions being mandated, there will never be the possibility of an equal relationship. As long as you are taking care of a selfish-person needs or desires they'll remain in relationship with you because those are their conditions. Their focus is not on adding to your life and making it better but their concern is what you are going to do to make their life better. A selfish person has a very narrow focus which is on getting what they want, when they want it, how they want it and where they want it!

A SELFISH PERSON ALWAYS BIRTHS LIES AND MANIPULATION.

A selfish person only sees how they can succeed in life but never takes into consideration how to help someone along the way even those whom they are in relationship with. They view the relationship as obstacles or hurdles to jump over and get around because they have the mindset to only birth lies and manipulation; to use and abuse whomever they are in relationship with because they are takers and not givers. Through their lies and manipulation they think only about helping themselves and about stepping on, using and abusing whomever they can. Rather than helping pull people up they would rather pull people down to get where they want in life.

A SELFISH PERSON WILL ALWAYS LEAD TO HURT.

A selfish person will abuse your heart to get whatever they are ultimately seeking. Once you can no longer provide what they want they will leave you. They had a selfish-motive and a hidden agenda for entering into your life which was to get all they can get and to take all they can take no matter the cost. Taking advantage of another individual in this way leads to hurt, disappointment, bitterness, delusional feelings and misguided love.

A SELFISH PERSON WILL ALWAYS BLOCK THE BUILDING OF TRUST.

When a selfish-person loves it is based upon conditions of selfishness that will never allow you to give them the benefit of the doubt. There will always be a block wall standing between you and them that will create distance and cause an inability to trust. A selfish-person always wants to have freedom to come and go in your life but they will lock you out of their life, only allowing you to come in when it's convenient for them, which is what causes the selfishness that blocks the building up of trusting a relationship.

A SELFISH PERSON IS ALWAYS ROOTED IN THE PAIN OF INSECURITY.

A selfish person focuses on covering themselves because deep down they really don't believe that anyone else will truly have their back. Their deep-rooted pain causes them to feel inadequate in every way. Instead of them getting help for their pain they will always suppress and numb their pain and live a life of denial. They convince themselves as well as others that they are someone they are not by trying to be more than they really are when in reality they live in self-denial and in a world where they have suppressed their feelings, emotions, hurt, pain and lies. They have deep rooted insecurities that cause them not to TRUST anyone else because in reality they don't trust themselves.

A SELFISH PERSON MAKES IT IMPOSSIBLE TO HAVE A REAL RELATIONSHIP.

A selfish person is impossible to live with, to have a relationship with, to be friends with, to talk to, to listen to and to have a future with. A selfish person has self-vision and self-vies. They are self-centered, self-focused and self-infatuated because they are in lust with themselves.

Selfish people expect you to be perfect when they are not perfect. They expect you to be mature when they are immature. They expect you to be forgiving when they are unforgiving. They expect you to change when they never change. They expect you to be better when they are not getting better. They expect you to get it right; when they never get it right. They expect you to have more in life; when they have lost everything in life. They expect you to understand everything they are saying when they never want to hear what you have to say. That's why you can never have a successful life with a selfish person. A selfish person is like dealing with an impossible challenge.

THE ANSWER AND ANTIDOTE OF THE STRONGHOLD OF SELFISH – DESIRES

The answer and the antidote to being delivered and set free from the stronghold of selfish-desires is to pre-determine the difference between what you love verses what you value. It is possible to be in a relationship with someone you love who may not value your future but rather rob you of your future. Be careful that the friends you love are not friends you can't value. Be sure the job you love is a job you can value because there's a difference in what you love and what you value. Many times people put their whole life, dreams, assignment and destiny into what and who they love and it may not be who they value for life!! There is a difference between what you love and what you value!

LOVE vs. VALUE

You will always know the difference between who you love versus what you value, because although who you love or what you love has caused you to become angry, upset, irritated, and frustrated; you understand because they add so much value to your present and an even greater value to your future. You can't afford to walk away from, break up with, quit, or give up on them because it's not only pre-determined but now pre-destined. You will discover it's not only someone or something that you love but it was destined to be someone or something you valued. When you discover what you value it will never depreciate or become a liability to you no matter how mad, upset, hurt, frustrated, and irritated you become with them.

So never allow yourself out of what you call love to make a permanent decision out of a temporary situation, unless you know its true value. You should first pre-determine if it's real love or lust. We find the difference in what we love and what we value in

> **JUDGES 16:4-6 NLV**
> **4 "After this Samson LOVED a woman in the valley of Sorek. Her name was Delilah.**
> **5 The leaders of the Philistines came to her, saying, "Tempt Samson to tell you the secret of his powerful strength. Find out**

how we can get power over him so we can tie him and hold him. Then we will each give you 1,100 PIECES OF SILVER."
6 So Delilah said to Samson, "I beg you. Tell me the secret of your powerful strength. Tell me how one can get power over you and tie you up and hold you."

We find in Judges 16:4-6, that Samson failed to pre-determine the difference between who he loved versus who he valued. Samson struggled with the stronghold of selfish-desire and he confused lust for love. In return it cost him everything. Delilah didn't love Samson but she lusted for the secret of his hidden strength, anointing and assignment on his life. Delilah became Samson's fatal attraction and fatal distraction!!!

Delilah didn't enter into Samson's life by accident; she was assigned by Samson's enemy to uncover his value called his strength and to destroy his relationship with God, his vision and the call on his life. We must pre-determine and fully understand the difference between what we love versus what we value because Samson loved Delilah more than he valued the call or assignment on his life.

The Bible starts off saying in Judges 16:4 that Samson fell in LOVE with a woman in the valley of Sorek. The name Sorek means the valley of decisions or the place of choices. Judges chapter 15 previously concluded that Samson just left (Gaza); which means the place of my stronghold where he allowed his Lust of the flesh to cause him to become drunk and to sleep with a prostitute then the enemy came in and attempted to attack him while he was naked, drunk, exposed and vulnerable. The Bible says God gave him strength to overcome his vulnerabilities and he snatched the gates off of (Gaza) the place of my stronghold.

Samson ends up falling in love with a woman named Delilah in Sorek. Delilah's name means my selfish-desires, my weakness and the one that will impoverish, break or destroy me. Which simply means that when Samson left (Gaza) he had just left his place of stronghold; then he came to Sorek the valley of decisions where he must now make new choices. Instead of making new choices he still makes the same decisions as he made in (Gaza) the place of his stronghold and gives his heart and his

LOVE to a woman named Delilah out of his selfish-desires. He didn't predetermine the difference between what he loved and what he valued.

Samson lost three things that he did not value and discovered what he thought he loved was really lust and it became his stronghold called selfish-desires.

1st It cost Samson his relationship with God. The Bible says when he went to shake himself as before; he discovered that his strength and anointing was not there. Samson lost his relationship with God and didn't know it

JUDGES 16:20 NLV

20 *"She said, "The Philistines are upon you, Samson!" He awoke from his sleep and said, "I will go out as I have at other times. I will shake myself free." But he did not know that the Lord had left him"*

2nd IT COST SAMSON HIS (VISION) – EYES.

JUDGES 16:21 NLV

21 *"The Philistines took hold of him and cut out his EYES."*

3rd IT COST SAMSON HIS ASSIGNMENT AND ANOINTING ON HIS LIFE.

JUDGES 16:21b NLV

21b *"They BROUGHT HIM DOWN TO GAZA and tied him with brass chains. Samson was made to grind grain in the prison."*

Now the same stronghold that God had delivered Samson from in Judges Chapter 15, the place called (Gaza) the place of my stronghold; we discover in Judges 16:21b when the enemy finally captured Samson he went right back to (Gaza) the place of his stronghold where God had just delivered him from. The woman Samson loved cost him everything! But Thank God for verse 22 that says the hair on Samson's head started to grow again after the enemy had cut it off. This is simply saying if we overcome the lust of the flesh, the lust of the eye and the pride of life and begin to pre-determine the difference in what we love versus what we value we will never again be so in lust with ourselves through selfish-desires that we will choose what we love or lust over but not what we value that determines our future.

Chapter 14

The Stronghold of Selfish-Ambitions
(Spiritual Disorder/Identity Crisis)

Moses' purpose and assignment was to bring deliverance to the people. Jesus' purpose was to save lives. What is our assignment? Our assignment is to be a blessing or to help somebody else, not yourself. So ask yourself, where and how did you go wrong? You made giving and doing about you.

Satan uses the stronghold called selfish ambition; which is a spiritual disorder and an identity crisis. He himself struggles with this spiritual disorder and an identity crisis because he tried to be God when he was only created by God to be an Arch Angel. Satan, through selfish-ambitions, tried to be more than he was created to be causing a spiritual disorder in the Heavens.

> **Romans 12:3 AMP**
> *3 "For by the grace (unmerited favor of God) given to me I warn everyone among you not to estimate and think of himself more highly than he ought [not to have an exaggerated opinion of his own importance], but to rate his ability with sober judgment, each according to the degree of faith apportioned by God to him."*

Ezekiel 28:14 talks about Lucifer (A.K.A. Satan) and says that out of selfish-ambitions he caused a catastrophic disorder in the cosmos. The Bible says he was ordained and anointed as the mighty angelic guardian who had access to the Holy Mountain of God (God's Holy Temple). Verse 15 says Lucifer you were faultless; in all this you did in the beginning. You walked in total perfection before God until the day you became selfish with ambitions and caused 1/3 of angels to become selfish like you. You quit being God-centered and became self-centered and fell from heaven to earth.

A selfish person makes choices and decisions that benefit and favor themselves rather than making a decision and choice that benefits and favors everyone else. A selfish-ambitious person always places their needs and wants above everyone else, they only have self-interest, and they only seek self-achievement and goals for themselves. They will undermine and destroy anyone that gets in their way while they are trying to get to the top. They will do anything in life to get the position they want, the job they want, the man they want, the woman they want, the money they want, or the life they want by lying, stealing, cheating and destroying others. Even if they have to do it illegally they'll do it my any means necessary. John 10:10; says "the thief comes not but to steal, kill and destroy."

The Greek word for steal means kleptomaniac or "klepto" which simply means a person that compulsively and repeatedly steals. So when Jesus quotes John 10:10; He's saying Satan is a kleptomaniac; but he's not only talking about Satan in John 10:10 but he's talking about kleptomaniac leaders that steal, kill and destroy from innocent people through selfish-ambitions to get to the top. These kleptomaniac leaders are operating out of spiritual disorder and an identity crisis.

James 3:14-16 NLT
"But if you are bitterly jealous and there is selfish-ambition in your heart, don't cover up the truth with boasting and lying. For jealousy and selfishness are not God's kind of wisdom. Such things are earthly, unspiritual and demonic. For wherever there is jealousy and selfish ambition, there you will find disorder and evil of every kind."

The stronghold of selfish-ambitions causes a person to develop nervous disorders, a demonic level of torment, to become delusional, dysfunctional, broken and moody. They suffer from uncontrollable crying. They are fussy and they have an uncontrollable take-over spirit. They always blame others when things don't go right. They develop patterns and cycle when things go wrong in their life they either talk about giving up or eventually give up. The person who struggles with selfish-ambitions will develop a habit of lying or become a pathological liar. The difference between the two is that a compulsive liar is someone who lies with ease and finds comfort in it but a pathological liar develops a spiritual disorder and struggles with mistaken identity. This simply means it's no longer them that is in control of their life but they are beginning to allow their mistaken identity through a spiritual disorder to dictate through satanic influences how they live.

John 8:44 AMP

[44] *"You are of your father, the devil, and it is your will to practice the lusts and gratify the desires [which are characteristic] of your father. He was a murderer from the beginning and does not stand in the truth, because there is no truth in him. When he speaks a falsehood, he speaks what is natural to him, for he is a liar [himself] and the father of lies and of all that is false."*

1 KINGS 22:22 GW

[22] *"The Spirit answered, 'I will go out and be a spirit that tells lies through the mouths of all of Ahab's prophets.' "The LORD said, 'You will succeed in deceiving him. Go and do it."*

The Stronghold of Selfish-Ambitions Symptoms, Signs and Side Effects

Therefore a person that has become a pathological liar operates out of the stronghold of selfish-ambitions is now influenced by the father of lies, the devil. They no longer know the truth so now they are in bondage to the stronghold of selfish-ambitions and the only way they can be free and delivered from this stronghold of selfish-ambitions and this spirit of lying is through John 8:32NIV which says "then you will know the truth, and the truth will set you free."

The 31 Self-Strongholds

John 8:32-37 AMP

32 "And you will know the Truth, and the Truth will set you free.

33 They answered Him, We are Abraham's offspring (descendants) and have never been in bondage to anybody. What do You mean by saying, You will be set free?

34 Jesus answered them, I assure you, most solemnly I tell you, Whoever commits and practices sin is the slave of sin. 35 Now a slave does not remain in a household permanently (forever); the son [of the house] does remain forever.

36 So if the Son liberates you [makes you free men], then you are really and unquestionably free.

37 [Yes] I know that you are Abraham's offspring; yet you plan to kill Me, because My word has no entrance (makes no progress, does not find any place) in you."

Selfish-Person verses a Selfless-Person

A selfish person takes.

A selfish person makes life harder for everybody else.

A selfish-person does what they do for what they can get out of it.

A selfish-person only plays life to win for them self.

A selfish-person becomes their rebel, renegade and superstar.

Selfless-Person

A selfless-person gives.

A selfless-person makes life easier and better for those that are around them.

A selfless-person does what they do so everyone else can get out of it.

A selfless-person plays life to win for the team.

A selfless person becomes a team player that sacrifices for the good of the team and makes the people that are in their life look better than they really are. Are you a selfish-person or a selfless-person?

> **Genesis 13:4-9 VOICE**
> *⁴ "He returned to one of the first altar tables he had made in the land, stopped there, and called on the name of the Eternal once again. ⁵ Lot, who had gone with Abram, also had flocks and herds and tents, ⁶ so the land was no longer large enough to support the two of them living together as one household. They each had so many possessions that they just couldn't stay together any longer. ⁷ Arguments erupted between Abram's and Lot's livestock herders as they tried to graze their flocks side-by-side. (During this time, the Canaanites and the Perizzites were living on this land too.) Abram (to Lot): ⁸ Let's not fight. I don't want there to be any animosity between you and me, or between our herders. After all, we're family. ⁹ A vast land is out there and available to you. It is time for us to go our separate ways. You choose your land. If you choose east, I'll go west. If you choose west, I'll go east—it's your call."*

A man named Lot struggled with the stronghold of selfish-ambitions. Lot was selfish and put his needs ahead of everyone else's. Abraham was selfless always putting everyone else's needs ahead of his own. The stronghold of selfish-ambitions cost Lot 3 things.

1. Lot's selfishness caused him to compromise. In Gen 13:5-10 we see that Lot compromised his values, character, beliefs, integrity, commitment and loyalty to Abraham and his covenant. As long as Lot had nothing he submitted and followed Abraham, but when Lot began to be blessed and to have more in life; he began to

compromise in all of these areas. Ask yourself, can God trust you to be blessed? Gen 13: 11 states "Then Lot chose for himself (selfish-ambitions) all the Jordan Valley and [he] traveled east. So they separated." Lot put his needs and wants ahead of his covenant and others.

2. Lot's selfishness cost him his blessings, family, the ability to lead as well as his covenant. In Gen 14:12 and Gen 19:20 and 26 the Bible says Lot left Abraham out of selfish-ambitions and chose to go to Sodom and Gomorrah to live. He thought the grass would be greener but like the Prodigal son, selfish-ambitions caused Lot to lose his blessings, family, and the ability to lead. Lot's selfishness caused him to lose all of his valuable possessions. He failed at trying to recover the blessing he lost, the family he lost and the leadership position he lost all because he left and separated from his covenant. God did not make the covenant promise to Lot, He made it to Abraham; therefore, Lot got what he wanted, but he lost what he had.

3. Lot's selfishness caused him to become contaminated. According to Gen 19:35-36, Lot became contaminated, got drunk and slept with his daughters and got them pregnant. Lot not only became contaminated but he birthed the spirit of perversion as well as the spirit of incest causing his bloodline and lineage to produce generation after generation of sons and daughters that continued to birth the spirit of perversion and incest.

First Lot compromised his values, belief, integrity and the ability to be loyal. Then he lost his blessings, family, covenant and relationship with God. Finally, he became contaminated; he was drunk with pride and birthed perversion and incest all as a result of the spiritual disorder and identity crisis called selfish-ambitions.

Gen 19:36-38 MSG
"Both daughters became pregnant by their father, Lot. The older daughter had a son and named him Moab, the ancestor of the present-day Moabites. The younger daughter had a son and named him Ben-Ammi, the ancestor of the present-day Ammonites."

Romans 4:22-24 AMP
[22] "That is why his faith was CREDITED to him as righteousness (right standing with God). [23] But [the words], It was CREDITED to him, were written not for his sake alone, [24] But [they were written] for our sakes too. [Righteousness, standing acceptable to God] will be granted and CREDITED to us also who believe in (trust in, adhere to, and rely on) God, Who raised Jesus our Lord from the dead,"

James 3:17-18 MSG
[17-18] "Real wisdom, God's wisdom, begins with a holy life and is characterized by getting along with others. It is gentle and reasonable, overflowing with mercy and blessings, not hot one day and cold the next, not two-faced. You can develop a healthy, robust community that lives right with God and enjoy its results only if you do the hard work of getting along with each other, treating each other with dignity and honor."

The stronghold of selfish-ambitions means self-seeking and always looking for one's own interest above the interest of anyone else. The Greek word for selfish-ambitions is (ERITHEA/ER'I'THE'A). It means to be full of one's self, to create strife, discord, confusion and unnecessary drama.

Chapter 15

The Stronghold of Self-Defeat/Self-Sabotage

(It's Only a Test/The Final Exit Exam)

Deuteronomy 8:18

[18] But you shall remember [with profound respect] the LORD your God, for it is He who is giving you power to make wealth, that He may confirm His covenant which He swore (solemnly promised) to your fathers, as it is this day.

The Stronghold of self-defeat/self-sabotage causes a person to struggle with personality disorders and have serial behavior dysfunctions. It causes them to sabotage everything that is good and positive in their life and to turn on themselves with dysfunctional thinking by convincing themselves that nothings ever going to go right for them ever again. This stronghold causes them to give up on what God has promised them in their seasons, dreams, goals and life. A person that struggles with the stronghold of self-defeat/self-sabotage takes on crippling patterns of self-defeating behaviors.

These patterns or cycles usually start with a person during their teenage stage of life and lasts through adulthood. They develop a pattern of always avoiding and undermining themselves, their relationships, the jobs that they get, in ministry and in their very own happiness. This person often avoids or undermines pleasurable experiences and they become attracted to and drawn into negative relationships.

The stronghold of self-defeat/self-sabotage causes a person to become afraid of committing themselves to happiness in a stable relationship because they are afraid to confront their past failures. They convince themselves that something is going to go wrong and that their life cannot be filled with happiness; so they intentionally sabotage and undermine themselves and the relationship that they are in. The reality is, they deliberately try hard not to get hurt by guarding and protecting themselves, but the truth is; not only did they end up getting hurt but they hurt the one that genuinely cared and loved them. This type of behavior is a result of "stinky thinking".

The Symptoms, Signs and Side Effects of the Stronghold Self-Defeat/Self-Sabotage:

A person that is under the influence of self-defeat/self-sabotage suffers from spiritual inflammatory nervous disorder. The word inflammatory means someone who is easily provoked to violence and someone that has strong emotions. A person that struggles with this stronghold becomes easily provoked, agitated, angry, easily distracted and the smallest things upset them, disturb them, or causes them to give up easily. They become fatigued, faint-hearted, disturbed and dysfunctional and take on a serial behavior dysfunction similar to that of a serial killer. Someone with serial behavior dysfunction goes on a serial relationship destroying spree; destroying and sabotaging any relationship that is good in their life. A person influenced by this stronghold will sabotage anybody that tries to help them, deliver them, and free them from their own mass destruction.

Someone that struggles with this stronghold constantly finds themselves always complaining, always speaking negative about themselves and others. They never find the good in themselves and neither do they find the good in others. They are always talking about what's wrong because they never see what has gone right and that's because of their serial behavior dysfunction. This person suffers from psychotic behaviors. They live their lives in remorse or guilt from what happened in their childhood and they have been exposed to and or lived in a hostile environment. They grew up in an emotionally, physically, sexually and spiritually abusive environment and they have experienced a life full of rejection, hurt, bitterness and pain which has caused them to struggle with the stronghold of self-defeat/self-sabotage.

EXODUS 14:11 ERV

[11] *"They said to Moses, "Why did you bring us out of Egypt? Did you bring us out here in the desert to die? We could have died peacefully in Egypt; there were plenty of graves in Egypt."*

NUMBERS 21:5 ERV

"They began complaining against God and Moses. The people said, "Why did you bring us out of Egypt? We will die here in the desert! There is no bread and no water! And we hate this terrible food!"

The people of God struggled with the stronghold called self-defeat/self-sabotage for 40 years. After God had delivered them out of the bondage and debt of Egypt they self-defeated and self-sabotaged their promise while God was trying to take them to the place of fulfillment that He had promised them. They kept missing their season; season after season because this spirit and stronghold caused them to complain, murmur and become easily distracted. For 40 years they found themselves going in circles and cycles of complaining to God and Moses asking have you brought us out in this wilderness to let us die. When a person constantly complains like this, they usually struggle with the stronghold of self-defeat/self-sabotage.

PROVERBS 18:21 KJV

[21] *"The tongue can speak words that bring life or death. Those who love to talk must be ready to accept what it brings."*

They can't see the positive for always talking about the negative. They can't see the good for always talking about the bad. They can never be thankful for what God has already done because they're always complaining about what God hasn't done for them; they can't get to the place where they need to be; because they're always going in cycles backsliding to where they've already been. These people of God missed their harvest season as well as promised season because they were complaining to God and the man of God. They failed to understand that it was only a test. This was their final exit exam and it was God testing them. He wanted to promote them, bless them, and empower them but for 40 years rather than being promoted they kept being demoted season after season. They couldn't appreciate being blessed because they allowed their trials, tribulations and persecutions to defeat and sabotage their purpose and assignment. It should have taken them 4 weeks or 4 months to get to their place of fulfillment or promise but it took 40 years because they kept failing the test. This is your final exit exam! This time you cannot afford to fail this test!!!

Gal 6:6-10 MSG

6 "Be very sure now, you who have been trained to a self-sufficient maturity, that you enter into a generous common life with those who have trained you, sharing all the good things that you have and experience. 7-8 Don't be misled: No one makes a fool of God. What a person plants, he will harvest. The person who plants selfishness, ignoring the needs of others ignoring God!—harvests a crop of weeds. All he'll have to show for his life is weeds! But the one who plants in response to God, letting God's Spirit do the growth work in him, harvests a crop of real life, eternal life. 9-10 So let's not allow ourselves to get fatigued doing good. At the right time we will harvest a good crop if we don't give up, or quit. Right now, therefore, every time we get the chance, let us work for the benefit of all, starting with the people closest to us in the community of faith.

Gal 6:9 AMP

9 "And let us not lose heart and grow weary and faint in acting nobly and doing right, for in due time and at the appointed season we shall reap, if we do not loosen and relax our courage and faint."

The answer to overcoming the stronghold of self-defeat/self-sabotage is to never allow your good work to turn into bad work. Never allow what you have sowed in your season turn into a seed of discord (Matt 13:24-25). This simply means you have self-defeated and self-sabotaged your own season of harvest because you allowed your serial behavior dysfunction to cause your good seed to be overtaken by seeds of discord within your own mind. These seeds of discord have convinced you God is not going to do what He's promised you.

Chapter five of the book of John talks about a man at a pool called Bethesda. He was surrounded by the sick, blind, crippled, paralyzed and impotent people. This man laid at this place called Bethesda for 38 years. The name Bethesda means the house of mercy, the place of my deliverance, the place of my outpour, healing and restoration. The man stayed in the same condition that robbed him of his purpose in life for 38 years and for 38 years he failed the test. The Bibles says that Jesus showed up and asked the man a question. Do you want to be healed and delivered? The man that suffered from the stronghold of self-defeat and self-sabotage who whenever it was his season he sabotaged his own healing and deliverance by saying every time it's my season something always goes wrong and it keeps me from being healed, delivered and set free. But in reality what was really going on with this man is that he suffered with an inflammatory nervous disorder; meaning every time his healing and deliverance was close to him he fainted in the face of victory.

For 38 years he accepted this defeat until the day Jesus confronted this stronghold and asked him, do you want to be healed? Do you want to be delivered? Do you want to be set free? Do you want to be blessed? Do you want to be used for the glory of God? If you are ready to come out of this unnecessary drama then get up and do something!! In laymen terms, Jesus was saying to this dysfunctional man, do something!

You have allowed your struggle with this stronghold of self-defeat and self-sabotage to cause you to fail the test. You have been in this same place for 38 years hanging out with the same people that are dysfunctional just like you. The same people that think just like you, that believe like you and that are living just like you. So, if you want your life to change this day, quit feeling sorry for yourself, quit complaining about what's not right in your life and GET UP AND DO SOMETHING! This man had been demoted for 38 years for failing the test but today it's time to be promoted to the next level and pass the test. This is your final exit exam for this season. This year ending it's time for you to be a game changer rather than a game complainer. You have to study to show yourself approved if you're going to pass this final exit exam.

2 TIMOTHY 2:15 AMP
¹⁵ "Study and be eager and do your utmost to present yourself to God approved (TESTED BY TRIAL), a workman who has no cause to be ashamed, correctly analyzing and accurately dividing [rightly handling and skillfully teaching] the Word of Truth."

This is our final exit exam and if God is testing us it's simply because He knows that He has prepared us with His instructions and He has equipped us by educating and empowering us with everything we need to pass the test. If you are taking the same test that you took last season it's an indication you failed the test. It indicates that you are on the same level as you were last season and you were demoted rather than promoted. If you are taking your test in this season and you're finding new challenges, new attacks, new struggles, new hurt, new suffering it is an indication this is your exit exam for new promotions, new assignments, and new blessings.

Chapter 16

The Stronghold of Self - Conflict

(How to Manage and Disarm Conflict)

Romans 12:3 AMP

³ For by the grace [of God] given to me I say to everyone of you not to think more highly of himself [and of his importance and ability] than he ought to think; but to think so as to have sound judgment, as God has apportioned to each a degree of faith [and a purpose designed for service].

The stronghold of self-conflict brings about a head on collision with two courses of destiny. One course is struggling to overcome the failures of your past and the other is conquering the promises of your future. This stronghold causes a person to live their life in dilemma, a state of confusion, wrestling between choosing the direction of good or bad, right or wrong. This stronghold leaves them at a place of should I or should I not do this or that.

The word conflict means a serious disagreement or argument, dispute, disharmony, or a head on collision. Conflict deals with the struggle of two opposing forces or problems and determining how they must be solved.

The Symptoms, Signs and Side Effects of Self Conflict

This stronghold causes a person to always make temporary decisions and never permanent decisions to become unstable, inconsistent, and indecisive about making a long term decision that will impact their future. A person that struggles with self confidence usually makes decisions out of impulse while trying to please everybody else. Instead of solving their problems they find themselves making temporary solutions like that of using, fix-a-flat. Fix-a-Flat is used for leaky tires that keep going flat. It is not a permanent solution for the leaky tire but it is just a temporary fix to an ongoing problem you just keep putting off. The fix-a-flat will never solve the tire problem and in the long run it will damage the rim and the tire. That's just similar to how the stronghold of self-conflict works when we keep putting off today what keeps confronting us tomorrow. Just deal with it. Never allow a simple problem that you can afford to fix today become a more expensive problem that you cannot afford to pay for tomorrow.

There are two types of conflict internal and external. Internal conflict occurs when a person is wrestling with one's conscious to decide between right and wrong with mixed emotions such as feeling happy one moment and disappointed at the same time. They can feel good about themselves one moment but in the same moment they are still stressed and worried about things not going right. This stronghold of self-conflict causes a person to struggle with self-image and conflicting identities.

Romans 7:15-24 GW (Internal Conflict)

[15] "I don't realize what I'm doing. I don't do what I want to do. Instead, I do what I hate.

[16] I don't do what I want to do, but I agree that God's standards are good.

[17] So I am no longer the one who is doing the things I hate, but sin that lives in me is doing them.

[18] I know that nothing good lives in me; that is, nothing good lives in my corrupt nature. Although I have the desire to do what is right, I don't do it.

[19] I don't do the good I want to do. Instead, I do the evil that I don't want to do.

[20] Now, when I do what I don't want to do, I am no longer the one who is doing it. Sin that lives in me is doing it.

[21] So I've discovered this truth: Evil is present with me even when I want to do what God's standards say is good.

[22] I take pleasure in God's standards in my inner being.

23 However, I see a different standard at work throughout my body. It is at war with the standards my mind sets and tries to take me captive to sin's standards which still exist throughout my body.
24 What a miserable person I am! Who will rescue me from my dying body?"

In Romans chapter 7, verses 15 - 24, the Apostle Paul is testifying to the church at Rome about his internal conflict. Apostle Paul is dealing with self versus self and an internal conflict that deals with self versus God. His testimony to the Church of Rome was about his early struggle of conflict in his life. When he chose to do good, he would find himself doing bad and what he should have done, he'd find himself not doing. He discovered that in the midst of his good, evil was still present all around him. We find another person suffering with internal conflict in Genesis. Jacob struggled with an internal conflict of identities.

Genesis 32:24-27 ERV
24 "Jacob was left alone, and a man came and wrestled with him. The man fought with him until the sun came up.
25 When the man saw that he could not defeat Jacob, he touched Jacob's leg and put it out of joint.
26 Then the man said to Jacob, "Let me go. The sun is coming up." But Jacob said, "I will not let you go. You must bless me."
27 And the man said to him, "What is your name?" And Jacob said, "My name is Jacob."

The second type of conflict is external. External conflict is the struggle between a person and outside forces. A person that is in external conflict may face several types of outside forces. The outside forces of conflict can be man versus man, man versus nature, man versus demonic spirits and man versus God. You can have conflict with

God internally as well as externally when God is trying to get you to say yes to His will and "yes" to His way. We find the definition of external conflict in the book of Chronicles.

2 Chronicles 20:1 NLT
[1] "After this, the armies of the Moabites, Ammonites, and some of the Meunites declared WAR on Jehoshaphat."

2 Chronicles 20:15-17NLT
[15] "He said, "Listen, all you people of Judah and Jerusalem! Listen, King Jehoshaphat! This is what the Lord says: Do not be afraid! Don't be discouraged by this mighty army, for the battle is not yours, but God's.
[16] Tomorrow, march out against them. You will find them coming up through the ascent of Ziz at the end of the valley that opens into the wilderness of Jeruel.
[17] But you will not even need to fight. Take your positions; then stand still and watch the Lord's victory. He is with you, O people of Judah and Jerusalem. Do not be afraid or discouraged. Go out against them tomorrow, for the Lord is with you!"

The enemy or opposing forces of evil tried to bring a conflict or attack against God's people by waging war. God sent a Word through the prophet to deliver and prophesy to the king and the people of God that in spite of your enemies waging the conflict of war against you this battle is not yours it's the Lord's and the Lord Himself will fight for you but position yourself to release total praise and sound the alarm! Conflict, whether it's natural or spiritual, internal or external is like a tyrant or a rebellious internal or external conflict that tries to destroy an individual whether inside out or outside in before they reach their full capacity or God-given potential to fulfill their assignment or their destiny in life.

There are 5 ways to manage and disarm conflict.

1. Accommodating the conflict

2. Avoiding the conflict

3. Confronting the conflict

4. Resolving the conflict

5. Partnering with the conflict

Accommodating the conflict

Accommodate means to make fit, to help, to assist and to serve, to provide suitable supply or to manage. It also means not to see the problem but to provide the solution to the problem. Accommodating simply means to do more with less and to take what's not enough and to make it more than enough. (Don't panic in the face of the conflict!!)

> **Matthew 14:17 - 21 NLT**
> *17 "But we have only five loaves of bread and two fish!" they answered.*
> *18 "Bring them here," he said.*
> *19 Then he told the people to sit down on the grass. Jesus took the five loaves and two fish, looked up toward heaven, and blessed them. Then, breaking the loaves into pieces, he gave the bread to the disciples, who distributed it to the people.*
> *20 They all ate as much as they wanted, and afterward, the disciples picked up twelve baskets of leftovers.*
> *21 About 5,000 men were fed that day, in addition to all the women and children!"*

Here we find Jesus managing and disarming the conflict. Jesus sees a multitude of people hungry and starving in the wilderness because they have followed His ministry. When Jesus asked His disciples to accommodate the conflict by feeding these struggling and hungry people the disciples panicked. They said to Jesus how can we accommodate the conflict when there are so many people to feed and we have so little money. Jesus accommodated the conflict by instructing His disciples to improvise and bring back some samples called "accommodation" (food). There was only one disciple out of 12 that brought back "accommodation", 2 fish and 5 loaves of bread. What he brought back was the starter blessing (the appetizer) but Jesus used it to accommodate and He turned the starter blessing into an all-day buffet meal by simply accommodating the conflict. Jesus took the 2 fish and 5 loaves of bread and caused them to multiply. Although accommodating means to take what's not enough and to make it more than enough, it's important to accommodate the conflict and not to panic because of the conflict. IMPROVISE!

Avoiding the Conflict

Avoid means to escape, to withdraw from, to stop yourself from doing something or to keep something from happening, to stay clear from, to declare disabled, to detour and to cut off. It also means no longer necessary. We must pick and choose our battles as we avoid conflict as it relates to managing and disarming the conflict. You should never choose to enter or to engage yourself in a battle, conversation, argument or controversy that has nothing to do with your tomorrow, which is called your "future". Avoid that conflict at all cost!

2 Timothy 2:23NKJV
23 "But AVOID foolish and ignorant disputes, knowing that they generate strife."

ACTS 16:16-18 ERV (TALKS ABOUT AVOIDING THE CONFLICT.)

16 "One day we were going to the place for prayer, and a servant girl met us. She had a spirit in her that gave her the power to tell what would happen in the future. By doing this she earned a lot of money for the men who owned her.

17 She started following Paul and the rest of us around. She kept shouting, "These men are servants of the Most High God! They are telling you how you can be saved!"

18 SHE CONTINUED DOING THIS FOR MANY DAYS. This bothered Paul, so he turned and said to the spirit, "By the power of Jesus Christ, I command you to come out of her!" Immediately, the spirit came out."

The Apostle Paul avoided the conflict. Acts chapter 16, deals with the Apostle Paul and Silas being led by God to do ministry in Philippi. While there they began to do outreach and evangelism but they were led to go into prayer and to intercede as intercessors over the assignment. The Bible says each day that they were going to the place of prayer to intercede over the assignment God had given them there was a demon possessed girl who for many days kept trying to bring distractions, confusion, commotion and disturbances against Apostles Paul and Silas. The Bible says for many days the Apostle Paul avoided the conflict until he had to face the conflict, rebuke the conflict, expose the conflict and bring deliverance to the conflict because there is a time and place for everything. Avoiding the conflict simply means we must pick and choose our battles.

Confronting the conflict

Confront means facing a situation that makes you uncomfortable or to say something to someone when you they really don't want to hear it. Confronting means coming face to face, to stand or come in front of. A head-on collision happens when the past confronts the present and the future confronts the past, a clashing of immaturity and maturity, a transformation from the negative to the positive or just facing the man in the mirror called "self". Confronting conflicts is breath taking because it's when we usually have to face an individual or a situation that we are not comfortable with.

Genesis 13:8-9 GW

[8] *"Abram said to Lot, "Please, let's not have any more quarrels between us or between our herders. After all, we're relatives.* [9] *Isn't all this land yours also? Let's separate. If you go to the left, I'll go to the right, and if you go to the right, I'll go to the left."*

Abraham had to confront an ongoing conflict that was of self-interest after frequently seeing Lot and his people daily arguing and fighting with Abraham's servants. Sometimes instead of dealing with the same conflict day after day, week after week, month after month and year after year, we have to do like Abraham did with Lot, you go your way and I'll go my way. If you go left, I'll go right. If you go east, I'll go west. We must in any type of relationship after unnecessary conflict come to the conclusion that it's not going to work and we must separate.

When it comes to confronting the conflict that faces our lives; we must eventually confront the conflicts that we keep putting off, as if they're going to get better. We have to come to the reality that some things are what they are and some people are who they are. We can keep praying about a situation, fasting about it, talking about it, fussing and fighting about it but until we confront it for what it is and realize that no matter what we say or do to help the situation get better; it's not going to change, nor is it going to work.

I Samuel 16:1 talks about God telling the Prophet Samuel to stop crying and praying to Him over King Saul because I (God) have rejected him. Some people and some things that we are trying to fix, help change, keep crying over, hurting over, going broke over, and about to lose our minds over, we just have to realize that God, Himself has already placed an "Out of Order" sign on them and it.

Resolving the Conflict

Resolve means to settle or to find a solution to a problem; to reach a decision or to bring an end to something that needs closure. As we manage and disarm the conflict we must also know how to resolve the conflict. We discover too many times that people can tell you about a problem, show you a problem, or even confront you with a problem but they don't know how to resolve the problem. The person that discovers that empowerment is not talking about what's wrong but fixing what's wrong. This is a person that God uses to take the baton, become a trendsetter, or a mover and a shaker. They become reformers that cause movements. People that only talk about problems become the problem but people that solve problems are the ones that are rewarded for being problem solvers.

The reason that you go to the doctor is because the doctor resolves medical problems. You go to a lawyer because they resolve legal problems and a mechanic to resolve mechanical problems. So what problem are you resolving? What problem do you have the answer too? Are you the one that causes the problem or the one that solves the problem?

> **I Kings 10:1-3 GW**
> *[1] "The queen of Sheba heard about Solomon's reputation. (He owed his reputation to the name of the Lord.) So she came to test him with riddles.*
> *[2] She arrived in Jerusalem with a large group of servants, with camels carrying spices, a very large quantity of gold, and precious stones. When she came to Solomon, she talked to him about everything she had on her mind.*
> *[3] Solomon answered all her questions. No question was too difficult for the king to answer."*

When we look at I Kings 10 we discover that King Solomon was a problem solver. Solomon knew how to resolve conflict so much so that kings and queens from around the world came to King Solomon and in return they brought him large cargos that were filled with precious gold, silver and other precious jewels. They came because they wanted to learn from his wisdom, how to resolve conflicts and to be a problem solver.

Partnering with the conflict

A partnership is an agreed upon method of working together for the benefit of a promissory, agreed upon by people that agree to do business together.

> **Amos 3:3 ERV**
> ³*"Two people will not walk together unless they have agreed to do so."*

To partner means to share responsibility as well as to become accountable to the work, the investment and the investor, to receive at the end the full and complete benefit of the reward.

> **Luke 5:6-10 GW**
> ⁶*"After the men had done this, they caught such a large number of fish that their nets began to tear.*
> ⁷*So they signaled to their PARTNERS in the other boat to come and help them. Their PARTNERS came and filled both boats until the boats nearly sank.*
> ⁸*When Simon Peter saw this, he knelt in front of Jesus and said, "Leave me, Lord! I'm a sinful person!"*
> ⁹*Simon and everyone who was with him were amazed to see the large number of fish they had caught.*
> ¹⁰*James and John, who were Zebedee's sons and Simon's PARTNERS, were also amazed. Jesus told Simon, "Don't be afraid. From now on you will catch people instead of fish."*

All conflicts are not negative or a bad problem. Some conflicts are positive and are good problems to have and to solve. But the only way we can solve some conflicts is that we must learn how to partner with other partners that understand what we are trying to do is greater than what we can do alone. If you confess that God has called you and assigned you to do anything and you think that God has called you to do it by yourself, it's not God. Whenever God gives a person an assignment he or she will have to begin to form a committee of partnerships because the call and the assignment is bigger than us.

When Jesus told Peter to cast his net back into the lake to catch fish; Peter misinterpreted the catch to be for a fish. Jesus' interpretation of throw your net back into the lake was not to catch a fish but to catch many fish.

With what we are about to catch in this season, we must learn how to connect and partner with the right people. We will no longer catch the season of not enough, no longer will we catch the season of just enough but with the help of partners we will catch the season of more than enough. While working with partners that we are called to network with, we will discover the net worth of our network.

The Bible says Peter and his brother Andrew were partners in a fishing business. They almost lost their harvest season of more than enough because they were looking to catch in this season what they caught in last season. In the last season they caught the fish called not enough and just enough without realizing that they had tapped into a new season called more than enough. The season of more than enough would have almost gotten away if they had not beckoned for their partners, collaborated and merged partnerships with James and John who also had a fishing business. They caught an abundance of fish as partners, so, what almost got away would have gotten away if they had not partnered with someone who understood partnering the conflict.

Chapter 17

The Stronghold of Selfish-Control

(Control Freak)

The stronghold of selfish-control is a spiritual and a natural stronghold that causes one's flesh and spirit to become distracted and hindered from their focus, purpose and assignment in life. This stronghold causes a person to become egotistical, greedy, hoggish, prejudice, stingy, self-centered, self-interested, narrow minded, out for #1 and wrapped up in one's self. A control freak is someone who feels justified in attempting to control everything and everybody and becomes aggressive in controlling every relationship that they enter into such as companionship, friendship and various auxiliaries they are placed in or over.

A person that's a control freak only hangs around people they believe are controllable, weak, fragile, naïve, or a push over. They are only attracted to people that refuse to think for themselves. A control freak is an insecure person with serious issues. If they are not in control they become angry, out of control, manipulative and obsessive with a takeover spirit. A person that struggles under the influence of selfish-control becomes such a control freak that it causes them to become a dictator, perpetrator, and violator of every relationship they are in. This stronghold causes a person to become a control freak by nature and has spiritual demonic tendencies that cause them to become physically, verbally and spiritually violent and abusive. The stronghold of selfish-control causes a person to lose complete mental and physical control.

Selfish-control verses Self-control

Selfish-Control

1. Selfish-control is seen in a person who only thinks about themselves and is abusive.

2. A selfish-control person tries to control the outcome.

3. A selfish-control person micro-manages. Micro means small, little, almost nothing.

4. A selfish-control person becomes distracted, aggravated, and frustrated by the smallest things because they operate in the minor not the major.

Self-Control

1. Self-control is defined as the ability to discipline one's self by controlling one's emotions, behavior and desires in the face of external demands and in order to function in society.

2. A self-controlled person has discipline and is always thinking about helping someone else by demonstrating disciplinary actions.

3. A self-controlled person plans the outcome.

4. A self-controlled person mega-manages. Mega means large, big, great and even important.

5. A self-controlled person becomes focused and in-tuned into the mega-management so they complete what they start because they major in the major, not the minor. They don't allow themselves to become distracted by unnecessary drama and they stay focused on their assignment.

   In psychology self-control is sometimes referred to as self-regulation which is essential in behavior to achieve goals and avoid impulse emotions that can prove to be negative.

Proverbs 25:28 MSG
"A person without self-control is like a house with its doors and windows knocked out."

2 Timothy 1:7 WEB
"For God didn't give us a spirit of fear, but of power, love, and self-control."

Proverbs 16:32 ERV
"It is better to be patient than to be a strong soldier. It is better to control your anger than to capture a city."

Proverbs 23:6 ERV
"Don't eat with selfish people. Control any desire you have for their finest foods."

Proverbs 29:11 ERV
"Fools are quick to express their anger, but wise people are patient and control themselves."

Psalms 8:6 ERV
"You put them in charge of everything you made. You put everything under their control."

A person that has selfish-control keeps things all for themselves with the primary concern being one's own interest, benefit, and welfare and not caring about anyone else. A person that struggles with the stronghold of selfish-control often times becomes very controlling and abusive. Their need for control is birthed from the spirit of fear that causes a person to become afraid of losing something or someone. It causes them to be abusive in every relationship they are in because of their own jealousy and fear. The worst type of abuse is not physical abuse but verbal abuse. Physical abuse causes wounds and wounds heal but verbal abuse causes mental abuse and mental abuse causes a person to become a slave to someone as well as being a slave to their own thinking. This type of abuse leaves a permanent wound in a person's mind that will never heal unless they break away from the person who has that influence and power over their mind. The person that exerts this control uses fear factors to dominate and control the mindset of the other person. They can cause a person to have mood swings during the day because of the things they say to them.

> **2 TIMOTHY 3:1-5 ERV**
>
> *"Remember this, There are some terrible times coming in the last day.[2] People will love only themselves and money. They will be proud and boast about themselves. They will abuse others with insults. They will not obey their parents. They will be ungrateful and against all that is pleasing to God.[3] They will have no love for others and will refuse to forgive anyone. They will talk about others to hurt them and will have NO SELF-CONTROL. They will be cruel and hate what is good.[4] People will turn against their friends. They will do foolish things without thinking and will be so proud of themselves. Instead of loving God, they will love pleasure.[5] They will go on pretending to be devoted to God, but they will refuse to let that "devotion" change the way they live. Stay away from these people!"*

THE SYMPTOMS, SIGNS AND SIDE EFFECTS OF THE STRONGHOLD OF SELFISH – CONTROL

The symptoms, signs and side effects of the stronghold of selfish control are evident when a person becomes a dictator, self-centered, greedy, self-seeking, or egotistic. They also struggle with being very territorial, having a takeover spirit and they become very crafty, cunning, manipulating, jealous and extremely abusive. The stronghold of selfish-control causes a person to become a control freak and to operate out of the spirit of fear that causes them to struggle with phobias and fear factors.

A person that appears to be the most dominant and strongest is usually the weakest. They only appear to be strong when they are in complete control but when they are not in control of their life or the lives of others, phobias and fear factors kick in because fear is torment. It creates horror that bring about devastation which brings forth anxiety, stress, nightmares and sleep disorders. Many people that struggle with selfish control also suffer from previous hurts and brokenness from past relationships that have caused them to have trust and consistency issues.

They try to move forward in life while at the same time they are still struggling to start a new relationship. If a person is still struggling from the break up of a previous relationship because of hurt, pain and brokenness then they are not ready to move forward with someone else in a new relationship. If they start a new relationship while still broken by the old relationship they will treat the new relationship like the old relationship because they are still struggling with a lack of trust and consistency as well as feelings of doubt, betrayal, being used and abuse.

JOSHUA 5:8 says the people of God were in pursuit of reaching the promise land (life of fulfillment) but they could not cross over into a place of newness until they were (healed) from their circumcision. Circumcision means the cutting away of the old flesh, cutting off, to bring closure and to bring something to an end. It's time to bring closure to relationships, situations and people from the past and give them the benediction!

THERE ARE 3 TYPES OF SELF – CONTROL STRATEGIES FOR OVERCOMING THE STRONGHOLD OF SELFISH – CONTROL

The first is called environmental strategies which involve changing surroundings, cultures, time, places or situations where one experiences problematic behavior. Environmental strategy changes cause us through self-control to change and or carefully choose our circle of people whom we socialize and hang out with. These changes help us to avoid pitfalls and setbacks that we have previously had because of a lack of disciplined behavior and failure to pick and choose the right people to share your time and day with. If you don't want these cycles to reoccur, you have to change your surroundings!

Learn how to make the necessary adjustments in the daily, weekly, and monthly scheduling of what you need to do instead what it is you want to do. Never allow your day to become so routine and habitual that you aren't accountable and responsible for being more productive and successful. Hold yourself accountable but also find someone within your circle to hold you responsible and accountable as well. Make adjustments in scheduling to ensure you don't form the pattern or cycle that causes you to talk more about what you want to do than produce results or have any evidence of what you have accomplished. These necessary adjustments of the responsibility and accountability will manifest creditability.

A behavioral strategy which consists of breaking cycles of bad habits is the second control strategy that can be used to overcome this stronghold. This strategy involves changing our patterns, routines and the stewardship of our money, relationships and our present which prepares us for our future by evaluating what we have done wrong to cause the bad habits that produces cycles of failure.

In order to break a cycle of bad habits we must begin developing a life of good habits such as implementing new ideas, plans, and strategies or surrounding ourselves with people that are as competent and serious about their life, goals and destiny as we are. Through researching, reviewing and studying what caused your bad habits that produced a cycle of failure we can turn them into good habits that lead to cycles of success. You can never change what you cannot understand! Bad decisions produce bad results, good decisions produce good results and you will never break your bad habits if you're still making the same bad decisions. So when you change what you do you will get a different result.

PROVERBS 4:7 AMP

"The beginning of Wisdom is: get Wisdom (skillful and godly Wisdom)! [For skillful and godly Wisdom is the principal thing.] And with all you have gotten, get understanding (discernment, comprehension, and interpretation)."

The 31 Self-Strongholds

Some good tips to use that will hold you accountable and help you to become consistent in developing good habits are to put your plans, your visions, your goals and your strategies in writing and put them in various places within your house to encourage you when you begin to feel vulnerable, weak, distracted and at the place of giving up and falling back into bad habits. Place on mirrors, the refrigerator, in the places where you are the most as well as your vehicles. You can use sticky notes, laminated papers or put your writings in picture frames. Flag yourself a daily reminder to stick to the plans, goals, strategy, the blueprint, promissory agreements, covenant or vows you've made with God or someone else that when you look at it you will be motivated and reminded not to give up!

You must learn how to encourage yourself when you are succeeding and overcoming at what you have failed at. You must also learn how to be self -disciplined and be true to yourself when you are failing at what you are trying to achieve. (2 SAMUEL 6:7-8)

Eliminate reoccurring behaviors that set you up to fail and remove all stumbling blocks that cause you to become weaker and not stronger. Write yourself a behavioral contract to hold yourself accountable for carrying out the 'Self-control Covenant'. This simply means daily you interview and grade yourself and at the end of the day determine how successful or unsuccessful you were. Grade yourself on your integrity, character, attitude, professionalism, love, forgiveness and patience was for the day. Use a scale of 1-10 each day and out of 7 days if you made less than 50 – 55 you fail for that week.

Thirdly, the functional and disciplinary behavior involves changing one's thoughts or beliefs or mindset toward a particular behavior. If you change the way you think you can change the way you live. In order to be functional you need to know four things:

1. Your IDENTITY (Who You Are)

2. Your CALL (What You Are Called To Do)

3. Your PURPOSE (How to Do It)

4. Your ASSIGNMENT (Where to Do It)

The 31 Self-Strongholds

Identifying who you are and understanding how to make adjustments in each season is vital for success in each new level of calling. Self- discipline and identify will help you to gain insight on the purpose and responsibility at your new level. Luke 12:48 says for much is given much is required which simply means the more we mature in our identity, calling and purpose the more responsibility or assignments God will add to us. We will always know when God is giving us a greater assignment that will enlarge our territory. It's when the place where we are in our life and seasons is no longer enough and it becomes too small for us. 2 KINGS 6:1 tells us about the Spiritual Sons of Elisha who discovered in their season that the place where they were was too small for them. They went to the man of God and said this place of assignment is too small so please give us our new assignment so we can we move forward. Elisha's new assignment for his Spiritual sons was to remove and cut down trees that was stagnating their growth. We must understand we cannot build anything massive or larger until we first cut down or remove some things. You can't go up until you remove or bring some things down first. In order to grow and increase in your season you must check out your surroundings to figure out what's preventing growth and development.

Elisha gave them instructions to go forward and cut down trees. There are some people in your life that have chosen to stay at the same level. These people are called temporary or scaffolding people and have been assigned only to be in your life for a season, to help start the process but they will never be able to finish it with you. Temporary or scaffolding people can be compared to scaffolding boards that are used at a construction site to start the building process but when the construction, the building and the work is finished the assignment is finished and the scaffolding boards are no longer needed. The scaffolding boards are then removed because they were never designed to stay there permanently but only temporarily. Too many people, when trying to understand the functional and disciplinary behaviors that produce self-control not selfish-control, get caught up in who's coming into our life instead of who's leaving our life. To help with understanding your new assignment we must do three things:

1. Be courageous enough to move when you need to move.
2. Remove people when you need to remove them.
3. Cut people out of your life when it's time to cut them off.

MATTHEW 14:22 NKJV

[22] *Immediately Jesus made His disciples get into the boat and go before Him to the other side, while He sent the multitudes away.*

Understanding the strategy of being functional and disciplined involves always knowing your identity, calling, purpose and assignment and knowing these things will always lead to knowing

1. Who am I?
2. What am I?
3. How am I?
4. Where am I?

If you don't know anything else, you need to know your identity (who you are). In Genesis 32:27 before God could bless Jacob He asked him the question, who are you? It took Jacob to almost lose everything because of the struggle of selfish-control for over 20 years to discover his identity (WHO HE WAS) because all of his life he not only struggled with identity but he also struggled with instructions. Before Jacob was born, his mother Rebekah, carried him and his twin brother Esau inside of her womb. God made a promise to Rebekah about Jacob's greatness and the man he would become in the future. So Jacob chased prophesy and a dream rather than chasing his identity. You can never fulfill prophecy for your life as well or the promise God made to you without understanding who you are.

God would not bless Jacob until he knew his identity so God asked Jacob, what is your name and who are you? Instead of trying to fulfill the promise made by God he tried to control the promise and cause it to come to pass without knowing his identity which caused him to struggle under the stronghold of selfish-control.

He was so manipulative, cunning, and crafty that he lied to his father Isaac about who he was when he claimed to be his brother Esau. He manipulated and took advantage of his brother Esau when he knew his brother was weak, vulnerable and about to give up in life that he influenced him with selfish-control. Jacob acted out of fear and ran away only to become homeless and to lose everything all because of the stronghold called selfish-control.

Another example of self-control is seen in the people who thought they were helping the man who was possessed with many demons. As soon as Jesus came with the disciples and got off the boat Legion came and threw himself at Jesus' feet. The man didn't know who Jesus was until the demon told him. The demon asked Jesus, have you come to torment us before our time? Jesus couldn't touch that man by law because he had been around dead things. Jesus was acting out of divine timing to bring healing, deliverance and salvation to the man as he does in our lives today. The man was controlled by religion, tradition and the people that were trying to control him couldn't help themselves. The reality is these people were never trying to help this man but trying to control him.

How to let go of self-control

The woman that broke the Alabaster box/jar filled with oil wasn't trying to control the flow nor was she trying to control how the oil came out but instead she broke the jar that caused the oil to run freely.

> MATTHEW 26:7 GW
> *"While Jesus was sitting there, a woman went to him with a bottle of very expensive perfume and poured it on his head."*

> LUKE 7:37 AMP
> *[37] Now there was a woman in the city who was [known as]a [e]sinner; and [f]when she found out that He was reclining at the table in the Pharisee's house, she brought an alabaster vial of perfume;*

MARK 14:3 EXB

[3] "Jesus was in Bethany at the house of ·Simon, who had a skin disease [[L]Simon the leper; [C]for leprosy, see 1:40; Simon may have been healed by Jesus]. While Jesus was ·eating there [reclining; [C]the posture for a banquet or dinner party; 2:15, a woman approached him with an alabaster ·jar [vial] filled with very expensive perfume, made of pure nard. She opened [broke open] the ·jar [vial] and poured the perfume on Jesus' head."

Although what this woman did caused the alabaster jar to become broken, crushed, shattered, and damaged, no longer in one piece or working order the broken jar did not change the value of the oil because the jar is replaceable. The oil represents treasure, the anointing and the power that changed the atmosphere because she did not try to control the moment but she learned how to flow in the moment by setting not controlling the atmosphere! When you're free from trying to control what's coming out you'll discover you're anointed to change the atmosphere as the woman did when she broke the jar of oil. The best thing God can do for us is to break or allow us to become broken in order for us to be delivered from fear.

2 CORINTHIANS 4:7

[7] *"Our bodies are made of clay, yet we have the treasure of the Good News in them. This shows that the superior power of this treasure belongs to God and doesn't come from us."*

If we're ever going to reach the treasure that's inside of us we must allow God to break the vessel because the vessel can be replaced but that which is inside the vessel called the treasure is priceless. Too many times we try in relationships, positions or in a place of authority to control the outcome by placing a bandage over the wounds or the hurt or by trying to glue something back together. We think that we're trying to preserve or hold on to what we call a precious memory by piecing, trying to tie or wrap things up but in reality we're just trying to control the situation. The best thing we can do is to allow God to break it!

Broken means to be crushed, wounded, or damaged and no longer in one piece or in working order. It also means changing directions. Jeremiah 18 talks about the potter's house where God takes the vessel that had become hard, brittle and stubborn and how the potter breaks it so He can use the same vessel that he had broken and make it something better. God's message to the prophet was that He did not try to control the situation or the condition that the vessel was in but he allowed it to be broken so he could make it better.

Chapter 18

The Stronghold of Self-Fear / Phobia

(Fear Factor – Don't Let Fear Win!)

The stronghold of self-fear causes one to become delirious or in a disturbed state of mind to have panic attacks. Self-fear causes a person to become paralyzed and mentally intoxicated when making right decisions. The stronghold of self-fear causes a person to go into a cycle of past failures which creates a pattern of repeated mistakes and failures that are caused by rejection.

The children of Israel wandered in the (cycle or circle) wilderness for 40 years because of fear. The spirit of fear caused them to miss their promise, purpose and assignment for 40 years. Fear caused them to panic and to begin talking about going back to Egypt, back to the old way of doing things; to the old way of life, old habits and old relationships.

Fear always causes a person to repeat their cycle of failures. The enemy, called Fear always tries to distract a person causing them to lose focus of their future by showing them the residue of their past. Residue means a small amount of something that remains after the main part has been taken away. Only 5% of the problem is residue but the other 95% of the problem is called fear. So fear always causes something minor to look like something major. Fear causes a person to exaggerate and to hallucinate by making a problem look bigger than it really is. Fear also causes a person to see and hear thing that don't exist. A person suffering from the spirit of fear begins having anxiety and panic attacks which causes them to begin operating out of order and to become dysfunctional.

There Are Two Kinds of Fear

The first is called phobia and second is called phobos or (yir'ah).

Phobia is a fear that causes a person to become irrational with fear of a specific thing or situation. This fear compels one to try to avoid the problem despite the awareness and reassurance that it is not dangerous. A phobia always causes a person to run away from the problem rather than confront the problem because of their fear.

The second type of fear is called phobos. Phobos or yir'ah means a Godly fear, honor, respect, loyal, alarm, reverence and a sense of awe. It also means to remove one's self, and lastly, it means it was not what I thought it would be, it turned out better than I thought. Genesis 28:17 talks about Jacob having a phobia and because of his fear he ran for his life as a fugitive from his brother Esau who was planning to kill him. In doing so Jacob became homeless and hungry; to a place in his life that he had nothing and no one.

The spirit of fear and phobias attacked his mind, identity, calling, purpose and assignment then God revealed unto Jacob a dream. In this dream, there was an open door to heaven and He let down a ladder and sent Angels to descend and ascend transporting supplies and provisions to Jacob. God's revelation and interpretation unto Jacob helped him to overcome his phobia and to discover that it was a PHOBOS moment. Jacob testified in verse 17 that what he thought was a phobia moment turned out to be a phobos moment and that this was an awesome place and he knew it not. Jacob didn't say that he was in an awesome presence but He said he was in an awesome place. He said this because phobia is a fear that creates an intangible presence but phobos is a Godly fear that reveals the manifest place.

The devil always tries to use phobias to get us out of the presence of God before God can manifest in the place, the secret place. So that we too may not discover that our going through, is not a phobia but a phobos, manifest place with God. Phobias are where Satan comes to steal, kill and destroy. Phobos is where Christ comes that we may have life and have it more abundantly.

The Symptoms, Signs and Side Effects of the Stronghold of Self-Fear

Luke 21:26 NKJV
"Men's hearts failing them from fear and the expectation of those things which are coming on the earth, for the powers of the heavens will be shaken."

The symptoms, signs and side effects of the stronghold of self-fear produces and brings about anxiety attacks, disorders, panic attacks, numbness and tingling in various places of your body, dizziness, chest pains, headaches, neck tension, upset stomach or nervous stomach, nausea, shortness of breath, electric shock feelings, shooting pains in the face, weakness in legs, seizures, heart attacks, strokes, death, inability to rest, sleeping disorders, satanic oppression, unnatural sickness, and feeling as if you are going crazy or losing your mind.

When we look at the root of the spirit of fear that comes from the enemy we learn that Satan's main strategy is to destroy a person's life by causing an anxiety disorder. An anxiety disorder causes anxiety attacks and panic attacks which Satan uses to attack your mind and contaminates your spirit.

2 Timothy 1:7 NKJV
"Timothy's mind was attacked by the spirit of fear. "For God has not given us a spirit of fear, but of power and of love and of a sound mind."

Anxiety is defined as a state of uneasiness, an uncertainty of your future. Anxiety occurs when we think and act in an apprehensive manner such as when worrying about things, people and problems that are beyond our control. Anxiety is not a medical, biological, chemical, or genetic problem but a mental one. It's when Satan attacks a person's mind and that person's mind becomes a battlefield and the individual struggles with mental breakdown because he or she cannot handle the pressures of life. Anxiety is a disorder that disrupts a person from being in order and causes a spiritual, physical and mental confusion in one's life. Anxiety that is birthed from fear, troubles one's state of mind and causes a dysfunctional disorder as well as a person to become paranoid about every little thing.

F. E. A. R. ACRONYMS

False	False	False	Forgive
Expectations	Experiences	Emotions	Everything
Appearing	Appearing	Appearing	And
Real	Real	Real	Run

Forgive	Finding	Failure	Forgot
Everything	Excuses	Expected	Everything
And	And	And	And
Remember	Reasons	Received	Relax

THE 5 TYPES OF SELF – FEAR/ PHOBIAS

1. THE FEAR OF PAIN

2. THE FEAR OF LOSS

3. THE FEAR OF NO GAIN/ OR THE FEAR OF NOT HAVING

4. THE FEAR OF UNCERTAINTY

5. THE FEAR OF FAILURE

THE FEAR OF PAIN

The fear of pain deals with pain, hurt and the extremities of pain that are excruciating. The fear of pain is a phobia that is called (Algo`phobia) which is a Greek word which means having the fear of pain. It is the fear of thinking about pain which causes the pain to be worse than it really is.

For example, you can have a physical pain in your body on a scale of 1-10. The level of pain could only be a 4 but the fear of pain or the phobia elevates the pain level to a 10 because the fear of pain is worse than the pain itself.

2 TIMOTHY 2:3-4 AMP

3 "Take [with me] your share of the HARDSHIPS and SUFFERING [which you are called to endure] as a good (first-class) soldier of Christ Jesus.
4 No soldier when in service gets entangled in the enterprises of [civilian] life; his aim is to satisfy and please the one who enlisted him."

The Apostle Paul tells his Spiritual son Timothy about being a good soldier, to toughen up, man-up and to endure hardness as a good soldier. Paul is bringing correction to his Spiritual son about how to endure hurt and suffering in battle. Timothy was the Pastor/Evangelist/Elder at the Church of Ephesus and the Ephesians along with Timothy had gone through spiritual warfare and attacks. The spirit of fear came over Timothy and this caused his faith to be so shaken that he began to doubt his identity, calling, purpose, and assignment.

Apostle Paul was in jail ministering a message of encouragement to a leader that had his freedom. What do you do when you are gifted, anointed, and still bound in bondage? Apostle Paul told Timothy that God has not given you the spirit of fear but the power of love and a sound mind, self-control; so man-up and endure the hurt, the pain and the suffering that you are going through as a good soldier would do. When a good soldier is wounded in battle he trains his mind not to focus on the pain or the battle that he is in but to look forward to how great the victory would feel beyond the pain and in the face of defeat.

A good soldier sees the end from the beginning and this is when he claims and celebrates the victory while the battle is still going on. So, don't wait until your battle, tribulation, or persecution is over shout now! Claim your victory!

THE FEAR OF LOSS

The fear of loss deals with being afraid to suffer a relationship loss as well as tangible loss such as a house, a car, a job or any materialistic things. The thought of losing what we have gained creates in our mind panic and desperation to guard and protect. The sense of loss is preceded by attachment in which we connect things and people to our sense of identity, making them an extension of ourselves. Loss then becomes a loss of self which relates to the fear of extension. We follow Job's example and not allow the attachments of people and things to define our identity.

JOB 1:20-21 AMP

20 *"Then Job arose and rent his robe and shaved his head and fell down upon the ground and worshiped*

21 *And said, Naked (without possessions) came I [into this world] from my mother's womb, and naked (without possessions) shall I depart. The Lord gave and the Lord has taken away; blessed (praised and magnified in worship) be the name of the Lord."*

JOB 3:25-26 ERV

25 *"I was afraid something terrible would happen, and what I feared most has happened.*

26 *I cannot calm down or relax. I am too upset to rest!"*

Satan would use Job's fear of loss to attack Job's identity, calling, purpose and assignment which is why Satan told God what Job would do.

JOB 1:9-11 ERV

9 *"Satan answered the LORD, "But Job has a good reason to respect you. (Phobos)*

10 *You always protect him, his family, and everything he has. You have blessed him and made him successful in everything he does. He is so wealthy that his herds and flocks are all over the country.*

[11] *But if you were to destroy everything he has, I promise you that he would curse you to your face."*

Satan attacked, killed and destroyed Job's sons and daughters, his cattle and his wealth which resulted in a type of fear called the fear of loss but it was not until Job overcame this fear of loss that he conquered the Spirit of fear. Thank God for Job chapter 42 where Job overcame the fear of loss and he began to pray for his friends. Job 42:12 says God gave Job double for his trouble! Double blessed!

THE FEAR OF NO GAIN/ OR THE FEAR OF NOT HAVING

This particular fear is the flip-side of the fear of loss and relates to losing everything you have gained. It causes you to believe that you are never going to have, achieve, or become anything in life and that who and what you are now is all you'll ever be. The thoughts and fears of not having can cause a person to have anxiety and panic disorders.

The fear of no gain or the fear of not having can be driven by anticipating loss. This means fear has convinced you that you are not good enough to have that man or you're not good enough to have that woman. You're not good enough to have that job or you're not good enough to have that friendship. This fear convinces you that you're not good enough to be blessed, you're not good enough to have the best and you're, not good enough to have that position that God has ordained you to walk in.

The fear of no gain or the fear of not having causes a person to be afraid to go through and to face pain because as we all know no "pain, no gain." If you are planning on having the best in life it will cost you some pain, hurt and some suffering but because you have paid the price at the end you will discover it was worth it all! So remember no pain, no gain!

2 CORINTHIANS 4:8-10 ERV

[8] *"We have troubles all around us, but we are not defeated. We often don't know what to do, but we don't give up.*

[9] *We are persecuted, but God does not leave us. We are hurt sometimes, but we are not destroyed.*

[10] *So we constantly experience the death of Jesus in our own bodies, but this is so that the life of Jesus can also be seen in our bodies."*

THE FEAR OF UNCERTAINTY

The fear of uncertainty deals with becoming disconnected between faith and doubt, believing and unbelieving, staying positive and being negative all at the same time. To overcome this fear we must bring balance to our life. In order to do that we must use a model called C.I.A. and we are not talking about the government's (C.I.A.) Central Intelligence Agency but instead we are talking about control, identity and access.

Our Sense of Control lets us know when we are safe and how to turn our environment into our purpose.

Our sense of identity tells us who we are and it keeps us from taking on a false identity no matter what state of mind or season we are in, good or bad. Your sense of identity will always keep you balanced and true to who you are.

Our sense of access lets us know we are approaching or entering a place; we have been given permission to approach open doors and the right or privilege to gain the secret password to what's locked in or what's locked out. Having access means to be profitable so when we understand the Sense of Access we will totally understand that no weapon formed against us will prosper. (Isaiah 54:17) We will also understand by the sense of access that Christ will open a door that no man can shut and will shut a door that no man can open (Revelation 3:8). When you have been granted the sense of access you receive wisdom, knowledge and understanding with divine instruction and a set of keys to the Kingdom of Heaven so that whatever you bind on earth will be bound in heaven and whatever you loose on earth will be loosed in heaven; and the gates of hell will not prevail against you. (Matthew 16:19)

THE FEAR OF FAILURE

The fear of failure convinces a person that they are going to fail before they even try. This spirit of fear tells people they can't or will ever be successful so don't try.

Failure means unsuccessful, nonperformance of something due, required or expected. This means you were expected to receive something but because you didn't participate or show up, nor did you attempt to succeed you disqualified yourself from the opportunity to win, to conquer and to be blessed. You disqualified yourself because of the fear of failure and never gave yourself a chance to be successful not because you couldn't just because you wouldn't even make an attempt to be successful. You caused yourself to be in default by your own delinquency or failure to appear.

The fear of failure means filing bankruptcy which means you were not penalized by someone else but you caused a foreclosure by filing bankruptcy on yourself when you still had good credit with God. You were a no-show and it was your time, your season, and your opportunity, to be successful, blessed and victorious but again you failed to appear. Your failure to appear caused you to be in default and disqualified you from being more than a conquer. The fear of failure also causes one to doubt and cancel out ones purpose and assignment in life.

> ### MATTHEW 14:28-31 ERV
> [28] *"Peter said, "Lord, if that is really you, tell me to come to you on the water."*
> [29] *Jesus said, "Come, Peter." Then Peter left the boat and walked on the water to Jesus.*
> [30] *But while Peter was walking on the water, he saw the wind and the waves. HE WAS AFRAID AND BEGAN SINKING into the water. He shouted, "Lord, save me!"*
> [31] *Then Jesus caught Peter with his hand. He said, "YOUR FAITH IS SMALL. WHY DID YOU DOUBT?"*

The 31 Self-Strongholds

When we look at Matthew 14:28-31, we discover that the fear of failure assigns and attaches itself to Peter's moment. While Peter was walking in the supernatural favor of God; he in that moment had already overcame the fear of the storm that they had encountered while on the boat. Now he had been given a command and divine instructions by Jesus to step out of the natural into the Spirit realm and walk by faith and not by sight. The Word of God says Peter was successfully walking on the water by the supernatural favor of God but he became distracted by the fear of failure which caused him to give up and to quit when he was experiencing success. How is it that God can at one moment reveal unto us how to win in our season, be blessed and to make progress in our season and just that quick we become distracted and lose our focus; especially since He has already proven to us that we can be successful. Although Peter allowed success to turn back into the fear of failure but he shows us a tool for recovering success at the moment of failure. Even though Peter became distracted and lost his focus and he began to sink he refused to drown because Peter had enough trust in Jesus to call out Him.

Peter did not allow his moment of distraction to cause a setback or to deny him because he understood he may be delayed in his assignment and success but he decided he will not be denied. So in the midst of failing caused by the spirit of fear he came to one conclusion, I may be sinking, and I may be failing, but I refuse to drown! Why? Because God made me a promise when I was on the other side and Jesus gave me divine instructions for my assignment. The divine instructions and the blueprint never said that he would drown so he refused too because he understood while trying to get to the next place or assignment, he would run into trouble, suffering, pain, setback, disappointment, sickness, some break ups and you might even be sinking in between here and there while you are trying to get to the other side but one thing was for certain. With the help of Jesus we will not drown!

Chapter 19

The Stronghold of Self-Depression

(Overcoming the Spirit of Depression)

The stronghold of self-depression occurs when the enemy creates a fortress against your mind that causes your mind to become a prisoner to satanic activities. When this stronghold attaches to your life it will cause a person's thoughts, behaviors, feelings, and sense of well-being to come under Spiritual Warfare. The stronghold of depression causes a person to become spiritually, physically, and mentally fatigued making them feel hopeless, helpless, worthless, guilty, and irrational and/or burned out.

Depression is dejection of the mind. It is darkness over one's life that causes feelings of being cast down, pressed down, discouraged and dishonored. People who suffer from depression have difficulty sleeping and changes in their appetite. Depression not only affects your emotions but also causes physical diseases. Chronically depressed people are at a greater risk of developing cancer. Survivors of heart attacks who also suffer from depression have an increased risk of dying within 6 months. Depression can come from grief, sorrow, and disappointment.

Isaiah 53:4 AMP
"Surely He has borne our griefs (sicknesses, weaknesses, and DISTRESSES) and carried our sorrows and pains [of punishment], yet we [ignorantly] considered Him stricken, smitten, and afflicted by God [as if with leprosy]."

Depression Statistics

1. Suicidal depression claims more lives than war, murder and natural disease all combined together.

2. 25 million Americans suffer from depression each year.

3. Over 50% of all people who died by suicide suffered from a major depression. If you include alcoholics and drug users that are depressed, the total goes up to 75%.

4. Depression affects nearly 50% of teenagers in America, between the ages 13-18 in a given year.

5. More deaths, murders, heart attacks, suicides, and sickness, are caused by depression than any other reason in the world.

80% to 90% of people with depression struggle with what is called shock, denial, disbelief and unbelief of their own steps to depression because they have suppressed their feelings, their hurt and their pain and are in denial that they have a problem with depression. That's why when you ask an average person when they are going through something, are you okay their response 80%-90% of the time is, I'm okay, I'm alright, it doesn't bother me. They also tend to say things like I'm not letting it get to me and I've moved past it but the reality is they haven't moved past anything.

They've just learned how to suppress the depression that has progressed into oppression and is elevating into a deeper obsession so much so that if they don't hurry and confront their inner fear, hurt and pain it will become a total demonic possession. A satanic influence will possess and take over their life and this influence leads to murder, suicides and sickness.

6 - STAGES OF SELF – DEPRESSION

1. Shock and denial (Matthew 26:34-35)

2. Entertaining suppressing thoughts (Luke 10:38-40)

3. Pain and hurt (1 Chronicles 4:9)

4. Anger and guilt (Genesis 4:8-11)

5. Acceptance (Romans 12:1-2)

6. Rehab and rebuilding from depression (Nehemiah 1:3; 4:6)

THE FIRST STAGE IS CALLED SHOCK AND DENIAL

The term shock means to be suddenly upset by suppressing situations and problems that a person has experienced. These problems or situations have been caused by the unexpected, the unexplained or the unplanned things that happen in a person's life. The term denial means a rehearsal of refusing to believe or to except something as truth. The first stage of depression is when the shock has taken place in a person's life that often causes them to be in denial and to refuse to believe or except what has happened to them is the truth. It makes a person almost feel like what's happening is a dream and that it cannot be happening to them.

THE SECOND STAGE IS CALLED ENTERTAINING SUPPRESSING THOUGHTS

The second stage of depression is to begin entertaining and suppressing thoughts that have brought confusion, hurt, and pain in their life.

2 CORINTHIANS 10:4-6 AMP

[4] *"For the weapons of our warfare are not physical [weapons of flesh and blood], but they are mighty before God for the overthrow and destruction of strongholds,*

[5] *[Inasmuch as we] refute arguments and theories and reasoning and every proud and lofty thing that sets itself up against the [true] knowledge of God; and we lead every thought and purpose away captive into the obedience of Christ (the Messiah, the Anointed One),*

[6]
Being in readiness to punish every [insubordinate for his] disobedience, when your own submission and obedience [as a church] are fully secured and complete."

The words entertain or entertainer means to perform or to an actor or actress it means to perform by playing a part. When we look at the stronghold of depression that deals with entertaining and suppressing thoughts; we see a person who suffers with this stronghold who begins to open up their mind to seducing spirits that have form strongholds in their mind and has caused them to become their own prisoner.

The influence of these seducing spirits and this stronghold causes a person to pretend or to perform as if they are something or someone they are not. Too many times when a person is going through the stages of depression they begin to entertain the wrong company of people, things and spirits. This is typically referred to as "misery Loves Company" and pain loves her hurt which results in the entertainment of seducing spirits that begin to placate our thoughts and conversations.

THE THIRD STAGE IS CALLED PAIN AND GUILT

Once shock and denial which is the first level of depression have set in; the entertaining and suppressing thoughts of level two bring about the pain and guilt of the 3rd level of depression. The third stage of depression takes on the tangible experience of pain and guilt and the enemy now begins to make a person feel guilty as if everything was their fault even when they were innocent.

Whenever we go through a traumatic experience the opportunity to process the experience emotionally will always be a delayed negative reaction because we live in a society that ignores the consequences of pain and guilt. The feelings of pain and guilt as well as trying to get past and cope with what has just left them devastated, broken, and confused are among the most common struggles of those dealing with depression. They now try to rationalize the pain and guilt or the depth of losing a love one, a divorce, a separation, a lay-off from a job, or the crisis that they are having by just trying to balance the thoughts of suppression and oppression. They experience a sense of pain and guilt, an inability to cope or to move on or they feel like they can't live because of the tragedy that has happened.

THE FOURTH STAGE IS CALLED ANGER OUT OF FEAR

The next stage of depression is one that consists of anger out of fear. Stage one shock and denial has happened. In stage two, you've entertained the wrong thoughts or counseling and in stage three the pain and guilt has now caused you to get to a place dealing with the fight between the thoughts of wanting to live and the thoughts of wanting to die. In stage four, anger out of fear causes a person to start becoming something or someone that they are not.

Although anger is a natural feeling when life doesn't go according to plan, what a person does with that anger from fear will determine if they can recover from the devastation or not.

When you study the nature of a snake that strikes or bites a person you will find that the snake doesn't bite or strike an individual out of offense or because he's that mean. It strikes and bites because it's afraid and it's on defense.

So many times when people lose a love one to death or had a relationship to end badly, they act out of character because of anger out of fear. They may angrily say things or do things that's not really who they are. During this fourth stage your anger is out of control because of fear.

THE FIFTH STAGE IS CALLED ACCEPTANCE

This stage of depression is called the acceptance or the remedy stage. It's called this because at this point you can still recover from the depression because this is the remedy and the antidote stage that can bring healing.

Acceptance occurs when a person acknowledges the reality and is ready to let go of the previous hurt, pain, anger and fear. It indicates that the person will no longer entertain the wrong thoughts, will move past the shock and denial and the anger resulting from fear because they now realize it's time to let it go. It's time to be delivered, healed or set free. It's time to let him or her, let the pain and hurt go, let the betrayal go and the lie go and choose to live through and after all of it.

They know acceptance is not how their story ends but it is just a closing of a chapter not the end of their life. They are able to say it's not the end of the book because only I control my biography and how the next chapter will go and now that I've accepted that it happened, that I can't change it and that it did hurt; I have to move past it. Now I realize I will stop trying to explain what I can't understand but I will start yearning to understand when I can't explain it.

Too many times we try to explain to our self and others what we don't understand but in the next chapter of your life learn how to move forward by learning how to understand what you can't explain such as I can't explain why I didn't lose my mind but I understand that this mind that's in me is the same mind that's in Christ Jesus. I can't explain how I made it through the sickness, break up, setbacks and hurt but I do understand if it had not been for the Lord who is on my side I don't know where would I be.

THE SIXTH IS KNOWN AS THE STAGE OF SELF – DEPRESSION REHAB AND REBUILDING FROM DEPRESSION (Nehemiah 1:3 & 4:6)

Rehab and rebuilding is the act of restoring something back to its original state. It's time to check into rehab for rehabilitation and in spite of all you've been through it's your combat season! It's time to rebuild the broken pieces of your life that caused you to go into your deep depression and to mentally, physically and spiritually fall apart. Nehemiah's assignment was to bring reconstruction and rebuilding to the city of Jerusalem.

NEHEMIAH 1:3 EXB

[3] *"They answered me, "·Those who are left [The survivors/remnant there in the province; [?] of Judah] from the ·captivity [exile] are in much ·trouble [DISTRESS; misery] and ·are full of shame [disgrace; humiliation]. The wall around Jerusalem*

*is ·broken down [ruined; breached], and its gates have been burned [*ᶜ²* either at the time of the Babylonian destruction of Jerusalem or later]."*

Nehemiah for 52 days brought rehabilitation and reconstruction not only to the city of Jerusalem but he also rebuilt the people through the process of rehabilitation. We must understand after we have overcome our shock and denial stage of depression, the entertaining suppressed thoughts stage, the pain and hurt stage and the anger out of fear stage, the fifth stage is to teach us acceptance, how to cope and how to check ourselves into rehab. The sixth and final stage of rehab and rebuilding teaches us not only that we accept what has happened but how to recover from it by first checking ourselves into a place of empowerment and teaching for full rehabilitation.

THE FIVE TYPES OF SELF – DEPRESSION

1st – PSYCHOTIC DEPRESSION

2nd – PERSISTENT DEPRESSIVE DISORDER

3rd – HOLIDAY DEPRESSION

4th – SEASONAL AFFECTIVE DISORDER DEPRESSION

5th – SITUATIONAL DEPRESSION

The first type of depression is psychotic depression. Psychotic depression is another name for psychosis which refers to an abnormal condition of the mind. This is also another term for the mental state of a person often described as involving a loss of contact with reality. Psychotic means temporary insanity or a mental collapse that causes nervous breakdowns, deranged moments such as temper tantrums, out of control screaming, cursing, fussing or fighting. This causes a person to have blackout spells in which they literally forget what they have done throughout certain parts of their day. Psychotic depression is also known as clinical depression and causes mental disorders characterized by a pervasive and persistent sense of insecurity. It is accompanied by low self-esteem and by a loss of interest and pleasure in life. Psychotic depression is a disabling condition that affects a person's family, work, school, sleep habits, eating habits and their general health.

Anxiety depression disorders are the most common mental illness in the U.S. affecting 40 million adults age 18 and older which amounts to a total 18% of the U.S. population being affected by some type of stress disorder. The cost related to anxiety depression disorders in the U.S. is more than $42 billion a year, almost 1/3 of the country's $148 billion total mental health bill, according to the *Economic Burden of Anxiety Depression Disorders*.

Psychotic depression has symptoms of major depression along with psychotic depression symptoms such as hallucinating (seeing or hearing things that aren't there), delusions (false beliefs) and paranoia (wrongly believing that others are trying to harm them).

1 KINGS 19:1-4 AMP
"Ahab told Jezebel all that Elijah had done and how he had slain all the prophets [of Baal] with the sword.
² Then Jezebel sent a messenger to Elijah, saying, So let the gods do to me, and more also, if I make not your life as the life of one of them by this time tomorrow.
³ Then he was AFRAID and arose and went for his life and came to Beersheba of Judah [over eighty miles, and out of Jezebel's realm] and left his servant there.
⁴ But he himself went a day's journey into the wilderness and came and sat down under a lone broom or juniper tree and asked that he might die. He said, It is enough; now, O Lord, take away my life; for I am no better than my fathers

1 KINGS 19: 7-9 AMP
⁷ "The angel of the Lord came the second time and touched him and said, Arise and eat, for the journey is too great for you.
⁸ So he arose and ate and drank, and went in the strength of that food forty days and nights to Horeb, the mount of God.

⁹ There he came to a cave and lodged in it; and behold, the word of the Lord came to him, and He said to him, What are you doing here, Elijah?"

The stronghold of depression doesn't discriminate neither is it prejudice or racist. Depression finds a victim in 1 Kings 19 who is a man of God, Prophet, and vessel of God named Elijah who is struggling and under attack by this stronghold of psychotic depression. For three years Elijah has served God through obedience by fulfilling his assignment to confront a corrupt system in a perverted kingdom being run by the perverted King Ahab and Queen Jezebel. Elijah prophesied that it would not rain until he said so. The man of God after 3 years watched the fulfillment come to pass but in the process he got burned out, stressed and struggled with psychotic depression.

1 KINGS 19:4 AMP

⁴ "But he himself went a day's journey into the wilderness and came and sat down under a lone broom or juniper tree and asked that he might die. He said, it is enough; now, O Lord, take away my life; for I am no better than my fathers."

God asked Elijah two things; first He asked Elijah, Do you know where you're at? The second thing He asked was what are you doing here, Elijah? God is asking many of us the same two questions, first being what are we doing here in a state of depression, the state of loneliness, the state of brokenness, the state of devastation, the state of backsliding and suicide. The second is do we know where we are? When God asked Elijah this question he was at a place and season where God was ready to promote and elevate him but Elijah was ready to give up and quit because of the psychotic depression.

The second type of depression is called persistent depressive disorder (PDD) which last for two years or longer and causes symptoms such as a change in your appetite that ranges from not eating enough to over-eating. It also can cause you to sleep too much or too little, a lack of energy or fatigue, low esteem, trouble concentrating or making decisions or feelings of hopelessness. PDD is a form of chronic depression that not only impacts an adult's life but also a child's life. This chronic depression from PDD attacks and afflicts a child the same as it afflicts an adult with chronic feelings of sadness or worthlessness, an inability to take pleasure and perform well in the activities of daily life.

PDD can go undetected over a long period of time usually because the person that is under this stronghold suffers from silent frustration, suppressing thoughts and depressing their frustration which leads to anger that has built up over a long period of time. After the anger has built up over a period of time when they finally let their anger, bitterness, hurt, and pain go it's like watching a live volcanic eruption with all the fiery lava exploding. The person that suffers from persistent depressive disorder is like a walking time bomb that is ready to explode at any moment on any given day.

The third type is called holiday depression and results from feelings of sadness, loneliness, depression and anxiety on and around HOLIDAYS that remind you there's a void in your life caused by the loss of family or loved ones that's no longer are in your life due to divorce, separation, a betrayal or someone turning on you. Being distant from home, struggling financially, job problems, unemployment or not making enough money to buy gifts for love ones such as children, family members or a companion also causes holiday depression.

Holiday depression causes a person to isolate themselves and to go into a deep dark place of seclusion. It causes a person to begin to act out of character so they begin to steal, act violently during rages of anger, and even become suicidal all because of the holiday season. Although it should be a time of thanksgiving, a time to be merry, joyous and a time to celebrate, this STRONGHOLD OF DEPRESSION binds people in their mind and spirit and causes them to lose focus on Jesus who is the reason for the season.

Seasonal affective depression disorder (SADD) is the fourth type of depression that most often occurs during the winter months when the days grow shorter and there is less and less sunlight.

JOHN 9:4 AMP

[4] *"We must work the works of Him Who sent Me and be busy with His business while it is daylight; night is coming on, when no man can work."*

Seasonal affective depression disorder (SADD) also known as winter depression, Winter Blues, summer depression and Summer Blues or seasonal depression is considered a mood disorder in which people's mindset becomes attacked by seasonal patterns or the reoccurrence of events, things or situations that show back up in cycles. It's these seasonal patterns that lets the enemy know when to show up and he does when it's your time and your season. In 1 SAMUEL 1:5-8 the Bible talks about two women, one named Hannah and the other named Peninnah. Peninnah (The Spirit of Peninnah) or the (Peninnah Syndrome) kept showing up every time it was Hannah's time and season to be blessed. The Spirit of Peninnah (The Peninnah Syndrome) causes Hannah for 7 years to be bound by the stronghold of SADD and for 7 years Hannah missed her season because she kept being distracted by her enemy that caused her to lose focus of her blessing and her season.

The fifth type which is called situational depression. It attacks a person's mind while the person is trying to manage stressful events in their life such as death, divorce, separation, losing a job, financial difficulties and or problems with their children. People in a leadership roles or positions are more likely to be attacked by this stronghold. Another name for it is adjustment disorder (AD) and occurs when an individual is unable to adjust or cope with a particular stressor like a major life event.

A symptom of situational depression (SD) or adjustment disorder (AD) is a person will begin developing a loss or interest in life and about things or people who at one time they had interest in. They allow their appearance and hygiene to go down; they stop cleaning their house and lose interest in the relationships they are in. They lose interest in how their children are doing in school and even in taking care of them. They stop taking care of responsibilities as far as going to work or even paying their bills simply because they are struggling under the stronghold of situational depression and adjustment disorder and it has caused them to have post-traumatic stress disorder (PTSD).

Statistics and research proves that more women struggle with and suffer from these particular depressions then men because women have a harder time making adjustments than men. The symptoms of situational depression and adjustment disorder are sadness, hopelessness, lack of enjoyment, crying spells, nervousness, anxiety, panic attacks, worry, stress, desperation, trouble sleeping, difficulty staying focused, feeling overwhelmed and thoughts of suicide.

Statistics also show there is a high percentage (60%-70%) of teenagers that struggle with situational depression and adjustment disorder with symptoms such as fighting, reckless driving, and ignoring important work at school or responsibility around the house. A teenager struggling with SD will begin to do anything to gain attention even if it means breaking rules, laws, or becoming rebellious or by any means necessary.

Situational depression causes adolescents to succumb to peer pressure and will start lying, avoiding family and friends, performing poorly in school, skipping school, vandalizing property and having sex. They begin to struggle with their identity in areas such as homosexuality and lesbianism, to join gangs, join occults and playing in witchcraft. They start messing around with sorcery, using known and unknown drugs such as smoking, drinking, pills, prescription medications, street drugs as well as over the counter medications because they keep looking for a new high to try to escape life's difficulties.

MATTHEW 17:14-20 NLT

[14] *"At the foot of the mountain, a large crowd was waiting for them. A man came and knelt before Jesus and said,*

[15] *"Lord, have mercy on my son. He has seizures and suffers terribly. He often falls into the fire or into the water.*

[16] *So I brought him to your disciples, but they couldn't heal him."*

17
Jesus said, "You faithless and corrupt people! How long must I be with you? How long must I put up with you? Bring the boy here to me."

18
Then Jesus rebuked the demon in the boy, and it left him. From that moment the boy was well.

19
Afterward the disciples asked Jesus privately, "Why couldn't we cast out that demon?"

20
"You don't have enough faith," Jesus told them. "I tell you the truth, if you had faith even as small as a mustard seed, you could say to this mountain, 'Move from here to there,' and it would move. Nothing would be impossible."

The father came to Jesus to help his teenage son who struggled with situational depression and adjustment disorder so bad that he tried to commit suicide. Matthew 17:15 says that this man told Jesus, I took my teenage son to your disciples to help my son but they couldn't help him because they didn't know what to do. What do we do when people are bringing their problems to the church and leaders that are supposed to be problem solvers cannot solve their problems? In reality they are causing problems and we are losing our children, teenagers and families to all types of depressions and we don't know what to do to bring deliverance to these teenagers' lives or bring deliverance and help to these families.

We've been caught up trying to impress people rather than trying to help people. Thank God for Jesus who told the man, bring your son to me and He delivered this young teenager from his situational depression and his adjustment disorder. This teenager learned how to exist and coexist in society, his home, with friends and it helped change his mind, decisions so that he no longer wanted to die but to live.

In Matthew verses 20-21, the disciples came to Jesus privately and asked him, why couldn't we help this teenage boy? Why couldn't we help free him, deliver him, counsel him, or empower him? Jesus told them this kind (these types of depression) can only be delivered through fasting and praying.

THE <u>SEVEN</u> SPIRITUAL DEMONIC STEPS OF DEPRESSION

1st – REGRESSION
2nd – REPRESSION
3rd – SUPPRESSION
4th – DEPRESSION
5th – OPPRESSION
6th – OBSESSION
7th – DEMONIC POSSESSION

Regression (backslidden condition) means to go backwards. Satanic attacks usually hits a person's life and causes them to go backwards by sending something or someone to hurt you, offend you, and or lie to you about something or someone to cause your life to go in reverse.

Repression (Backslidden tendencies which means picking back up old habits) means to squeeze, to hold back or push down to restrain, to keep under, to put down, to banish, to become unconscious, to backslide, and a pattern of repeated cycle.

Suppression causes a person to be in denial of their backslidden ways and denying that they have a problem with old habits and new addictions. Suppression means to keep numb; to bring down by force, to crush, to subdue, to smother, to hold down by force, to stop and to leave out.

Depression (totally backslidden) is defined by medical doctors as a mental state of altered mood characterized by feelings of sadness, despair, discouragement, and disappointment. Depression causes you to think that you are losing control of your life, your ability to think rationally and that something or someone else is thinking for you. Depression causes a person to feel that they're losing their mind, going crazy, that someone or something is controlling their life by hypnotics or charmed by enchanting spells.

Oppression means to be weighted or to try to carry unnecessary burdens caused by unnecessary drama. Oppression means to press against or upon, to smother, to overwhelm, to distress, to treat with cruelty and to load with a heavy burden. Oppression or demonic oppression (beginning to allow demonic influence to make decisions for you) is worse than human depression because in this state the devil creates major confusion in your life to cause mistaken identity and as Satan grows bolder you grow colder.

Obsession (being attracted and lusting for bad and evil desires more than good ones) is a compulsive preoccupation with a fixed idea or an unwanted feeling or emotion often accompanied by symptoms of anxiety. Luke 22:31 says Jesus told Peter that Satan desires (he is obsessed with) to sift you him as wheat. The word desires means obsessed with obsession. Obsession occurs when a person's personality is being progressively destroyed. Satan's obsession with a person causes an individual to become jealous, full of hatred, and to not forgive forcing them to do things out of character.

Demonic possession (Your body and soul is now under the influence of demon possession) means to be controlled by demonic and satanic influence. It also means no longer being who you are but becoming something or someone else that is demon possessed. It is the entering into and the controlling of a person that occurs because they have given their permission and consent to the devil. After giving into the obsession and demonic influences, strongholds can now possess a person's body and take over their mind completely.

LUKE 22:3 NKJV
³ "Then Satan entered Judas, surnamed Iscariot, who was numbered among the twelve."

TEN SYMPTOMS AND SIGNS OF DEPRESSION

1. SADNESS
2. GUILT/ SHAME
3. IRRITATION/ FRUSTRATION
4. MENTAL INCAPACITIES
5. PHYSICAL ILLNESSES
6. LOSS OF ENERGY
7. LOSS OF INTEREST

8. SLEEP DISORDER FROM DEPRESSION
9. EATING DISORDER FROM DEPRESSION
10. SUICIDAL THOUGHTS

Sadness is a symptom of depression that may include feelings of hopelessness and emptiness. You may find that no matter how hard you try you just can't control the negative thoughts and find yourself crying for no obvious reason.

Guilt/shame is a sign of severe depression that causes one to feel that they are worthless and helpless. They may even see this depression as a sign of weakness and begin self- doubting, developing low self – esteem and having even more insecurities.

Irritation/frustration is a sign of depression that may cause a person to become angry easily, very anxious about nothing or become seriously depressed often by developing unnecessary aggression or reckless behavior. This sign exposes itself by becoming violent and out of control.

Mental incapacities are symptoms that show up in a person having trouble focusing and who is easily distracted. They have trouble making decisions and remembering details. These symptoms cause a person to feel that their thought process has slowed down and they are losing faculties or their ability to think clearly.

Physical illnesses are symptoms that persons with physical depression often have such as aches, pains, headaches or digestive problems. A person that struggles with physical depression develops unnatural sicknesses 50% of which doctors can't explain because they did not come from natural sickness but something unnatural which is why they don't show up on an X-ray or an M.R.I. but will show up on a stress test. This is why doctors ask the questions, what is bothering you, are you under severe stress?

Loss of energy is a result of depression that causes you to have a lack of energy or makes you feel tired all the time. They will feel that their physical abilities have slowed down and wake up tired, go through the day tired, and lay back down tired because they struggle from being burned out, and spiritually, mentally, and physically dehydrated.

A loss of interest is a sign of depression that causes a loss of interest in pleasurable activities like sex, hobbies, or social interaction. This loss of interest also shows up to cause a person to neglect their responsibilities of taking care of themselves in ways such as bathing, brushing their teeth, working and to even lose their spiritual interest and relationship with God. Sleep disorder symptoms cause a person not to be able to sleep or to sleep too much. More than 40 million Americans suffer from chronic long term sleep disorders and an additional 20 million report sleeping problems due to stress and anxiety disorder caused by abnormal sleep patterns that interfere with physical, mental and emotional functioning. This depression not only impacts how much you are sleeping or not sleeping but it impacts your everyday living.

Eating disorders is a result of eating too much or not enough and often goes hand in hand with one or more medical illnesses such as depression or anxiety due to negative feelings and a person's low self-esteem. They work differently with each individual for example, a depressed person who weighs 200 lbs., the eating disorder may cause them not to eat and within one month they may lose up to 40-50 lbs. and go from 200 lbs. to 160-150 lbs. Another depressed person that struggles from this same eating disorder may weigh 200 lbs. and within one month they may pick up 40-50 extra pounds because this same depression causes them to eat too much so they go from 200 lbs. to 240-250 lbs.

Suicidal thoughts are acts of premeditated torture and affliction to bring devastation and destruction to end one's life because demonic attacks and satanic influences have caused strongholds and spiritual warfare upon a person's mind. A person having thoughts of harming them self is a serious sign of depression and they always need to be taken seriously. These attacks convince a person they have nothing to live for because their better days are behind them and their worse days are in front of them but the devil is a liar! You will live and not die and your future will be better than your past!

Chapter 20

The Stronghold of Selfish-Vain Imagination

(No More Throwing Shades/ No More Shades)

The meaning of acting shady in urban terminology is being disrespectful (dissin'), illegitimate behavior (trippin') and to judge someone unfairly because of jealously (player hating).

No more throwing shades came from the saying "to cast shadow," and it's when someone throws shades on who and what you have, where you're going in life or when someone deliberately tries to throw darkness in your day or throw a storm into your sunshine. It's similar to someone throwing hate on your love, a curse on your blessing and or negative on your positive. Tell the devil and your enemies to "stop throwing shades!"

The stronghold selfish-vain imagination deals with Satan forming a stronghold or fortress over the mind of an individual causing it to become a mind or house with wrong thinking. Satan causes the mind to struggle with selfish-vain imagination by planting wrong thoughts in a person's thinking. The Greek word for thought is noema which means a plot, plan, or design by something calculated. Satan orchestrates schemes, traps, and pitfalls that are designed for a believer to fall into.

He forms this stronghold of selfish-vain imagination by planting the seed of doubt in a person's mind which causes them to begin entertaining wrong thoughts. Satan forms images and imaginary pictures within the mind to cause a person or believer to not only question themselves but to begin questioning God, and everything and everyone that has ever been a positive influence in their life. Vain imagination becomes the gatekeeper and doorkeeper of our mind and not only produces wrong thinking but wrong images that produce bad thoughts and creates bad habits along with addictions. The Greek word for thoughts means device; it also means to form images and imagination which produces vain imagination. Vain imagination forms ideas and mental pictures that create imaginary fantasies, unreal worlds or virtual worlds. It creates an animated world full of deception and deceit that fills the mind with thoughts, pictures, and images that are not real. Vain imagination forms lies within our mind as if they are the truth.

Imagination comes from the root word image which means a reproduction or imitation of something or someone that is a counterfeit. It is a reflection of something or someone's likeness but in reality it's not real. It's only the negative (image) of what reflects the positive. This is how Satan forms the stronghold of vain imagination in a person's mind. Satan is always manipulating the negative image through vain imagination as if it's the positive image deceiving a person to believe what they see and hear is really God speaking and revealing it to them. Selfish-vain imagination is the same deception that he used on Eve in the Garden of Eden and that vain imagination perception births the wrong conception that causes spiritual abortion or premature spiritual death.

Look at the photographer's development process of a picture. The photographer takes a picture with his or her camera. The camera snaps the picture and causes the flash from the camera to go off. Simultaneously the lens opens, reaches out and captures the person or objects reflection and brings back the image from the picture that it captured and places it on the film. Now the photographer takes what is called the negative and starts developing the proof or the positive after which he takes the negative film into a dark room or what is sometimes called a green room uses developer and creates a positive proof of what was captured.

This process is similar to what God does in our lives. He did the same process for Adam in Genesis 3. He formed man from the negative, called the ground or the dirt; He then placed the negative (man) into His dark room until man's negative image was developed into His likeness; God's positive proof. God caused man's negative image to no longer reflect man's vain imagination. The positive proof is what God framed as a picture and created a mirror for man so that every-time man looked in a mirror he would be able to see God's positive proof, the image that reflects who God is, not the negative image of man. When we look in the mirror we should never be able to see ourselves, the old us, or the reflection of who we use to be but we should be able to see who we're becoming.

Satan uses Spiritual Warfare against the mind of a believer which is called creating arguments within a believers mind and it causes them to form wrong thinking or wrong thoughts. Experts estimate that the mind thinks between 60,000 to 80,000 thoughts a day. An average person thinks about 2,500 to 3,300 thoughts per hour. But according to these experts, 98% of an average person's thinking is recycled and reprogrammed. The mind reproduces the same thoughts that it had the day before. So are you an average thinker? Because if you're saying the same things that you always say that means 98% of the time you're still doing the same things you've always done!!! Maybe that's why your life has not changed!

Scientific studies of the mind through the field of neuroscience, psychology, and physics experts have determined that 80% of an average person's thinking is negative which simply means on a daily basis an average person's thoughts are only 20% positive. This also means that an average person only lives 20% of their life thinking positive thoughts and the other 80% of their life is spent thinking on the negative. Such large percentage of negative thinking causes an average person to self-sabotage their life and produces negative living.

PROVERBS 23:7 NKJV
"For as he THINKS in his heart, so is he."

2 CORINTHIANS 10:4-6 AMP
4 "For the weapons of our warfare are not physical [weapons of flesh and blood], but they are mighty before God for the overthrow and destruction of STRONGHOLDS,
5 [Inasmuch as we] REFUTE ARGUMENTS and theories, reasoning and every proud and lofty thing that sets itself up against the [true] knowledge of God; and we lead every THOUGHT and purpose away captive into the obedience of Christ (the Messiah, the Anointed One),

6 Being in readiness to punish every [insubordinate for his] disobedience, when your own submission and obedience [as a church] are fully secured and complete."

Satan uses the stronghold of vain imagination to create arguments, confusion and doubt as warfare in the mind of a person to bring them into bondage so they can evict the truth and live with the lie as if they're living in truth. Psalms 23:4 states that David declared "yea though I walk through the valley of the shadow of death, I will fear no evil." The word shadow is an image that reflects the person or object that it gets its image from but a shadow cannot form its own image.

A shadow gets its power from the light that it reflects and has no power or light of its own. When David said he was in the valley of the shadow of death and he feared no evil it was because regardless of how dark it may get in your life, if we can see our shadow there must be light coming from somewhere because in the midst of the darkness without light there wouldn't be a shadow or an image to reflect.

The shadow or the negative images always appears bigger than it really is. In reality there would not be a shadow or a negative image without the likeness of the positive proof so the negative image or shadow isn't real but only a reflection of the person or object's likeness. So David discovered what we all must discover and that is our shadow, our image or our negative can't hurt us because it's just a shadow. It only exists because you're there; it only has the power that you give it through fear which is why David said I will fear no evil for God you are with me.

When David wrote the 23rd Psalms he was in a dark place and time in his life. David quoted in the 23rd Psalms verse 4, *"even though I walk through the valley of the shadow of death, I will fear no evil*; for you God are with me; your rod and your staff comfort me."* David is saying that even though the enemy is trying to create fear through the stronghold of selfish-vain imagination in this moment of his life Satan could have only created a shadow or image in the darkness from the light. Without light the enemy couldn't throw shades and he couldn't cast shadows because shadows and images only come from a reflection of the light. So David is saying even though the enemy is throwing shades and tripping and it feels like you're in your valley of the shadow of death just know what David revealed and declared, the Lord is with me.

For the Lord is with me; his rod and staff they comfort me means God is with you even in the midst of the darkness and in the dark places in your life. John 8:12 says Jesus is the light of the world and that means we have light within us but the enemy is trying to create vain imagination to cause us to lose focus, to reflect and see the negative, not the positive. By throwing shades and causing us to fear we see the negative image rather than the positive proof. We need to see and know that "If God be for us, He is more than the world against us." ROMANS 8:31.

The enemy tries to throw shades (cast a shadow) to cause you to fear what's in front of you called your future and because of fear he wants you to run back to your past. Tell your enemy that's throwing shades and creating confusion from fear that God said the reflection from this shadow represents my light and reminds me when I look at what's ahead of me through this gigantic shadow I see what my future looks like. I'm looking ahead and planning for my future. I'll be bigger than I am right now because my shadow will always magnify my greatness, God's excellence, His promise and blessings ahead for me.

> **COLOSSIANS 2:17 GW**
> *17 "These are a SHADOW of the things to come, but the body that casts the SHADOW belongs to Christ."*

FIVE CHARACTERISTICS OF A PASSIVE MIND OF VAIN IMAGINATION

The first is called PASSIVE WILL
The second is called PASSIVE MIND
The third is called PASSIVE IMAGINATION
The fourth is called PASSIVE JUDGMENT
The fifth is called PASSIVE SPIRIT

1. Passive will is seen in a person who is indecisive and tortured and tormented because of shame and embarrassment from struggling with low self-esteem as a result of some insecurity.

2. Passive mind is one that is inactive and unstable with a lack of confidence, judgment and focus and that cannot remember well.

3. Passive imagination is portrayed by someone that's gazing with the eyes of an evil look, someone that has a lack of vision, bound in their thinking, contaminated from negative thinking and or someone who fantasizes in an unreal world.

4. Passive judgment causes a person to be unable to make clear judgment calls on issues because of hypocritical thinking, seeing, hearing, doing and speaking of things from a negative perspective.

5. Passive spirit causes one to be weak and poor in the spirit because of wrong thoughts. They are bound in the spirit and have an unwilling filthy and impure spirit. A person with a passive spirit can easily become attached or bound to an ungodly soul-tie relationship.

7 TYPES OF IMAGINATIONS

1. EFFECTIVE IMAGINATION
2. CONSTRUCTIVE IMAGINATION
3. IMAGINATIVE OR IMAGINARY FANTASY IMAGINATION
4. STRATEGIC IMAGINATION
5. EMOTIONAL IMAGINATION
6. DREAMY IMAGINATION
7. MEMORY RECONSTRUCTIVE IMAGINATION (M.R.I.)

Effective imagination is combining information together to synergize new concepts and new ideas; however, effective imagination always needs to be enhanced, modified and elaborated upon. It can be guided or triggered by random thoughts used and stimulated by what a person experienced in their past that relates to their present and plans for their future. Effective imagination causes a person's mind to construct concepts, ideas, and active scenarios and enables flexibility in our thinking.

The 31 Self-Strongholds

In Genesis 1 we find an example of effective imagination in the fact that God, who in the beginning synergized new concepts and ideas by being innovative through constructive concepts, spoke a Word and framed it through a constructive word called light. In Genesis 1 God said let there be "light" and there was "light."

The Bible says in John 8:12 states "And He was the light of the world." So when God said let there be light because of effective imagination, God was saying, let there be Jesus on the 1st day because the natural light, the sun, the moon, and the stars didn't come until the 4th day according to Genesis 1:14-16.

When Satan fell from Heaven he left a dark void in the earth that caused catastrophic disorder. When God speaks through effective imagination, He declares the end from the beginning in Isaiah 46:10. God said let there be light and through effective imagination the world that was in darkness brought forth light because of God's new concepts and ideas through His innovative effective imagination.

Constructive imagination is the ability to take a person's life that has been devastated, broken, left in ruins and try to put the broken pieces of their life back together again. We find a constructive imagination exemplified in Jeremiah 18 as he talks about the potter's house and the clay. God gives the Prophet an illustration of constructive imagination in the story about The Potter, who is God taking the pottery vessel that had become hard and fragile in His hand. Then the Potter (God) breaks the vessel and through constructive imagination He takes the same vessel that's broken and makes it into a better vessel. Constructive imagination helps us to use our imagination in a positive way and to look past all of our flaws, mistakes, and wrong doings to become more constructive in our imagination and to make the brokenness in our life better.

Imaginative or imaginary fantasy imagination gives us the ability to create and develop stories, pictures, stage plays, fictions and fantasies in our mind. Look at the pattern of satanic attacks that usually targets a child's life from the ages of 3-12 years old used by imaginative or imaginary fantasy imagination in certain toys, television, movies, books, video games, magazines and music used to entertain children. Our imagination is a gift from God but Satan takes the gift from God by trying to influence the good and to pervert it into evil.

For example, the game Dungeons and Dragons is one of children's favorite animated cartoons/games that the enemy uses to create strongholds through vain imagination in the mind of the children that play it. Dungeons and Dragons is an animation that entails dragon lords, a Tyrant of Dragons, unleashes evil queen dragons, from their prison to create a new dragon empire. What is so innocent and harmless about our children being caught up in dragons and dragon empires which entail dragons escaping a bottomless pit?

This is a picture of Lucifer or Satan escaping the bottomless pit of hell and building a dragon lord empire (Revelation 12 and Revelation 13:1-4). Dungeons and Dragons teaches demonology, witchcraft, voodoo, murder, rape, blasphemy, suicide, assassination, insanity, sexual perversion, and Satanic worship – demons summoning, and sacrificing humans. The Dungeons and Dragons game can cause a child to take on a demonic personality.

The biggest influences in a child's life are his or her parents so it's important that the parents know and understand the subtle things that Satan uses to attack their mind. We cannot as parents become blinded by satanic attacks against our children through vain imagination also called imaginary fantasy or animation of a child's virtual world. Satan is targeting the same things that parents think is innocent and harmless and at the same time it is damaging, hurting and harming our children at an early age through animation or selfish-vain imagination.

Another example is Rainbow Brite and Sprite doll that presents a cute little girl which has magical powers that can cast spells and use mind control. This cartoon series is filled with cult symbolism and disembodied spirits.

Care Bears produced toys, movies; television shows audio tapes and greeting cards from 1983-1987 and became America's top Teddy bear company. They sold over 40 million Care Bear toys, published and sold over 45 million books and created over 70 million greeting cards so imagine how many homes have entertained this demonic stronghold called transferring spirit from the 80's to 90's alone.

The innocent and cute little Care Bears are designed by Satan to disturb the relationship between a parent and a child by transferring the love and security of a parent to an initial object. Satan used this cartoon to cause transference of intimacy through dark heart casting of spells. So the child begins to fantasize and imagine Care Bear will protect them causing the child to begin forming an ungodly soul-tie attachment to the object.

The Cabbage Patch Doll creates a demonic soul-tie with a child by means of a covenant oath which is issued with each doll. It comes as a promissory note (birth certificate) requiring a signature indicating that the owner has agreed to the adoption of this doll. This simply means making covenant with something or someone through ungodly soul-ties.

In the early 1980's these dolls came on the scene. The humanizing of these dolls is taken to the point that a child views the doll as a real person and causes them to develop and form attachments that are ungodly.

Harry Potter is a cute-face teenager that portrays an innocent young boy when in reality he's a sorcerer that does enchantment, cast spells, works black magic and he communicates with the dark world. Harry Potter is one of the most watched movies as well as books sold in the last decade.

The enemy always portrays these people and things as harmless and innocent and for many it's only a movie or a picture being made. The reality is that is true, but it is a movie, a picture, an image, of vain imagination that hypnotizes the mind of the viewers, especially children into thinking that it's okay to join an occult, play with Ouija boards, to become a sorcerer, a witch, to cast spells, and to sell your soul to the dragon lord when in reality the dragon according to the book of Revelation is Satan, the devil, the serpent. Revelation 12:9

This causes a child to open their mind and soul to accept a familiar and demonic spirit. Also the humanizing of these toys, animated cartoons and movies make a mockery of life, death, adoption, and all the things that are truly good in life. Many toys, games, cartoons, animated pictures and video games are tools used by Satan to attack the child. The majority of these toys, games, and cartoons present a picture of devils, dragons, mythical gods, wizards, warriors, magical powers, black princesses, magic droll, evil monsters, curses of death, evil spirits, black magic, druids, witchcraft, evil wizards, sorcery, demons, curses, monsters, magical spells, enchantment, and blood shedding.

Strategic imagination is one's ability to recognize and evaluate opportunities by turning defeat into victory, seeing the benefits and identifying and acquiring the necessary resources required for accomplishing any particular actions because of their ability to count up the cost of what they're trying to strategically accomplish. The person with a strategic imagination has a sense of vision that guides them into turning a liability into an asset. Strategic imagination is an imagination that causes a person to still strategize and plan their exit strategy in spite of their circumstance, crisis, problems and or what they're going through.

> **2 KINGS 7:4 AMP**
> *If we say, We will enter the city—then the famine is in the city, and we shall die there; and if we sit still here, we die also. So now come, let us go over to the army of the Syrians. If they spare us alive, we shall live; and if they kill us, we shall but die.*

2 Kings 7, talks about 4 lepers that have to use their strategic imagination while they're facing a crisis of life and death. They determine that if we go back in the city we will starve to death and if we stay here we will die. Their strategic imagination saved their life and it exemplifies how we too must look ahead strategically. Strategic imagination forces us to look ahead to our future while making destiny decisions today.

Emotional imagination deals with manifesting emotional dispositions and causing them to escalate into something that it's not. Emotional imagination manifests feelings, moods and confusion caused by fear. A person who shows excessive emotional imagination displays psychotic tendencies. Emotional imagination is one of the most powerful types of imagination. It dominates a person's thinking process.

The 31 Self-Strongholds

EXODUS 17:3 AMP

3 But the people thirsted there for water, and the people murmured against Moses, and said, Why did you bring us up out of Egypt to kill us and our children and livestock with thirst?

The people of God struggled with emotional imagination every time trouble, problems, or controversy appeared they panicked. Their emotional imagination always caused them to see the negative, to begin thinking the negative and to live their life in fear by going back in a cycle because of their emotional imagination. They should have arrived in the promise land anywhere from 4 days to 4 months but it took them 40 years to get there and only those that were 20 years or younger made it there. Those that were older died in the wilderness because they allowed their emotional imagination to paralyze and cripple them from moving forward as did Lot's wife. Because of emotional imagination she turned into a pillar of salt and was paralyzed and could not move forward to escape her past.

Dreams called imagination causes an unconscious form of the imagination made up of images, ideas, hopes, and determination to help a person to stay positive in times when negative things are happening in their life. Genesis 37 talks about a Dreamer named Joseph who had a dream, a glimpse and a foresight of his future at the age of 17 years old. He went through a process of trouble, tribulation persecution, rejection, being lied on and mistreated but he held to his dreams. Joseph watched his dream become a reality and what the devil meant for evil God meant for good. Joseph's dream took him from being a slave to becoming the 2nd in charge of all the Kingdom of Egypt. Joseph never stopped dreaming and you should never give up on your dream.

Memory reconstructive imagination (M.R.I.) is the process of retrieving our memories of people, objects and events. Our memory is made up of prior knowledge consisting of a mixture of truth, belief, and influences from our past and present experiences. The process of memory reconstruction imagination (M.R.I.) reoccurs within our subconscious mind which emerges into our conscious mind without us, really being aware of what's totally happening. M.R.I. is assimilated to construct new knowledge out of random facts, beliefs and experiences and gives us new insight.

M.R.I. in medical terms means Magnetic Resonance Imagining and is a technology that uses a magnetic field and radio waves to create detailed images that reveal pictures and imaging of the inner body that cannot be seen with the naked eye. When we look at memory reconstructive imagination we know that it deals with rediscovering what you lost that you failed to value from the beginning and now you have come to your senses and remembered what you once had was good and priceless and you traded it for something that had less value.

LUKE 15:17-18 AMP

[17] Then when he came to himself, (M.R.I.) he said, How many hired servants of my father have enough food, and [even food] to spare, but I am perishing (dying) here of hunger!

[18] I will get up and go to my father, and I will say to him, Father, I have sinned against heaven and in your sight.

The lost son had a M.R.I. experience in which he remembered the covenant relationship he had with his father in the father's house. The Prodigal Son got up, redirected and reconstructed his memory back home to his covenant because he saw three stages of deliverance before he acted on it.

1st - The Prodigal Son through his imagination remembered how well he had it in the beginning at the father's house.

2nd – The Prodigal Son imagined if he would get up and repent to God and Heaven and to his father and father's house that he could be delivered and restored back to his original state (which means reconciliation).

3rd – The Prodigal Son through M.R.I. visualized being restored to his covenant, inheritance and the benefits he had lost. Through repentance he began to imagine his deliverance before delivery. The Prodigal Son not only remembered what he lost but through M.R.I. it was revealed how to get it back because he recognized he got what he wanted but he lost what he had.

Reconstruct means to rebuild what has been torn down, destroyed, or lost. The Prodigal Son recognized from repentance he needed to change the way he thought. After he repented saw what he did differently and knew he needed to reconstruct, restore, and rebuild the relationship that he messed up with his father and not only his father, but with his father's house.

Repentance gave this Prodigal Son forgiveness from God as well as his father, renewed the covenant relationship and gave the son the privileges and benefits that come with the covenant. A complete benefit package is what the father gave him which includes first of all, a robe which represents covering. Secondly, the father threw him a party which represents a celebration of newness and victory. Thirdly, the father gave him sandals for his feet which represents that his son is no longer in bondage or debt physically, mentally, spiritually or financially. Last but not least of all, the father gave him a ring which represents his identity, power, authority and favor.

Chapter 21

The Stronghold of Self-Righteous

(Toxic Relationship and Toxic Leadership)

TOXIC RELATIONSHIPS AND TOXIC LEADERSHIP

TOXIC means poisonous, dangerous, contaminated, life threatening and deadly. Toxic relationships and toxic leaderships are parallel to one another. For example, a person that ends a bad relationship and becomes bitter, hurt, and full of hatred and then goes out and starts a new relationship now brings that contamination and poison from the old relationship into the new relationship. This causes the new relationship to become just as toxic as the old relationship.

Often times we discover this same thing happening in churches. A person leaves a church, hurt, bitter, broken, angry, full of toxins and poison just to go to another church with that same toxin of hurt, pain, anger, and brokenness, and starts the toxic contamination process all over again in a new relationship with a new ministry. If they would have taken the time to be healed and rehabilitated from the toxic and poisonous condition that left them contaminated, they could have started the new relationship afresh rather than dysfunctional. They really thought if they left the place of pain, hurt, and anger; left those who had left them broken; they then could escape the toxic relationship. However, running away from your past doesn't allow you to heal. It's only when you confront the hurt and pain of the toxic relationship that the process of rehabilitation begins the healing of the past. So, in reality, you may have left the place of what hurt you, but the place didn't leave you. So you can't start a new relationship when you're still carrying old toxins. Self-righteousness is refusing to change what is wrong. A self-righteous person is prideful and self-serving. A self-righteous person always see the fault and wrong in someone else, but never sees their own faults and wrongness. A self-righteous person always tries to change another person, but refuses to change themselves. Their excuse is, this is just who I am. Self-righteous is defined as being self-satisfied. It means to be hypocritical and pious, to pretend to be more than you are. Self-righteous people will take their wrong, and present it, as if it was right. Then they will take someone else's right and make that person feel that they were wrong. A self-righteous person operates out of mood swings tendencies and patterns. They always make excuses when they do things that appear to be out of character, when in reality their bad attitude, their temper tantrum, unprofessionalism, and judgmental comments were not out of character for them, that's who they really are. When a self-righteous person doesn't get their way, they throw such a bad temper tantrum, that it changes the environment that they are in. They allow what has gone wrong in their day, to now effect the surrounding of everyone else.

THE SIGNS TO LOOK FOR IN TOXIC RELATIONSHIPS

Toxic relationships are relationships characterized by behaviors and patterns that are emotionally, and physically damaging to one another. These relationships drain and contaminate individuals by poisoning their life either slowly or suddenly. The signs that you are in a toxic relationship are evident:

1. When it seems like you can't do anything right.
2. When everything is always about them and never about you.
3. When you find yourself unable to enjoy the good moments in a relationship and you experience more negative than positive times.
4. When you become uncomfortable being yourself around the person you are in relationship with.
5. When the relationship doesn't allow you to grow or change.
6. When you begin blaming the relationship for your own emotions, hurt and pain rather than taking the responsibility that you have not yet moved on.

7. When a person talks more about what has hurt them in their past, rather than talk about how to stop what can hurt them in their future.

THE SIGNS TO LOOK FOR IN TOXIC LEADERSHIP

1. Toxic leadership is more interested in controlling and taming you rather than training and empowering you.
2. Toxic leadership spends more time trying to build their own personal kingdoms, rather than instruct people how to build the Kingdom of God.
3. Toxic leadership bullies people rather than help people.
4. Toxic leadership tries to control people in the direction they want them to go, rather than give people instructions on how to reach their destiny.
5. Toxic leadership creates more questions than answers.
6. Toxic leadership causes problems but does not solve problems.

THE STRONGHOLD OF A SELF – RIGHTEOUS/ RELIGIOUS SPIRIT

Self-righteousness is a spiritual sin not a natural sin that births a religious spirit.

> **PROVERBS 6:16-19 ERV**
> *"16 The Lord HATES these seven things:*
> *17 eyes that show PRIDE, tongues that TELL LIES, hands that KILL innocent people,*
> *18 hearts that PLAN EVIL THINGS TO DO, feet that RUN TO DO EVIL,*
> *19 witnesses in court who TELL LIES,*
> *and anyone who causes family members to FIGHT."*

The stronghold of self-righteousness originated in the Heaven, with Lucifer (A.K.A.) Satan. Lucifer was one of the Arch Angels of God that was assigned and ordained by God to be over, praise and worship; but Satan became self-righteous, was lifted up in pride, and believed that he was equal with God. Because of Lucifer's self-righteousness and pride he was evicted from Heaven. He was fired and demoted from his position because he believed that he was the only one entitled to the position. (GOD ALWAYS HAS SOMEONE ON RESERVE TO TAKE OUR PLACE!!!!!!)

   Lucifer, (A.K.A.) Satan, birthed what is called a religious spirit. This religious spirit caused him to become insubordinate, rebellious, and not submissive before God. When Lucifer was created by God, he was ordained by God, to be the Arch Angel over worship that manifests the glory before the presence of God. God testified according to Ezekiel 28, that righteousness and beauty were found in Lucifer from the beginning; until Lucifer, (A.K.A.) Satan, took the righteousness of God, and conformed it into his own Self-righteousness. Lucifer committed a spiritual sin before God and the Heaven. God then gave the Arch Angel, Michael permission to evict Satan from the Heaven. When Lucifer was fired from his position from being over worship and praise, God gave Man Satan's position to lead praise and worship. From that moment, Satan has looked for an opportunity to get back at God, and to destroy Man, who took his place.1

> **PSALMS 8:3-6 NLV**
> *"3 When I look up and think about Your heavens, the work of Your fingers, the moon and the stars, which You have set in their place,*
> *4 What is man, that You think of him, the son of man that You care for him?*
> *5 You made him a little less than the angels and gave him a crown of greatness and honor.*
> *6 You made him to rule over the works of Your hands. You put all things under his feet:*

EZEKIEL 28:14-18 TLB

14 I appointed you to be the anointed Guardian Angel. You had access to the holy mountain of God. You walked among the stones of fire.

15 "'You were perfect in all you did from the day you were created until that time when wrong was found in you.

16 Your great wealth filled you with internal turmoil, and you sinned. Therefore, I cast you out of the mountain of God like a common sinner. I destroyed you, O Guardian Angel, from the midst of the stones of fire.

17 Your heart was filled with pride because of all your beauty; you corrupted your wisdom for the sake of your splendor. Therefore, I have cast you down to the ground and exposed you helpless before the curious gaze of kings.

18 You defiled your holiness with lust for gain; therefore, I brought forth fire from your own actions* and let it burn you to ashes upon the earth in the sight of all those watching you."

Self-righteousness causes one to become prideful, arrogant, and so self-centered that they convince themselves that they are the center of the universe, and everything in life revolves around them. Self-righteousness leads to division (that's why Satan through self-righteousness caused division in the Heaven, so much so, that a third of the angels followed Satan and this is why it's important in church that we don't allow self-righteous people to be leaders, because they will cause a division in the House of God due to their Self-righteousness, pride and religious spirit. A self-righteous person is un-teachable they become very defensive when being corrected by authority.

In Genesis 4, the Bible talks about Cain being in the presence of God while worship was taking place. God began to minister a Word of counseling to Cain about his attitude. God asked Cain why was he in His presence of worship with a bad attitude. He told him to repent and do what's necessary, that I may bless you, as I have blessed your brother Abel. The Bible tells us that Cain became so self-righteous, prideful and full of such a religious spirit that he left out of praise and worship, and from the presence of God without repenting. You should never leave the presence of God when God has exposed your wrong especially if you have become prideful, stubborn like Cain and still refuse to repent. The definition of repent means to change the way you think.

God had forewarned Cain. If you leave out of My presence and this place of praise and worship, after I have exposed to you what's wrong with you and what has kept you from being blessed, sin now waits at the door. Because of Cain's disobedience, caused by self-righteous, he disobeyed God, and allowed his anger cause him to kill his brother Abel.

THE SYMPTOMS OF A SELF – RIGHTEOUS OR RELIGIOUS SPIRIT

1st – Very Judgmental

2nd – Religious pride

3rd – Very critical with criticism

4th – Legalism

5th – Very controlling

6th – Very divisive and manipulative

7th – Sows seeds of discord to bring division. They operate in error (through doctorial falsehood).

8th – They convince others of how much faith and belief they have but the truth is, they are doubters and unbelievers. They operate with a spirit of confusion by always being an agitator and an instigator because they are like their father Satan, the author of lies and confusion. JOHN 8:44

A self-righteous person has these symptoms: they are very argumentative and always using condemnation to belittle, judge and destroy a person's confidence because they need power to control and dictate a person's life. In Luke 18:9-14 MSG, Jesus explains what a self-righteous/religious person is;

" 9-12 He told his next story to some who were complacently pleased with themselves over their moral performance and looked down their noses at the common people: "Two men went up to the Temple to pray, one a Pharisee, the other a tax man. The Pharisee posed and prayed like this: 'Oh, God, I thank you that I am not like other people—robbers, crooks, adulterers, or, heaven forbid, like this tax man. I fast twice a week and tithe on all my income.'

13 "Meanwhile the tax man, slumped in the shadows, his face in his hands, not daring to look up, said, 'God, give mercy. Forgive me, a sinner.'"

14 Jesus commented, "This tax man, not the other, went home made right with God. If you walk around with your nose in the air, you're going to end up flat on your face, but if you're content to be simply yourself, you will become more than yourself."

THE 8 TYPES OF SELF – RIGHTEOUS PERSONALITY DISORDER

1st – PASSIVE/ AGGRESSIVE PERSONALITY DISORDER

2nd – POWER DRIVEN PERSONALITY DISORDER

3rd – ENTITLEMENT PERSONALITY DISORDER

4th – AVOIDANT PERSONALITY DISORDER

5th – PRETENDING TO BE A SHEEP PERSONALITY DISORDER

6th – BULLY PERSONALITY DISORDER

7th - OBSESSIVE - COMPULSIVE PERSONALITY DISORDER

8th - PARANOID PERSONALITY DISORDER

1st – PASSIVE/ AGGRESSIVE PERSONALITY DISORDER

This is a type of behavior or personality characterized by indirect rebellion to demands of authority, which causes a self-righteous person to procrastinate, pout and to have depressing and stressing moments. They begin feeling sorry for themselves; while being tormented by demonic attacks. Also, developing out of control anger disorder caused by a (Distressing Spirit) that troubles and torments a person. 1st Samuel 16: 14-17, talks about a man named King Saul, who was self-righteous and struggled with passive/aggressive personality disorder. King Saul was not only passive and aggressive but also insecure and jealous. This caused him to have emotional breakdowns, to be inconsistent and to be an unstable leader that became toxic and poisonous to his leadership and followers. King Saul struggled with mood swings and a demonic spirit that caused him to create a hostile environment. Thank God for David, who was able to minister unto King Saul's troubling and unclean spirit, until it brought him back into the presence of God. We all need someone in our life that knows how to reach the Throne of God in a time of trouble.

2nd – POWER DRIVEN PERSONALITY DISORDER

A self-righteous person always thinks it's necessary for them to be over something and to control everything. They become bossy, fussy, and aggressive just to have their own way. They are like a child that throws a tantrum when things don't go the way they want it too. This power driven personality disorder person is like a child that has toys, that is not playing with the toys, but when another child starts to play with their toys, the child begins to run and snatch their toy away, when the child wasn't even playing with the toy.

This happens too many times in church. When a self-righteous power driven personality disorder individual ignores their ministry, ignores their position and ignores the responsibility of their assignment, and as soon as someone else picks up and begins to take their responsibilities and to do what it is they were assigned to do, they begin to throw temper tantrums like a child. They operate from this power driven personality disorder and they begin to ask the person that's doing what they should have done in the beginning, "why are you doing this, this is what I was put over" as this self-righteous/religious spirit pushes their weight around. They are telling people, "this is what I'm supposed to be doing. You are out of order because this is my ministry, and my position."

A self-righteous person that operates with this power driven personality disorder begins to sow seeds of discord with other members or people who made them look bad. People that struggle with the power driven personality disorder are very territorial, anytime they sense someone is coming anywhere near their position or place, they will begin to become very argumentative. But in reality, it's like the example of the child with the toys. When one child picks up another child's toy, that they are not playing with and the child that owns the toy begins to throw a tantrum. This similar to the reality that plays out within church. The person that's over the ministry neglects their responsibility and what they were assigned to do, and when someone else comes along and picks up their responsibility, the person that neglected their ministry throws a tantrum like a child. They were not hurt or devastated because of their ministry lacking, they were hurt, devastated and embarrassed because someone stepped up to do what they should have done from the beginning.

1 CORINTHIANS 13:11 NCV
"11 When I was a child, I talked like a child, I thought like a child, I reasoned like a child. When I became a man, I stopped those childish ways.

1 CORINTHIANS 13:11 ERV
11 When I was a child, I talked like a child, I thought like a child, and I made plans like a child. When I became a man, I stopped those childish ways."

3rd – ENTITLEMENT PERSONALITY DISORDER

Self-righteous people believe that they have seniority, or special privilege for positions, places and things in life. They believe they should be given superior treatment, regardless of their own contribution to the relationship, the job, the ministry, the situations, or circumstance. The person that struggles with the self-righteous, entitlement personality disorder believes that everybody owes them something. Luke 15, talks about the Prodigal Son that told his father, give me what belongs to me. This prodigal son was an immature person that felt he was entitled to the father's estate or money.

Entitlement makes a person believe that they are worthy and deserving with special privilege for something he or she did not help make, build, work, or sacrifice for, but they still believe they got a right to it.

LUKE 15:25-32 ERV
[25] "The older son had been out in the field. When he came near the house, he heard the sound of music and dancing.
[26] So he called to one of the servant boys and asked, 'What does all this mean?'
[27] The boy said, 'Your brother has come back, and your father killed the best calf to eat. He is happy because he has his son back safe and sound.'
[28] "The older son was angry and would not go in to the party. So his father went out and begged him to come in.
[29] But he said to his father, 'Look, for all these years I have worked like a slave for you. I have always done what you told me to do, and you never gave me even a young goat for a party with my friends.
[30] But then this son of yours comes home after wasting your money on prostitutes, and you kill the best calf for him!'
[31] "His father said to him, 'Oh, my son, you are always with me, and everything I have is yours.
[32] But this was a day to be happy and celebrate. Your brother was dead, but now he is alive. He was lost, but now he is found.'"

This older son was self-righteous and struggled with the entitlement personality disorder. The younger son struggled with immaturity, operating in flesh and being worldly. The older son tolerated his brother but he wouldn't celebrate his brother's deliverance. So now he's pouting, feeling sorry for himself, acting very immature and sensitive like a spoiled child. So much so that his father, had to leave his younger son's party, go out into the field, and expose his older son, that needed unnecessary attention because he felt like he was the son that should have been celebrated, appreciated and recognized.

Too many times we see in everyday life as well as in the church, a person that has been saved for many years and a person that just got saved, and the person that has been saved for many years acts more immature than the person that just got saved. The person that just got saved walks with more consistency, stability, and integrity than the person that has been saved for years.

4TH – AVOIDANT PERSONALITY DISORDER

The avoidant personality disorder causes a person that is out of order, to avoid anyone in leadership or authority. They avoid anyone that can hold them accountable and responsible and anyone who has the ability to bring exposure to them for who they really are. This individual suffers from social anxiety. They are sensitive to criticism, disapproval, social isolation and they have a fear of rejection. They are always seeking attention, affection and acceptance. The person that struggles with avoidant personality disorder distances themselves from strong saints and believers and they become attracted to weak saints and struggling believers so they can take advantage of them. A person with avoidant personality disorder is a person that experiences inconsistency, feelings of inadequacy and they are extremely sensitive to what others think about them. This person develops a pattern of shyness, insecurity, and instability. They become very sensitive to rejection because they lack the confidence to rule their own life and home so they take their power from their own authority given through self-righteousness and then they take this self-righteousness to rule someone else's life and home.

1 SAMUEL 3:11-14 AMP

"11 The Lord told Samuel, Behold, I am about to do a thing in Israel at which both ears of all who hear it shall tingle.
12 ON THAT DAY I WILL PERFORM AGAINST ELI ALL THAT I HAVE SPOKEN CONCERNING HIS HOUSE, FROM BEGINNING TO END.
13 And I [now] announce to him that I will judge and punish his house forever for the iniquity of which he knew, for his sons were bringing a curse upon themselves [blaspheming God], and he did not restrain them.
14 Therefore I have sworn to the house of Eli that the iniquity of Eli's house shall not be atoned for or purged with sacrifice or offering forever."

This passage of scripture talks about a High Priest named Eli, who suffers from avoidant personality disorder. Eli has no problem being a leader and a High Priest, judging everyone else's house, but Eli avoids judging and correcting his own house. He judged Hannah in the temple, when he thought she was intoxicated and drunk but in reality she was caught up in the Spirit of God and was slain in the Spirit. Eli had no problem judging all the other people of Israel and their house when they did wrong by condemning and belittling them before the people; but when it came time to judge his house and his two sons that God told him to deal with, Eli refused to rebuke and judge his own house.

1 SAMUEL 2:22-25 AMP
"22 Now Eli was very old, and he heard all that his sons did to all Israel and how they lay with the women who served at the door of the Tent of Meeting.
23 And he said to them, Why do you do such things? For I hear of your evil dealings from all the people.
24 No, my sons; it is no good report which I hear the Lord's people spreading abroad.

25 If one man wrongs another, God will mediate for him; but if a man wrongs the Lord, who shall intercede for him? Yet they did not listen to their father, for it was the Lord's will to slay them."

Too many times we have so many self-righteous people that know how to judge everyone else's family, and everyone else's sons and daughters, by always telling someone else how to fix their relationships, children and problems, but in reality they are hypocrites and self-righteous individuals who can't fix their own life or family.

5th – PRETENDING TO BE A SHEEP PERSONALITY DISORDER

Pretending to be a sheep when in reality they are a wolf dressed up in sheep's clothing.

MATTHEW 7:15 AMP
"15 Beware of false prophets, who come to you dressed as SHEEP, but inside they are devouring wolves."

The self-righteous sheep personality disorder occurs when this religious spirit disguises itself as being harmless, innocent and humble. It pretends that it has the sheep's best interest but in reality this wolf or self-righteous/religious spirit has disguised itself as being all of these things but this individual is not harmless but toxic and has been sent by Satan to contaminate your life and to rob you of your future.

2 Corinthians 11:14 NKJV talks about how Satan transformed himself into an angel of light; pretending to be Christ like, but he's in disguise, the antichrist, which means he's against everything that Christ stands for and died for.

6th – BULLY PERSONALITY DISORDER

A bully is a person who uses strength or power to harm or intimidate those who are weaker by trying to intimidate, dominate or destroy people's lives. This self-righteous bully personality disorder finds weak Christians, vulnerable broken people, which have been violated and confused in life. This bully personality disorder is one of Satan's tactics used on passive saints and believers. A bully senses weaknesses and vulnerability in a person. They take advantage of these weaknesses by becoming physically and mentally abusive. They use manipulation, intimidation and domination to bring fear over another person.

THERE ARE 5 TYPES OF BULLYING.

1ST - PHYSICAL BULLYING which means kicking, hitting, punching, fighting

2ND - VERBAL BULLYING which simply means name calling or trying to belittle someone's value of confidence.

3rd - RELATIONAL AGGRESSION BULLYING which is intentional sabotage to a relationship.

4th - CYBER BULLYING by using the internet and social media such as Facebook, Twitter, cell phones through text or other technology, to harass, threaten, embarrass or target another person.

5th - SEXUAL BULLYING which means taking advantage of another person's unwanted sexual tendencies, by trying to fulfill your own desires.

> *1 PETER 5:8 TLB*
> *"8 Be careful—watch out for attacks from Satan, your great enemy. He prowls around like a hungry, roaring lion, looking for some victim to tear apart." (BULLY)*

Notice, in 1 Peter 5:8, it says Satan comes at a believer like a roaring lion, which means he roars like a lion, but he's not a lion, that's just what bullies do. They try to intimidate their victim with fear, but this is how you handle a bully when they approach you. You stand up to the bully, regardless of the outcome. You confront that bully and cause that bully to recognize that you will no longer be intimidated. Because the reality that comes when dealing with a bully 98% of the time is that their bark is louder and more dangerous than their bite.

7th – OBSESSIVE – COMPULSIVE PERSONALITY DISORDER

The self-righteous obsessive-compulsive personality disorder causes an individual to become compulsive, excessive, pathological, and an inescapable individual. This disorder causes a person to be a stalker, someone that is a dictator and someone who is controlling. They try to control the outcome of everything that is being said, and what any other person is doing. This religious spirit becomes a taskmaster that tries to convince a person they are only looking out for their best interest, but in disguise they are manipulating people to get what they want for themselves. Obsessive-compulsive personality disorder is an anxiety disorder in which people have unwanted and repeated thoughts, feelings, ideas and sensational obsessions. Someone whose behaviors make them feel driven to do something out of compulsion. This disorder of self-righteousness causes a person to repeat a pattern of cycles of unnecessary impulses which produce what is called the cycle of sin.

> *JUDGES 2:18-19 TLB*
> *"18 Each judge rescued the people of Israel from their enemies throughout his lifetime, for the Lord was moved to pity by the groaning of his people under their crushing oppressions; so he helped them as long as that judge lived.*
> *19 But when the judge died, the people turned from doing right and behaved even worse than their ancestors had. They prayed to heathen gods again, throwing themselves to the ground in humble worship. They stubbornly returned to the evil customs of the nations around them."*

The cycle of sin caused the people of God, 22 times from Chapter 1 to Chapter 4 of the Book of Judges, to go in a circle of sin. Because they struggled with this obsessive-compulsive personality disorder it caused them to keep missing season after season. Every time God would deliver them from their debt of bondage and bring them out, they repeated the same cycle of sins and went right back doing what they were doing. It's like a dog that vomits, and the same dog walks away from its vomit and comes back later, licks, and eats the same vomit that it threw up earlier.

> *PROVERBS 26:11 AMP*
> *"11 As a dog returns to his vomit, so a fool returns to his folly.*

> *2 PETER 2:22 ISV*
> *22 The proverb is true that describes what has happened to them: "A dog returns to its vomit," and "A pig that is washed goes back to wallow in the mud."*

8th - PARANOID PERSONALITY DISORDER

The self-righteous person with paranoid personality disorder suffers from rejection and brokenness from their past which still affects them in the present. The paranoid personality disorder causes a person to struggle with distrust and suspicion. It causes them to always question the loyalty of friends, their spouse, leadership in the ministry and everything and everybody they are connected to. Paranoid personality disorder always causes a person to believe that someone's out to get them, trying to hurt them, talking about them, lying on them, and taking advantage of them. This disorder causes a person to see what's not there and to hear things that are not being said because tormenting spirits, through demonic activities are trying to scare this person away, from their season of harvest and cause them to vacate what's theirs. We find in 1 Samuel 18:6-11 AMP, that King Saul struggled with this self-righteous stronghold of paranoid personality disorder because he was intimidated by the anointing on David's life. King Saul being an insecure leader becomes paranoid that David is going to take his place as the new king in the Kingdom. When in reality David only takes King Saul's place as the next king, because King Saul disqualified himself, through self-righteousness, disobedience, rebellion, stubbornness, and selfish pride. All of the things that God hates are all spiritual sins.

PROVERBS 6:16 AMP
"16 These six things the Lord hates, indeed, seven are an abomination to Him..."

King Saul is an unstable and insecure leader, so much so that he is jealous of David and seeks an opportunity to kill him. This is the same King Saul that would not stand up and fight the giant called Goliath, but sends this same young boy named David to fight for him. We see this all too often in life in which the people, that you help and assist in life, will later turn and bite the hand of the person that saved and helped them in life and it's all because of this paranoid personality disorder.

Chapter 22

The Stronghold of Self-Games

(Church Games)

A stronghold called self-games is evident when a person plays with someone else's love, emotions, mind, life, future, money and destiny. The stronghold of self-games is a predator spirit that Satan uses to target vulnerable people that have a "victim spirit".

This stronghold or "predator spirit" aligns itself through demonic partnership agreements to target individuals that have been abused, raped, misused and violated. The demonic spirit enters through the door of victimization and trauma that has been unintentionally left open in a person's life and gives the demonic predator or self-games spirit access to take advantage of a person's fragilities, weakness, brokenness, rejection, relationship drama, and financial difficulties. It is important that these open doors be slammed shut, that this demonic spirit no longer partners with other demons to continue to have access, in and out of your life, your mind, your heart, relationships or your finances.

REVELATIONS 3:7 MSG
"7 Write this to Philadelphia, to the Angel of the church. The Holy, the True—David's key in his hand, opening DOORS no one can lock, locking DOORS no one can open—speaks:..."

A person with a "victim spirit" has lost their faith, hope, had their confidence destroyed and will always settle for less. The person who embraces the 'victim' mindset keeps the victimization pattern reoccurring unless it is broken. This mindset opens the door for demonic activities. If this "victim spirit" is not dealt with, and deliverance doesn't take place, this self-games stronghold, predator, and demonic spirit will come back through the open door.

MATTHEW 12:43-45 MSG

[43-45] *"When a defiling evil spirit is expelled from someone, it drifts along through the desert looking for an oasis, some unsuspecting soul it can bedevil. When it doesn't find anyone, it says, 'I'll go back to my old haunt.' On return it finds the person spotlessly clean, but vacant. It then runs out and rounds up seven other spirits more evil than itself and they all move in, whooping it up. That person ends up far worse off than if he'd never gotten cleaned up in the first place. That's what this generation is like: You may think you have cleaned out the junk from your lives and gotten ready for God, but you weren't hospitable to my kingdom message, and now all the devils are moving back in."*

Many times a Victim will stay in an abusive relationship, because they have been brain washed through mind control, manipulation, verbal, physical, and mental abuse by the individual that is struggling with self-games from the predator spirit. The predator spirit asks these questions and makes these statements:

1st - How are you going to live without me?

2nd - You have no life without me!

3rd - Nobody wants you!

Self-games is a stronghold spirit that targets an individual's life and causes a person to become a manipulator in order to get what they want from someone by taking advantage of a person's vulnerabilities, weaknesses, or by being charming with craftiness, mind control, brain washing and a hypnotic demonic influence.

The 31 Self-Strongholds

This stronghold of self-games targets its victim because this predator spirit always senses its prey. The spirit finds them and victimizes them from a place of total disadvantage and destroys their self-confidence by robbing them of their future, stealing their identity and taking over their life.

A self-gamer is a player, hustler, schemer, manipulator, predator, imitator, a non-originator and someone who tries to be more than they are. Self-game occurs when someone tries to use a person's disadvantages to their advantage through the use of mind control and brain washing. They do this by controlling a person's mind in the way they want them to behave, act, or by playing with a person's emotions, heart, and future. The stronghold of self-game is a perpetrator who carries out or commits a harmful, illegal, or immoral act.

> **GENESIS 25:28-31 AMP**
> *[28] "And Isaac loved [and was partial to] Esau, because he ate of Esau's GAME; but Rebekah loved Jacob. [29] Jacob was boiling pottage (lentil stew) one day, when Esau came from the field and was faint [with hunger]. [30] And Esau said to Jacob, I beg of you, let me have some of that red lentil stew to eat, for I am faint and famished! That is why his name was called Edom [red]. [31] Jacob answered, Then sell me today your birthright (the rights of a firstborn)."*

Jacob in the beginning of his life, operated under the stronghold of self-game. Jacob had the gift of gab which caused him to be immature and manipulating and always trying to take advantage of everyone else's weaknesses, vulnerabilities when they are going through struggles and having problems in their life. Jacob was a hustler, a trickster and a schemer. The Bible says in GENESIS 25 that Jacob took advantage of his brother Esau. The Bible says, Esau became vulnerable, he was at a disadvantage of his life, and was also hungry and about to faint, and his brother Jacob propositioned him with an ultimatum. He would give him something to eat if Esau would sell him his birthright which means giving up his inheritance and identity. But in reality Jacob did more than cook game for his brother Esau, he through the gift of gab sold him "game", called self-game. We also find in

GENESIS 27:1-7 MSG

"When Isaac had become an old man and was nearly blind, he called his eldest son, Esau, and said, "My son." "Yes, Father?" 2- 4 "I'm an old man," he said; "I might die any day now. Do me a favor: Get your quiver of arrows and your bow and go out in the country and hunt me some GAME. Then fix me a hearty meal, the kind that you know I like, and bring it to me to eat so that I can give you my personal blessing before I die." 5-7 Rebekah was eavesdropping as Isaac spoke to his son Esau. As soon as Esau had gone off to the country to hunt GAME for his father, Rebekah spoke to her son Jacob. "I just overheard your father talking with your brother, Esau. He said, 'Bring me some GAME and fix me a hearty meal so that I can eat and bless you with God's blessing before I die."

GENESIS 27:11-12 MSG

11-12 "But Mother," Jacob said, "my brother Esau is a hairy man and I have smooth skin. What happens if my father touches me? He'll think I'm playing GAMES with him. I'll bring down a curse on myself instead of a blessing."

Years later Jacob is still under the stronghold of self-game. Although years have passed, Jacob is still hustling, manipulating, procrastinating and pretending to be something and someone he's not. The Bible says, through the stronghold of self-game Jacob hustled and tricked his father Isaac, who had gotten old in age. Isaac was nearly blind and had lost his vision, but Jacob through self-game disguised himself, by imitating, and pretending to be his brother Esau. Jacob convinced his father that he was Esau, through the manipulation of self-game. Isaac released the blessing of impartation into Jacob's life because he thought he was Esau. Jacob not only cooked up self-game, but he sold his father self-game, through false identity, pretending to be someone he wasn't by taking advantage of his blind father.

When you deal with a person that is under the influence of self-game they always try to take, steal and hustle, to get what's someone else's, rather than going out in life and possessing what is theirs. Instead of becoming an originator they become an imitator. They'd rather be a cheap copy of someone else than the originator of the best they can be.

In GENESIS 29:21-25, we discover that Jacob is not the only one, that struggles with self-game. In case you didn't know, game recognizes game! The Bible says, Jacob's uncle Laban is also under the influence of the stronghold called self-games. He used manipulation and deception to get Jacob to work for him for seven years for free. The Bible says, that Jacob agreed to work for Laban but in return he would receive Laban's daughter Rachel to marry. Laban being a self-gamer deceived Jacob for seven years, making him work for free to receive Rachel to be his wife. Not only did Jacob work for free but he did not get Rachel in the first seven years. What goes around comes around!

Jacob deceived Esau his brother, Isaac his father, and others in his family. But now years later Jacob himself got played, used, and hustled for seven years by Laban with an additional seven more years totaling 14 years without a pay check.

GENESIS 29 also talks about how Laban played self-games with his two daughters called Leah and Rachel. He tricked Jacob into marrying his daughter Leah. Because of her father, Leah had a messed up mind and life causing her for years to have low self-esteem, to be broken, confused, insecure, and so bitter that even when Leah begins to birth children it affected their lives. Leah struggled with ungodly soul-ties until she birth her 4th child and called his name Judah. Laban gave his daughter Leah to Jacob in marriage by manipulating Jacob through the wedding reception and causing Jacob to get caught up in the celebration of drunkenness and intoxication. Jacob was so drunk when he married Leah; he thought he was really marrying her sister Rachel. It was the Jewish custom to throw the reception before the actual wedding. The Bible says, after Jacob had committed his vows he went in to Leah and had sexual intimacy with her. Jacob discovered the next morning that he didn't sleep with Rachel but had slept with her sister Leah.

So, what do you do when you discover that because of your sexual desires, at your drunken stage of decision making, that when you finally sober up and come to your right mind, you realize that you were with and have committed your life and future to the wrong person? The person you thought was your soul-mate and dream come true, turned out to be a total nightmare. You need to wake up before you discover it's too late. The answer and solution is to never become the "victim" or become "victimized" by those that operate under the influence of self-game or is a self-gamer.

Self-gamers also target people that have just ended a broken relationship, or is still in a vulnerable relationship, friendship, ministry, church, business or job or etc. They will also target people with financial problems, by taking advantage of them with some "Get Rich Quick Scheme." The self-game stronghold or self-gamers target any and everybody that they can use. It makes no difference, if it's their mother, father, sister, brother, children, friends, husband, wife, companion etc. Anyone that is a self-gamer through the stronghold of self-game will use and abuse, by trying to rob you and to steal your identity so they can get ahead in life at your expense.

The answer and solution to overcoming a self-gamer, is to never become the victim, or be victimized by self-game. You avoid becoming the victim by doing self appraisals and understanding the value of your net worth. A self-appraisal is the act of estimating or judging the value and worth or your true net-worth. The word appraisal means assessment, evaluation, or an estimation to determine one's value and worth. There are five processes to performing your self-appraisal, and determining your true net-worth.

5 Processes for determining net-worth:
1st – is BE REALISTIC
2nd – is BE SPECIFIC
3rd – is BE HONEST
4th – is BE CLEAR
5th – is BE CONSTRUCTIVE

The 1st process for developing self-appraisals and net-worth:
Be realistic as you evaluate yourself as objectively as possible, by being able to talk and communicate on your values, goals, ideas, of what can be achieved or expected. This process includes showing total awareness by focusing on reality, by estimating the cost of what it will take for you to accomplish and achieve what you have purposed and envisioned for your life. You must be realistic when doing anything to build, discover and to define what you want your future to look like, through your own uniqueness and creative imagination. Whether it's business, relationship, ministry, anything of value, you must always know the four "C" factors.

The 4 "C" Factors:
1st – COMMUNICATE
2nd – COLLABORATE
3rd – COORDINATE
4th – CORPORATE

1st – Communication means to share or exchange information, news or ideas and understanding how to net-work will be exchanged for net-worth.

2nd – Collaborate, Ecclesiastes 4:12 NLT says, *"12A person standing alone can be attacked and defeated, but two can stand back-to-back and conquer. Three are even better, for a triple-braided cord is not easily broken."*

3rd – Coordination means to organize, order, arrange, harmonize, synchronize and to bring what you envision to reality.

4th – Corporate means teaming up, joining forces and power. The Greek meaning of corporate is building a power structure or dynasty that becomes a legacy, and a succession of winners, royalty and a house of wealth.

The 2nd process for developing self-appraisals and net-worth:

To be specific means to always be able to clearly define your identity, your purpose, your goals, calling, or your assignment and strategy from beginning to end, from A – Z. It is important that you understand self-evaluations, by identifying what you are doing, how you are planning on doing it, and who you are partnering with to do it. Being SPECIFIC helps you to identify with the details.

The 3rd process for developing self-appraisals and net-worth:

Being honest is extremely important. To be truthful and honest with yourself will keep you from ever overstating your accomplishments or taking more credit for a project, or assignment, than you really earned which will always cause you to have a setback in life. For Example: Never say, you are priceless or worth millions, when in reality you don't have a million dollar dream, a million dollar plan, or a million dollar strategy. Honestly, you can never be worth anymore, than you can plan or strategize for. Honesty helps you to consider your strengths and weaknesses. Always evaluate a list of your strengths and weaknesses that it may help you to identify how to strategize what to do and what not to do. Here are some honesty questions and things you should remember to ask yourself going forward.

1. Where would you like to be in five years?
2. What research will it take for you to be successful in the next five years of planning?
3. Determine your gaps and create a five year career development plan.

4. Determine how much distance, time, and money you are lacking to accomplish your five year plans.

LUKE 14: 28 NLT
28 "But don't begin until you count the cost. For who would begin CONSTRUCTION of a building without first calculating the cost to see if there is enough money to finish it?"

The 4th process for developing self-appraisals and net-worth:

Be clear. You must always have clarity and understanding of what you are doing and how you are doing it. Do self-evaluations on what you are planning to do, and the goals you have set to do them. You have to determine how much it will cost to see your dreams become a reality. How long will it take to see or witness the intangibles becoming the tangibles? Being clear deals with understanding the plan, the blueprint, the product, and the location by doing what is called self-inspection. You must know with total confidence and certainty this is what you are called and destined to do in life because there is a difference in what you are destined to do and what you desire to do.

2 PETER 1:10 AMP
"10 Because of this, brethren, be all the more solicitous and eager to MAKE SURE (to ratify, to strengthen, to make steadfast) your calling and election; for if you do this, you will never stumble or fall."

2 PETER 1:10 EXB
"10 [Therefore] My brothers and sisters, ·try hard [make every effort; strive] to ·be certain that you really are called and chosen by God [confirm your calling and election]. [For] If you do all these things, you will never ·fall [stumble]."

The 5th process for developing self-appraisals and net-worth:

Be constructive. You must identify who you are by doing a self-analysis on who you are partnering with as well as on those net-working with you because the greater the network, the greater your net-worth. But what you must be able to do is to handle constructive criticism. The people that are your partners in life will help determine your net-worth. They must be able to point out your weaknesses, your negativity, your flaws and your errors, to keep you accountable, and responsible for what you're trying to accomplish in life.

PROVERBS 27:17 AMP
"17 Iron sharpens iron; so a man sharpens the countenance of his friend [to show rage or worthy purpose]."

The Bible says, in the book of Nehemiah, that Nehemiah was able to start construction rebuilding the walls within the city of Jerusalem by identifying all of his partners and assigning them to work specific areas within the city walls. Being realistic, Nehemiah assigned those who could handle certain things within the building process by identifying their value and net-worth, by being honest with each leader, family and individual, and by identifying what they were good at instead of what they failed at. Nehemiah before he ever began rebuilding the walls, brought forth clarity by making it clear to each person that partnered in the assignment, that he had counted up the cost, and that he understood how much money it would take to complete the walls. Nehemiah had also planned, calculated, and estimated, how much time it would take to rebuild the walls, which turned out to be 52 days.

The 5 Steps of Self-Appraisal

1st STEP - Understand your self-appraisal or net-worth.
2nd STEP - Identify your accomplishments.
3rd STEP - Understand your challenges and opportunities for improvement.
4th STEP - Focus on the future.
5th STEP - Make it easy on yourself for the next time.

The 31 Self-Strongholds

Step 1- Understand your self-appraisal or net-worth.

The 1st step is to understand how self-appraisal or net-worth will be used. You must ask yourself do you understand your vision, goals and plans in life. What is it that you're trying to do? Do you understand how to do it? Is it worth doing? Is there a return or residual on your money? Is there equity in the investment for the sacrifice and the time you have or will invest? Do you know what residual means? Residual simply means the remaining, leftover, unused or revolving surplus; whether it is money, money multiplying, or additional capital gains. It simply means your money gaining interest, no longer you gaining interest for your money but your money gaining interest for you. In understanding your self-appraisal or net-worth you will realize that you must determine whether or not it deals with something that you desire to do or something that you are destined to do.

> **JEREMIAH 1:9-12 AMP**
> *"9 Then the Lord put forth His hand and touched my mouth. And the Lord said to me, Behold, I have put My words in your mouth. 10 See, I have this day appointed you to the oversight of the nations and of the kingdoms to root out and pull down, to destroy and to overthrow, to build and to plant. 11 Moreover, the word of the Lord came to me, saying, Jeremiah, what do you see? (WHAT IS IT THAT YOU UNDERSTAND)? And I said, I see a branch or shoot of an ALMOND TREE [the emblem of alertness and activity, blossoming in late winter]. 12 Then said the Lord to me, You have seen well (YOU UNDERSTAND CORRECTLY), for I am alert and active, watching over My word to perform it."*

> **ACTS 8:30 NLT**
> *"30 Philip ran over and heard the man reading from the prophet Isaiah. Philip asked, "Do you UNDERSTAND what you are reading?"*

Step 2 - Identifying your accomplishments.

Identifying your accomplishments in order to know what you're going to do next. First identify what you have already done, that's considered an accomplishment in your life. When you research and audit your past returns, previous investments and sacrifices, you'll always know what you've accomplished. To learn more about your accomplishments, ask yourself, what goals have I accomplished? What goals do I still need to accomplish? What are two or three things that I consider my greatest accomplishments? Then you need to articulate your accomplishments and relate them to your individual goals and organizational goals. Identify and describe the opportunities and highlights of what you have done in your past and present successfully. Let you, be the marker to help you, identify what you need to continue to do, that was successful, and an accomplishment versus what you need to stop doing that was a failure.

Step 3 - Understanding your challenges and opportunities for improvement.

Never play down your challenges and opportunities for improving performance. Take time to think through the challenges you have encountered in the past and present seasons of your life. Never settle for being average or mediocre when you can be extraordinary and excellent, being the best at what you do; not the less of what you've done. Always evaluate what you have done by troubleshooting what needs to be improved, by taking advantage of new opportunities of what you have already done. Never feel good when you know you didn't give 100%, but always be challenged within yourself by asking, what could I have done differently or better?

Step 4 - Focus on the Future

The reason so many people fall in life and become a victim or become victimized by the self-game is because they allow themselves to become vulnerable, fragile, unstable, and distracted by their past. So, many individuals never really plan where they're going, their future, because they have been distracted by their past failures, disappointments and losses in life and it causes them to become a liability to their own future. So they allow life to continue to cause them to stay the victim, rather than plan, strategize and stay focused on the future of where they're going instead of where they've been. When you understand true self-appraisal and your true net-worth you'll begin to identify every high risk person and every liability in your life. You will begin to write off people, things and places that will try to interfere and distract you. You won't allow anything or anyone to rob you of your goals, plans, ideas, sacrifices, suffering and hurt that will deter you from the focus on your future.

Step 5 - Make it easy on yourself for the next time.

Making it easier simply means to have succession planning. Succession planning embodies two phrases. The first is "If it's not broke, don't fix it". The origin of this phrase means that if there's no evidence of a real problem, then fixing a problem that was really not a problem in the beginning causes a person to waste time and energy on something and someone needlessly. When in reality the problem that needed to be fixed, the thing that was broken, you ignored, and what was already fixed, you broke it. You spent too much of your time and energy fixing what was not broken, and not enough time on fixing what was broken. The second phrase is "Quit trying to re-invent the wheel, when the wheel is already working. Learn how to work with the wheel that has already worked for you, and it will always excel or accelerate your new stage or season of your next or new assignment.

You look back through the consistency of your life and do a self-evaluation to determine what worked for you and what didn't. After recognizing the things you've done successfully and the things you've failed at; you begin to strategically design what is called a patent. A patent is a license or authority that is proven evidence that what you have already done has worked. The patent makes you the author, the originator and is proof of your achievement.

Chapter 23

The Stronghold of Self-Works

Selfish-Works vs. Self-Worth
(Perpetuity of Success)

The perpetuity of success means that it last forever; it's everlasting or the eternal health and wellness benefit package. It's an annuity in which periodic payments are given, indefinitely without limits. It is the Law of Restriction which means paid for life.

The Stronghold of Selfish-Works

There are two types of works; good works and dead works. Good works means repenting from Dead Works. Good works are an assignment from God with a complete benefit package that gives you an opportunity to receive "Perpetuity for Success" (success that lasts a lifetime). We find good works in Hebrews 6:1 AMP, Philippians 1:6NLT, Ephesians 2:10 GW, and Matthew 5:16 NLT.

> **Hebrews 6:1 AMP**
> *"Therefore let us go on and get past the elementary stage in the teachings and doctrine of Christ (the Messiah), advancing steadily toward the completeness and perfection that belong to spiritual maturity. Let us not again be laying the foundation of Repentance and abandonment of Dead Works (dead formalism) and of the faith [by which you turned] to God,"*

PHILIPPIANS 1:6 NLT

"And I am certain that God, who began the Good Work within you, will continue his Work until it is finally finished on the day when Christ Jesus returns."

EPHESIANS 2:10 GW

10 God has made us what we are. He has created us in Christ Jesus to live lives filled with Good Works that he has prepared for us to do."

MATTHEW 5:16 NLT

"16 In the same way, let your Good deeds shine out for all to see, so that everyone will praise your heavenly Father."

What is Repentance? Repentance is a change of attitude, mind and actions. Repentance also means to change the direction of your life. So in order to understand how to be delivered from selfish – works or dead works we must repent from dead works. The stronghold of self-works is the same as dead works according to...

James 2:20 NKJV

"20 But do you want to know, O foolish man, that faith without Works is Dead?"

James 2:26 NKJV

"26 For as the body without the spirit is Dead, so faith without Works is Dead also."

Dead works mean any attempt to find favor, earn acceptance, or be made righteous before God by one's own effort, ability or willpower. Dead works is a dead end without detours; it lacks depth, substance, stability, purpose and identity. Dead works is works without life, a job without meaning, purpose and benefits. Dead works is hard labor, a job without compensation or any type of coverage.

Selfish – works is dead works which is simply a job without pay, that doesn't equal your net-worth. Satan uses the Stronghold called selfish – works when we find ourselves doing more complaining, arguing, and fighting about what we're doing and we forget why we're doing it. This brings about more confusion than harmony.

Luke 10:38-42 talks about two women; one by the name of Martha and the other by the name of Mary. Martha struggled with the stronghold called selfish – works. She started off doing good, doing good works, she served Jesus as a servant with passion but soon became distracted. Then she began serving less and began more selfish-works, so much so until she began to complain and bring a distraction to the whole house. That's when her good became evil spoken of. Anytime you take on an assignment and serve with passion; you'll never allow what you are doing to become a distraction to you or others. You will always know, when you have allowed your self-worth to be devalued, by the distraction of your selfish-works because selfish-works is when a person allows the influence of strongholds through dead works to become vain glory or self-glory rather than giving complete glory unto God.

Vain glory means worthless glory, or emptiness, caught up in excessive vanity or one's self. Vanity is the quality of being worthless, fruitless, and useless. It is caused by the stronghold of selfish-works. which causes a person to become boastful and prideful and get caught up in their own agenda through self-righteousness and being self-centered.

The 31 Self-Strongholds

The symptoms, signs and side effects of the stronghold Selfish-Works

Selfish-works, vain glory and self-glory is a result of a person becoming arrogant, boastful, over confident and caught up in one's own self-importance. This type of person will find themselves becoming big headed by beginning to take on their own agenda in life, rather than the assignment God has given them. Like Martha, they become busy doing work, rather than doing their ministry. The reason Martha became so frustrated and aggravated is because she created her own agenda and false identity while Jesus was in her house. She made it about herself through a hidden agenda and got caught up in her own self-glory. Jesus had to expose Martha by telling her; Martha, you are distracted and worried about the wrong things. He told Martha that she should be focused on doing her ministry, but instead she had become distracted in doing her own selfish-works. Whereas her sister Mary was in true worship, and working, giving me the glory; Martha through selfish-work, rather than giving Jesus the complete glory, she was caught up in her own self-glory. Martha should have asked Jesus, what else can I do to serve you while you are in my house as an honored guest; rather Martha interrupted worship and distracted Jesus. She said unto Jesus, tell my sister Mary to stop worshipping and serving you, and come help me.

2 TYPES OF WORKS.

Dead works in Hebrew are called a-vo-dat and abad. Good works in the Hebrew language are called a-vo-dah and er-gon. Abad means dead work, becoming a slave to a job, bondage, burden, enslaved, subject to hard labor or to be in debt. It means working hard to have it, and struggling hard to overcome it. The word dead works (abad) means emptiness, and brokenness. Avodat occurs when dead works become false worship, and false labor. This in turn causes someone who through selfish-works fails to get ahead in life to always find themselves in false worship, which produces false labor. Avodat also means taking on your own assignment rather than it being assigned by God.

The 31 Self-Strongholds

A pregnant woman can have false labor although she believes she is ready to give birth. She immediately is rushed to the hospital or doctor, to give birth to her baby, just to discover she had false labor due to unnecessary pain from contractions. Many that operate through the stronghold of selfish-works find themselves doing the right thing the wrong way. When they could birth what's in their season and what has been promised by God, they find themselves in false worship, combined with false labor and when it is time to give birth or bring forth promise they miss their season.

The second type of 'Work' is called Good Works which means repentance from dead works. The Hebrew word for good works is a-vo-dah and ergon. The word avodah means true worship and to serve within the beauty of your assignment and ministry. The word ergon comes from good works and means action, accomplishment and title deed. It also means complete, to do business, to do ministry and to reach one's destiny.

GENESIS 2:15 EXB
"15 The Lord God [⁑took and] put ·the man [or Adam] in the garden of Eden to ·care for [or till] it and ·WORK [take care of; look after] it."

This verse reveals God's original plan for man in the beginning when God assigned man to the Garden of Eden, to work known as avodah. The first assignment of work that God gave man was to care for it, which means to serve (stewardship). His second assignment of work which God gave man in taking care of the garden was to manage or oversee it and to be successful. The third assignment of work that God gave man was to look after it which means to worship and to adore the beauty and the glory of God's creation, that He, God; had set man over. This was God's original plan for man according to Genesis 2:15. God took man from the world and put him in an environment called Eden to do good work. The first good work God gave man in the Garden of Eden was to care for the environment by being a good servant and/or a good steward.   Second, man was to improve the environment by managing and being successful. Man was to be fruitful, multiply, replenish and bring forth increase through development and promoting growth. The third good work God gave man in Eden was to look after the environment in the garden; which is avodah, by giving true worship by beholding the beauty of the Lord and offering God praise and worship and by acknowledging God as being The Creator of Heaven and earth.

Your seed works for you, and your seed is your ministry that becomes an agent and a partner to help promote growth in the ground. Your seed works for you, you don't work for your seed. God offered Adam a packaged deal to 'work'; to accept the responsibility of doing ministry and to complete his assignment.

GENESIS 1:28 AMP
"28 And God blessed them and said to them, Be fruitful, multiply, and fill the earth, and subdue it [using all its vast resources in the service of God and man]; and have dominion over the fish of the sea, the birds of the air, and over every living creature that moves upon the earth."
This was the package deal God made with man.

If you choose to work for a system or a company, the work you do is labor; typically they will offer you their own package deal. They tell you that you will receive a check or seed according to the length of time and hours that you work or provide labor. You then must decide or determine are you working for your seed or is your seed going to work for you. If you're working for your seed, then you are in pain and suffering from the lack, as a slave suffers, because your seed dictates the outcome. If your seed is working for you; then you dictate the outcome because the seed understands your value and your net-worth. So, you will never have to work for money because money will always work for you. Your money will always be the answer to your problem. (Ecclesiastes 10:19 MSG)

PERPETUITY FOR SUCCESS

    1st - Perpetuity – means success that last forever, it's everlasting or eternal health and wealth benefit package.

    2nd - It's an annuity in which periodic payments are given indefinitely.

    3rd – It is the law of restriction which means, paid for life.

    God's original plan for man in the beginning. God being the C.E.O. (Chief Executive Officer), hired man to be His C.F.O. (Chief Financial Officer) over the Garden of Eden estate. Man's assignment and responsibility was to cause the Garden of Eden to be fruitful and multiply.

GENESIS 1:28 AMP

" 28 And God blessed them and said to them, Be fruitful, multiply, and fill the earth, and subdue it [using all its vast resources in the service of God and man]; and have dominion over the fish of the sea, the birds of the air, and over every living creature that moves upon the earth."

    The contract that God and man agreed upon according to Genesis 2:15 was to work the Garden of Eden in the avodah, true worship, or ergon. Man was to care for, to take care of and to look after the garden. God's agreement with man through his eternal contract was that man would, faithfully abide by God's promissory agreement plan, and in return, God would give man perpetuity for success which meant forever, eternal success. He had given man an eternal health and wealth benefit

The 31 Self-Strongholds

package. The health benefit plan meant that man would never get sick or die and the wealth benefit plan was for man to never be broke a day in his life, as long as he didn't break the promissory agreement. But in In Genesis 2:17-19 ERV, man broke the promissory agreement.

> *"17 Then God said to the man, "I commanded you not to eat from that tree. But you listened to your wife and ate from it. So I will CURSE the ground because of you. You will have to WORK hard all your life for the food the ground produces.*
> *18 The ground will grow thorns and weeds for you. And you will have to eat the plants that grow wild in the fields.*
> *19 You will WORK hard for your food, until your face is covered with sweat. You will WORK hard until the day you die, and then you will become dust again. I used dust to make you, and when you die, you will become dust again."*

Man gave up the perpetuity of success that caused him to be forever blessed and out of disobedience through selfish–work man turned his forever blessing of perpetuity to cursing, simply because he traded in avodah, true worship, for avodat, false worship, false labor, and false identity. Because man broke the promissory agreement, produced dead works in place of good works he lost his benefit plan for life. (James 2:20)

Chapter 24

The Stronghold of Self-Praise

The Model and Formula for Success

The stronghold of self-praise is the act of expressing approval or admiration through self-appreciation. It is a person's admission of their self-importance. Self-praise is evident when a person without proof claims to be someone through their own self-entitlement. A person that struggles with the stronghold of self-praise becomes arrogant, boastful, self-inflated, self-centered, self-important and self-proclaimed by attempting to establish or build their own kingdom.

> **Genesis 11:4-5 GW**
> *"⁴ Then they said, "Let's build a city for ourselves and a tower/ kingdom with its top in the sky. LET'S MAKE A NAME FOR OURSELVES (so that we won't become scattered all over the face of the earth.")*
> *⁵ THE LORD CAME DOWN TO SEE THE CITY and the tower/ kingdom that the descendants of Adam were building."*

The stronghold of self-praise is an unclean spirit that assigns and attaches itself to a person's life and tries to use its demonic influence to cause the individual to take credit for their own success. For all the good things that has ever happened in their life.

> **James 1:17 AMP**
> *"¹⁷ Every GOOD gift and every perfect (free, large, full) gift is from above; it comes down from the Father of all [that gives] light, in [the shining of] Whom there can be no variation [rising or setting] or shadow cast by His turning [as in an eclipse]."*

A person under the influence of the stronghold of self-praise allows the enemy or an unclean spirit to convince or deceive them into believing that they are worthy or desiring of what they have accomplished in life or what God has blessed them to have.

This stronghold of self-praise is a demonic influence that manipulates through deception. The spirit of deception charms a person to get caught up in self-entitlement. This is the same type of deception that Satan uses in Genesis 3:1-4 when he used the snake to deceive the woman by the stronghold of self-praise to eat from the forbidden tree which caused man and woman to lose their perpetuity of success. The stronghold of self-praise makes you believe you are more than you are or somebody you are not. Satan convinced the woman through deception and self-praise that she was equal to God. He said to the woman, if you eat of this tree your eyes will be open and you will be just like God. (EQUAL to GOD)

THE SYMPTOMS, SIGNS & SIDE EFFECTS OF THE STRONGHOLD OF SELF – PRAISE.

Things to monitor or look for when a person struggles with self-praise.

1st – The individual can handle failure better than success. When facing failure they humble themselves before God but in the face of success they exalt themselves above God.

2nd – A person forgets how they got blessed and that it was God that gave them favor and power to become successful.

> **Deuteronomy 8:18-19 NLT**
> *"18 Remember the Lord your God. He is the one who gives you power to be SUCCESSFUL, in order to fulfill the covenant he confirmed to your ancestors with an oath.*

19 "But I assure you of this: If you ever forget the Lord your God and follow other gods, worshiping and bowing down to them, you will certainly be destroyed."

3rd – The individual focuses more on the blessing than the giver of the blessing, God. They become more consumed with receiving things from God rather than having a relationship with God.

Job 1:20-21 AMP
"20 Then Job arose and rent his robe and shaved his head and fell down upon the ground and Worshiped.
21 And said, Naked (without possessions) came I [into this world] from my mother's womb, and naked (without possessions) shall I depart. The Lord gave and the Lord has taken away; Blessed (PRAISE and magnified in Worship) be the name of the Lord!"

4th – An individual does what they do only to be recognized, seen and esteemed, by being lifted up by the praise of people, rather than the praise of God (miss prioritizing their life). Always remember to prioritize and have everything in the right perspective by keeping the main thing, the main thing!

Matthew 4:8-11 MSG
"8-9 For the third test, the Devil took him to the peak of a huge mountain. He gestured expansively, pointing out all the earth's kingdoms, how glorious they all were. Then he said, "They're yours—lock, stock, and barrel. Just go down on your knees and worship me, and they're yours."
10 Jesus' refusal was curt: "Beat it, Satan!" He backed his rebuke with a third quotation from Deuteronomy: "Worship the Lord your God, and only him. Serve him with absolute single-heartedness."

The 31 Self-Strongholds

¹¹ The Test was over. The Devil left. And in his place, angels! Angels came and took care of Jesus' needs."

Satan was full of self-praise and wanted to be worshipped. That's why he told Jesus, I will give you this kingdom and world if you bow down, praise and worship me. As one that self proclaims, he gave himself what is called, self-entitlement. Self-entitlement means to give yourself permission to be God, King, and Lord, by your own decisions, and to self-proclaim your own position.

He exalted himself to be God and king over the earth because he was caught up in his own self-praise. The only entitlement that God gave Lucifer/ Satan was the title and position of Arch Angel over praise and worship, to carry and bring forth the Ark of God that would produce the glory and the presence of God in heaven. The Ark of God symbolizes the presence of God, the security of God, the protection of God, the victory of God and the blessings of God. So when Satan in his own mind became self-entitled, he gave up his position, his assignment and the benefit package for his own self-praise rather than to honor and worship God. When Satan lost his focus, became distracted and quit doing his assignment; God not only demoted Satan/ Lucifer, he fired him and evicted him from Heaven.

Lucifer's name means the keeper and the carrier of Morning Glory, but when he stopped being who God had made him to be, when he stopped being a praise and worshipper and Glorifying God it cost him the privilege of staying in the Presence of God. When Satan was fired, God created and hired man to become the new praise and worship leaders that would carry the Ark of God and manifest total glory unto God. Not only did man become the new praise and worship leader, man also received the perpetuity benefit package that Satan once had.

Man received the benefit package for perpetuity which entitled us to the ability to be in the presence of God, to receive the security and protection of God, (God placing a hedge around man and keeping him in a secret place), man received victory from God in the time of battle, 2 Chronicles 20. As part of this benefit package, man received favor and blessings from God, along with total healing from God. Had Satan stayed in his entitled position he would have known what man was now benefiting from. He would have known to be someone that praises and worships allows you to stay in the presence of God.

Daniel 4:28-34 ERV

"28 All these things happened to King Nebuchadnezzar.

29-30 Twelve months after the dream, King Nebuchadnezzar was walking on the roof of his palace in Babylon. While on the roof, the king said, "Look at Babylon! I Built This Great City. It Is My Palace. I Built This Great Place by My Power. I Built This Place to Show How Great I Am." (SELF – PRAISE)

31 The words were still in his mouth when a voice came from heaven. The voice said, "King Nebuchadnezzar, these things will happen to you: Your power as king has been taken away from you.

32 You will be forced to go away from people. You will live with the wild animals and eat grass like an ox. Seven Seasons Will Pass Before You Learn Your Lesson. Then you will learn that God Most High rules over human kingdoms and gives them to whoever he wants."

33 These things happened immediately. Nebuchadnezzar was forced to go away from people. He began eating grass like an ox. He became wet from dew. His hair grew long like the feathers of an eagle, and his nails grew long like the claws of a bird.

34 Then at the End of That Time, I, Nebuchadnezzar, Looked up Toward Heaven, and I was in my right mind again. Then I Gave

Praise to God Most High. I gave honor and glory to him who lives forever. God rules forever! His kingdom continues for all generations."

The Bible says King Nebuchadnezzar began to walk and look over the kingdom of Babylon that he ruled and said aloud to all those that was around him; look at what my hand has built. King Nebuchadnezzar through self-praise caused God to visit him in a dream and when he awoke the next morning and called for his royal administration to interpret his dream, no one in his royal administration could, but Daniel came and told King Nebuchadnezzar that the God whom he served, the creator of the heavens and the earth had blessed him to be king. But now through the stronghold of self-praise he had forgotten how far God had brought him in life. The king had now provoked God to take it all away from him because he got caught up in his own vain and self-glory rather than giving God the glory. Daniel told the king, God is going to come and take all this away from you because of your self-praise and vain glory. You are about to lose everything. King Nebuchadnezzar not only lost the kingdom but he also lost his mind.

Daniel 4:33-34 ERV
"33 These things happened immediately. Nebuchadnezzar was forced to go away from people. He began eating grass like an ox. He became wet from dew. His hair grew long like the feathers of an eagle, and his nails grew long like the claws of a bird.
34 Then at the end of that time, I, Nebuchadnezzar, Looked up Toward Heaven, And I Was in My Right Mind Again. Then I Gave Praise to God Most High. I gave honor and GLORY to him who lives forever. God rules forever! His kingdom continues for all generations."

Acts 12:21-24 GW

"21 The appointed day came. Herod, wearing his royal clothes, sat on his throne and began making a speech to them.
22 The people started shouting, "The voice of a god and not of a man!"
23 Immediately, an angel from the Lord killed Herod for not giving GLORY to God. Herod was eaten by maggots, and he died.
24 But God's word continued to spread and win many followers."

King Herod also struggled with the stronghold of self-praise. The king forgot how he gained success and authority to rule his kingdom. The stronghold of self-praise caused King Herod to become arrogant and prideful, so much so that he began to rob God of the praise, worship, and glory that belongs to God. Acts 12:23 says, when King Herod allowed the people to worship him rather than worship God. God sent an angel to bring sickness, and then death, over the life of King Herod. The Bible says, maggots begin to eat away at his body, for stealing the Glory from God.

The Model and Formula for Success

In order to understand the model and formula for success, you must understand success will always attract trouble, pass failures, setbacks, disappointments, controversy, and enemies, and a lot of criticism. We find the antidote, model and formula for success in:

Genesis 39:2-5 AMP

"2 But the Lord was with Joseph, and he [though a slave] was a SUCCESSFUL and PROSPEROUS man; and he was in the house of his master the Egyptian.
3 And his master saw that the Lord was with him and that the Lord made all that he did to flourish and SUCCEED in his hand.

⁴ So Joseph pleased [Potiphar] and found FAVOR in his sight, and he served him. And [his master] made him supervisor over his house and he put all that he had in his charge.

⁵ From the time that he made him supervisor in his house and over all that he had, the Lord blessed the Egyptian's house for Joseph's sake; and the Lord's BLESSING was on all that he had in the house and in the field."

THE MODEL AND FORMULA FOR SUCCESS

1ST - DREAM IT – Joseph's Dream (Genesis 37:5 & 9 AMP)

2ND - BELIEVE IT – The Blueprint (Genesis 37:10-11 GW)

3RD - SEE IT – Interpret the Dream (Blueprint) (Genesis 41:15 AMP)

4TH - PLAN IT – Who I Am, What I Am & Where I Am
(Genesis 41:34-37 AMP)

5TH – TELL IT – Promote & Market/If You Can't Tell It, You Can't Sell It!
(Genesis 41:55 GW)

6TH - WORK IT – You Got to Sow It to Grow It (Genesis 41:46-49 GW)

7TH – ENJOY IT – When A Dream Becomes A Reality (Genesis 41:56-57 MSG)

DREAM IT –

(Genesis 37:5 AMP)
"⁵ Now Joseph had a DREAM and he told it to his brothers, and they hated him still more.

(Genesis 37:9 AMP)
⁹ But Joseph DREAMED yet another DREAM and told it to his brothers [also]. He said, See here, I have DREAMED again, and behold, [this time not only] eleven stars [but also] the sun and the moon bowed down and did reverence to me!"

BELIEVE IT –

(Genesis 37:10-11 GW)

"*10 When he told his father and his brothers, his father criticized him by asking, "What's this DREAM you had? Will your mother and I and your brothers come and bow down in front of you?" 11 So his brothers were jealous of him, BUT HIS FATHER KEPT THINKING ABOUT THESE THINGS."*

SEE IT –

(Genesis 41:15 AMP)

"*15 And Pharaoh said to Joseph, I have DREAMED a DREAM, and there is no one who can INTERPRET it; and I have heard it said of you that you can understand a DREAM and INTERPRET it."*

PLAN IT -

(Genesis 41:34-37 AMP)

"*34 Let Pharaoh do this; then let him select and appoint officers over the land, and take one-fifth [of the produce] of the [whole] land of Egypt in the seven plenteous years [year by year].*
35 And let them gather all the food of these good years that are coming and lay up grain under the direction and authority of Pharaoh, and let them retain food [in fortified granaries] in the cities.
36 And that food shall be put in store for the country against the seven years of hunger and famine that are to come upon the land of Egypt, so that the land may not be ruined and cut off by the famine.
37 And the PLAN seemed good in the eyes of Pharaoh and in the eyes of all his servants."

TELL IT -

(Genesis 41:55 GW)
"⁵⁵ When everyone in Egypt began to feel the effects of the famine, the people cried to Pharaoh for food. But Pharaoh said to all the Egyptians, "Go to Joseph! Do what he TELLS you!"

WORK IT -

(Genesis 41:46-49 GW)
"⁴⁶ Joseph was 30 years old when he entered the service of Pharaoh (the king of Egypt). He left Pharaoh and traveled all around Egypt.
⁴⁷ During the seven good years the land produced large harvests.
⁴⁸ Joseph collected all the food grown in Egypt during those seven years and put this food in the cities. In each city he put the food from the fields around it.
⁴⁹ Joseph stored up grain in huge quantities like the sand on the seashore. He had so much that he finally gave up keeping any records because he couldn't measure it all.'

ENJOY IT -

(Genesis 41:56-57 MSG)
"⁵⁶⁻⁵⁷ As the famine got worse all over the country, Joseph opened the store-houses and sold emergency supplies to the Egyptians. The famine was very bad. Soon the whole world was coming to buy supplies from Joseph. The famine was bad all over."

THE ANTIDOTE, MODEL AND FORMULA FOR SUCCESS

The first time Joseph dreamed he shared it with his brothers. The second time Joseph dreamed, he shared it with his father. When you share your dream with a person of immaturity, they will become jealous and full of hatred. They will spend more time trying to kill your dream rather than supporting and celebrating your dream for success. The biggest mistake that a person can make is to share their dreams with the wrong people. Joseph should have shared his dream with his father first because his father represented a person of maturity, and a person that had already proven, he favored him. The Bible says in Genesis 37:3, his father favored him and made him a coat of many colors. In Genesis 37:4-5, the Bible says, when Joseph shared his dreams with his brothers, they hated him and could not speak personally or professionally to him. According to Genesis 37:4, before Joseph even shared his dreams with his brothers, they already hated him and could not speak to him personally or professionally all because Joseph's father had made him a coat of many colors that represented Joseph being multi-gifted, multi-talented and having an abundant perpetuity of success.

Genesis 37:5; Joseph's brothers conspired among themselves how they would kill him. You should never share the intimacy of the dreams that God has given you to develop and promote for growth. Joseph was 17 years old when his dreams began (Genesis 37:2) and he was 30 years old when his dream began to become a reality (Genesis 41:46). This means that it took Joseph 13 years to witness the 6 steps of a Transformation for Change.

6 STEPS FOR TRANSFORMATION OF CHANGE
- PRE-CONTEMPLATION - Not ready for change
- CONTEMPLATION - Getting ready for change/ Thinking about change

The 31 Self-Strongholds

- PREPARATION or DETERMINATION – Ready for change/ Planning to change/ Making an exit strategy
- THE ACTION or THE WILL POWER – Commitment to Change/ The person modifies their behavior because of their experiences.
- MAINTENANCE the CHANGE – Maintain the steps you have taken to prevent a relapse. Make the necessary adjustments. Put the right people in your life to prevent you from having a relapse.
- TERMINATION – Destroy bad habits and replace them with good habits (Good Works). Destroy bad relationships and replace them with good relationships.

Chapter 25

The Stronghold of Selfish-Prayers

(Prayer Blockers / Breaking the Stronghold of Selfish-Prayers)

People that struggle with selfish-prayer, always pray under the "I" syndrome. For example, when these people pray it's always asking God to bless me, heal me, work it out for me; and my family, and look over my house. A person that struggles under the stronghold of selfish-prayer loves reminding God what they have done for Him, Heaven, the earth, the world, and people. When they pray the selfish-prayer they often remind God of their sacrifice, and all they have given up to follow Jesus.

> *Mark 10:28-30 GW*
> *[28] Then Peter spoke up, "We've given up everything to follow you." [29] Jesus said, "I can guarantee this truth: Anyone who gave up his home, brothers, sisters, mother, father, children, or fields because of me and the Good News [30] will certainly receive a hundred times as much here in this life. They will certainly receive homes, brothers, sisters, mothers, children and fields, along with persecutions. But in the world to come they will receive eternal life.*

Selfish-prayers are prayers in which a person begins to pray for their own desires rather than God's will. Selfish-prayers cause prayers to go unanswered. The stronghold of selfish-prayers causes a person to pray to God, out of the will of God, through a negative petition or an appeal that is forbidden and prohibited before God. Selfish-prayers occur when someone illegally tries to reach the throne room of God, without God's permission or God giving them access.

Hebrews 4:16 NKJV

"16 Let us therefore come boldly to the throne of grace, that we may obtain mercy and find grace to help in time of need.

Hebrews 4:16 AMP

16 Let us then fearlessly and confidently and boldly draw near to the throne of grace (the throne of God's unmerited favor to us sinners), that we may receive mercy [for our failures] and find grace to help in good time for every need [appropriate help and well-timed help, coming just when we need it]."

Prayer is petitioning God, it is a request for permission to come before Him and to litigate His will. A selfish-prayer is trying to go before God in your own name and will. This is contempt before God, and if you're in court it is contempt before the Judge. Contempt means to disrespect, to have a lack of reverence, to be out of order or to be insubordinate.

Selfish-prayers or prayers with selfish-desires hold a person in contempt with God and cause God to throw the prayers out of Heaven. Even though these types of prayers presented their petitions and have gone through the process of appeals and have been litigated before God. They have done so with a lack of reverence, lack of respect, and a lack of evidence (faith). Having a lack of evidence stops or blocks ones prayers from being answered. Selfish-prayers not only cause a person to be a prayer blocker but selfish-prayers also cause a person to become a blessing blocker all because they pray with wrong motives and out of selfish-desires.

What is a prayer blocker?

A prayer blocker is anything or anyone that can hinder prayers that are offered up, from reaching the Altar of God and is the result of bad or poor communication during litigation. This type of litigation causes God Himself to place a restraining order on the selfish-prayer that is blocking the prayer.

> **James 4:3 AMP**
> *"³ [Or] you do ask [God for them] and yet fail to receive, because you ask with wrong purpose and evil, SELFISH motives. Your intention is [when you get what you DESIRE] to spend it in sensual pleasures.*
> **James 4:3 NKJV**
>
> *³ You ask and do not receive, because you ask AMISS, that you may spend it on your pleasures."*

James 4:3 talks about selfish-prayers, unanswered prayers, prayer blockers, and blessing blockers that were in the churches of Jerusalem. James is writing and talking to believers that are struggling with their faith which is causing them to grow weary. Many of them began to fall out of fellowship with God and the church. They began to lose their faith, their focus, to become distracted and to doubt the prayers they prayed unto God.

Selfish-prayers will cause God to look through the 'prayer caller I.D.', and place a blocked call notification on and prohibit them from getting through. James begins to inform these believers that they were praying through the stronghold of selfish-prayers and this stronghold caused their prayers and blessings to be blocked by God.

These believers were praying wrong because they were praying with hidden agendas and selfish-motives causing God to place a block on their selfish-prayers. James says in chapter 4:3 to the church of believers that the reason they were not receiving the approval and blessings from God when they prayed was because they asked amiss.

The Greek word for amiss is Kakos which means something that is bad or wrong. It also means asking wrongly, badly, or inappropriately. Kakos also means, to be in contempt, and insubordinate. Praying in amiss or Kakos disqualifies your prayers before God because they no longer follow right procedures and policies. Your prayers have disqualified you and your right to petition and appeal your case by presenting your lack of evidence before the court of law.

When we look through scripture we find many people that struggled with selfish-prayers and that Jesus himself encouraged His disciples to never pray the prayers of selfish-prayer before God.

We find selfish-prayers in:

Luke 18:10-13 NLV
"10 Jesus said, "Two men went up to the house of God to PRAY. One of them was a proud religious law-keeper. The other was a man who gathered taxes.
11 The proud religious law-keeper stood and PRAYED to himself like this, 'God, I thank You that I am not like other men. I am not like those who steal. I am not like those who do things that are wrong. I am not like those who do sex sins. I am not even like this tax-gatherer.
12 I go without food two times a week so I can PRAY better. I give one-tenth part of the money I earn.'
13 But the man who gathered taxes stood a long way off. He would not even lift his eyes to heaven. But he hit himself on his chest and said, 'God, have pity on me! I am a sinner!"

Luke 18:10-13 VOICE
"10 Imagine two men walking up a road, going to the temple to PRAY. One of them is a Pharisee and the other is a despised tax collector.
11 Once inside the temple, the Pharisee stands up and PRAYS this PRAYER in honor of himself: "God, how I thank You that I am not on the same level as other people—crooks, cheaters, the sexually immoral—like this tax collector over here.

[12] Just look at me! I fast not once but twice a week, and I faithfully pay my tithes on every penny of income."
[13] Over in the corner, the tax collector begins to PRAY, but he won't even lift his eyes to heaven. He pounds on his chest in sorrow and says, "God, be merciful to me, a sinner!"

THERE ARE 7 TYPES OF PRAYERS

1ST – THE PRAYER OF FAITH

2ND – THE PRAYER OF AGREEMENT

3RD – THE PRAYER OF CONSECRATION AND DEDICATION

4TH – THE PRAYER OF PRAISE AND WORSHIP

5TH – THE PRAYER OF INTERCESSION

6TH – THE PRAYER OF BINDING AND LOOSING

7TH – THE PRAYER OF BREAKING AND DESTROYING UNGODLY SOULTIES

THE PRAYER OF FAITH

The first type of prayer is called the prayer of faith and we find it in

Mark 11:24 GW
" [24] That's why I tell you to have FAITH that you have already received whatever you PRAY for, and it will be yours.

Mark 11:24 AMP
[24] For this reason I am telling you, whatever you ask for in PRAYER, believe (trust and be confident) that it is granted to you, and you will [get it]."

The prayer of faith is also known as the petitioning prayer. The prayer of faith is prayer that will always get answered by God.

Matthew 18:19-20 GW
"20 He told them, "Because you have so LITTLE FAITH. I can guarantee this truth: If your FAITH is the size of a mustard seed, you can say to this mountain, 'Move from here to there,' and it will move. Nothing will be impossible for you.""

HEBREWS 11:1 AMP
"Now FAITH is the assurance (the confirmation, the title deed) of the things [we] hope for, being the proof of things [we] do not see and the conviction of their reality [FAITH PERCEIVING as real fact what is not revealed to the senses]."

THE PRAYER OF AGREEMENT

The second type of prayer is called the prayer of agreement, corporate prayer.

Matthew 18:19-20 GW
"19 "I can GUARANTEE again that if two of you AGREE on anything here on earth, my Father in heaven will accept it. 20 Where two or three have come together in my name, I am there among them.""

Mark 2:3-5 NCV
*"3 Four people came, carrying a paralyzed man.
4 Since they could not get to Jesus because of the crowd, they dug a hole in the roof right above where he was speaking. When they got through, they lowered the mat with the paralyzed man on it.*

⁵ When Jesus saw the faith of these people, he said to the paralyzed man, "Young man, your sins are forgiven."

The paralyze man didn't have faith, the 4 men carrying him had faith, and they corporately touched and agreed through the prayer of agreement that this paralyze man would be healed.

THE PRAYER OF CONSECRATION AND DEDICATION

The third type of prayer is the prayer of consecration and dedication.

LUKE 22:41-43 ERV

"⁴¹ Then Jesus went about 50 steps away from them. He knelt down and PRAYED,

⁴² "Father, if you are willing, please don't make me drink from this cup. But do what you want, not what I want."

⁴³ Then an angel from heaven came to help him."

The prayer of consecration and dedication is evident when you're no longer praying for God to stop, to vacate or to interrupt the hurt, the pain and the suffering you're going through but like Jesus you are praying the Father's will be done because you're consecrated and dedicated. The word consecration comes from the word consecrate which means to make, or declare, to be sacred, or set apart, or to be dedicated to the assignment that's been given to you. The word dedicate is the root word for dedication which means a person that is devoted and committed to their call or purpose and committed to walk with integrity and loyalty. Such a person will be steadfast, relentless, faithful, and true to the call and purpose of their assignment.

Jesus prayed this prayer unto God his father; if it is possible let the suffering and crucifixion that awaited Him to be cancelled, but because of Jesus' consecration and dedication to His assignment, He prayed again and the second time it was the prayer of consecration and dedication, not my will but thy will be done.

During the prayer of consecration and dedication, it was the only time Jesus prayed to God concerning Himself, His assignment, and the suffering and the pain He was going through. The prayer of consecration and dedication is not about praying to God out of self-pity, or sorrow, but you are praying to God to strengthen or restore your strength so you can complete your assignment.

In verse 43, God honored Jesus' request of the prayer of consecration and dedication and God sent angels to minister and strengthen Jesus. This helped Jesus to be renewed and strengthened and to finish His assignment on the cross of Calvary. At the end of Jesus' assignment, while being crucified, Jesus said it's finished, I've completed my assignment through the prayer of consecration and dedication.

THE PRAYER OF PRAISE AND WORSHIP

Luke 2:20 AMP
"20 And the shepherds returned, glorifying and PRAISING God for all the things they had heard and seen, just as it had been told them."

We also find the prayer of praise and worship in.......

2 Chronicles 20:5-6 NLT
(There was a 3 part process; 1st Prayer, 2nd Praise, 3rd Worship)
"5 Jehoshaphat stood before the community of Judah and Jerusalem in front of the new courtyard at the Temple of the Lord. 6 He PRAYED, "O Lord, God of our ancestors, you alone are the God who is in heaven. You are ruler of all the kingdoms of the earth. You are powerful and mighty; no one can stand against you! "
2 Chronicles 20:18 NLT

"¹⁸ Then King Jehoshaphat bowed low with his face to the ground. And all the people of Judah and Jerusalem did the same, WORSHIPING the Lord."

2 Chronicles 20:21 NLT

"²¹ After consulting the people, the king appointed singers to walk ahead of the army, singing to the Lord and PRAISING him for his holy splendor. This is what they sang:
"Give thanks to the Lord; his faithful love endures forever!"

THE PRAYER OF INTERCESSION

2 Chronicles 7:14-16 ERV

"¹⁴ and if my people who are called by my name become humble and PRAY, and look for me, and turn away from their evil ways, then I will hear them from heaven. I will forgive their sin and heal their land.
¹⁵ Now, my eyes are open, and my ears will pay attention to the PRAYERS PRAYED in this place.
¹⁶ I have chosen this Temple, and I have made it a holy place. So I will be honored there forever. I will WATCH over it and think of it always. "

Ezekiel 33:6 ERV

"⁶ But if the WATCHMAN sees the sword coming and does not blow the trumpet and the people are not warned, and the sword comes and takes any one of them, he is taken away in and for his perversity and iniquity, but his blood will I require at the WATCHMAN'S hand. (AS LONG AS THE WATCHMEN SOUND THE ALARM, THEN THEIR WORK IS NOT IN VAIN)."

Acts 12:5 AMP

"[5] So Peter was kept in prison, but fervent PRAYER for him was persistently made to God by the church (assembly)."

THE PRAYER OF INTERCESSION

1 Timothy 2:1-3 AMP
"First of all, then, I admonish and urge that PETITIONS, PRAYERS, INTERCESSIONS, and THANKSGIVINGS be offered on behalf of all men,
[2] For kings and all who are in positions of authority or high responsibility, that [outwardly] we may pass a quiet and undisturbed life [and inwardly] a peaceable one in all godliness and reverence and seriousness in every way.
[3] For such [PRAYING] is good and right, and [it is] pleasing and acceptable to God our Savior."

The Apostle Paul tells his spiritual son Timothy that there are four levels of prayer that he should pray about.

1st - **Petitioning** - going before God appealing the Word of God's Law.

2ND – **Prophesying** - praying into the future. It's occurs when you pray with the ability to foretell, foreknow, and foresee by proclaiming and declaring.

3RD – **Intercession** - coming together corporately to intercede, interrupt and intercept, any principalities, strongholds, powers of darkness, rulers of darkness, and spiritual wickedness in high places, that have planned against a country, state, city, community, a people, or a person for a complete turnaround, restoration, restitution and healing.

4TH – **Thanksgiving** - It's when you are thankful to God for His goodness, mercy, grace and favor.

THE PRAYER OF BINDING AND LOOSING

Matthew 16:17-19 NKJV

"^{17} Jesus answered and said to him, "Blessed are you, Simon Bar-Jonah, for flesh and blood has not revealed this to you, but My Father who is in heaven.

^{18} And I also say to you that you are Peter, and on this rock I will build My church, and the gates of Hades shall not prevail against it.

^{19} And I will give you the keys of the kingdom of heaven, and whatever you BIND on earth will be BOUND in heaven, and whatever you LOOSE on earth will be LOOSED in heaven."

Binding and loosing are legal terms that represent in a spiritual realm what we call keys. When Jesus says unto Peter, I will give you keys to bind and loose. He is indicating to Peter that he has the authority to bind and loose on earth and in heaven. Binding and loosing are (1) keys to the kingdom, (2) keys of power and authority, (3) keys of knowledge, and (4) keys of understanding. All four keys are representative of the law of earth and the law of heaven and with these keys the gates of hell will not prevail against you.

THE PRAYER OF BREAKING AND DESTROYING UNGODLY SOULTIES

1 Chronicles 4:9-10 MSG

" $^{9-10}$ Jabez was a better man than his brothers, a man of honor. His mother had named him Jabez (Oh, the pain!), saying, "A painful birth! I bore him in great pain!" Jabez prayed to the God of Israel: "Bless me, O bless me! Give me land, large tracts of

land. And provide your personal protection—don't let evil hurt me." God gave him what he asked."

The Jabez prayer teaches us that a person may be disabled but not disqualified. Jabez's name means my pain, my sorrows, my grief, my burden, and my trouble. He understood the stronghold, the pattern, the cycle and the root of what caused his ungodly soul-ties. It came from his mother's own hurt and pain that she had experienced through her ungodly soul-ties in relationships that she attached to and was attracted to her life. These soul-ties bound and broke her spirit and left her life with a void. But the prayer of breaking and destroying ungodly soul-ties is the beginning of litigation and petitioning God through the process of appeal. In this process you expose the enemy and the stronghold that created the ungodly soul-ties.

Proverbs 6:31 NIV
"31 Yet if he is caught, he must pay sevenfold, though it costs him all the wealth of his house."

In Matthew 6, Jesus gives us a prayer that we ought to model. This was not to be the only way we pray but to effectively remember that we are petitioning heaven, praying prophetically, interceding for others and giving thanks.

Matthew 6:9-13 NLT
"6 But when you PRAY, go away by yourself, shut the door behind you, and PRAY to your Father in private. Then your Father, who sees everything, will reward you.
7 "When you PRAY, don't babble on and on as people of other religions do. They think their PRAYERS are answered merely by repeating their words again and again.

[8] *Don't be like them, for your Father knows exactly what you need even before you ask him!*

[9] *PRAY like this: Our Father in heaven, may your name be kept holy.* [10] *May your Kingdom come soon. May your will be done on earth, as it is in heaven.* [11] *Give us today the food we need,* [12] *and forgive us our sins, as we have forgiven those who sin against us.* [13] *And don't let us yield to temptation, but rescue us from the evil one."*

Chapter 26

The Stronghold of Selfish-Success
(The Price for Success)

There are two types of success, bad success and good success. Selfish-success is another name for bad success and it leads to addictions, broken relationships, broken people, greed, desperation, and the pressures of life, the loss of sleep, health problems, and high levels of stress, bondage and debt. Bad success always leads to selling your identity; the person you are, for what someone wants you to be. Don't gain the world and lose your soul all in the name of bad success. Bad success causes a person to become someone they are not. Selfish-success is the stronghold for bad success and is the satanic influence used by Satan to offer a person that struggles with it greed, impatience, materialism, stardom, fame, and the riches of this world. Satan comes along and offers a person a 5, 10 or 20 year contract to receive counterfeit success in exchange for their soul.

1 Samuel 10: 6-7 ERV (Good Success)
"⁶ Then the LORD'S SPIRIT will come on you with great power. You will be CHANGED. You will be like a DIFFERENT man. You will begin to prophesy with these prophets.
⁷ After that happens, you can do whatever you choose to do, because God will be with you."

1 Samuel 16:14-15 AMP (Bad Success)
"¹⁴ But the Spirit of the Lord departed from Saul, and an EVIL SPIRIT from the Lord tormented and troubled him.

15 Saul's servants said to him, Behold, an EVIL SPIRIT from God torment you."

THE DIFFERENCE BETWEEN GOOD SUCCESS & BAD SUCCESS

In the beginning Saul was a humble man. He reverenced and feared God and the Spirit of God came upon him. He was a changed man. King Saul was one that received good success, brought forth power, authority, influence, and great materialistic success, but from 1 Samuel chapter 10 to 1 Samuel chapter 16, King Saul's good success turned into bad success because he did not know how to implement the model and the formula for success. So this same Saul that was humble in the beginning also followed God's instructions in the beginning, had no reputation or image to uphold, no house or palace, no chariots or horses, no wealth or money, no prestige, position or title. He stayed humble and operated out of good success, but once he accumulated all the finer things in life, the materialistic things in life; position, power and authority, his good success turned into bad success because he did not have a succession plan.

Succession planning is identifying and developing a person's potential to become a successor. The criteria for succession planning is having the ability to manage what you already have, become more successful while taking the success you have already accomplished to a new level of power and authority. It propels your current success to a new position of responsibility and elevation. Succession planning also means taking success to a new place called succession for promotion by moving and managing from one level of success to a greater level until your latter is greater than your beginning.

Luke 12: 47-48 NLT
47 "And a servant who knows what the master wants, but isn't prepared and doesn't carry out those instructions, will be severely punished. 48 But someone who does not know, and then

does something wrong, will be punished only lightly. When someone has been given much, much will be required in return; and when someone has been entrusted with much, even more will be required."

BAD SUCCESS

We find examples of bad success in Matthew 16:26 AMP,

"26 For what will it PROFIT A MAN if he gains the whole world and FORFEITS his life [his blessed life in the kingdom of God]? Or what would a man give as an EXCHANGE for his [blessed] life [in the kingdom of God]?"

Psalms 21:11 GW

"11 Although they scheme and plan evil against you, they will not succeed."

Psalms 37:7 GW

"7 Surrender yourself to the Lord, and wait patiently for him. Do not be preoccupied with an evildoer who succeeds in his way when he carries out his schemes."

GOOD SUCCESS

Joshua 1:8 NKJV

"8 This Book of the Law shall not depart from your mouth, but you shall meditate in it day and night, that you may observe to do according to all that is written in it. For then you will make your way prosperous, and then you will have good success."

Joshua 1:5-8 NLT

"5 No one will be able to stand against you as long as you live. For I will be with you as I was with Moses. I will not fail or abandon you.

[6] "Be strong and courageous, for you are the one who will lead these people to possess all the land I swore to their ancestors I would give them.

[7] Be strong and very courageous. Be careful to obey all the instructions Moses gave you. Do not deviate from them, turning either to the right or to the left. Then you will be SUCCESSFUL in everything you do.

[8] Study this Book of Instruction continually. Meditate on it day and night so you will be sure to obey everything written in it. Only then will you prosper and succeed in all you do."

Questions we must answer to be successful.

1st – What is success to you?

2nd – What are you looking to get or receive from success?

3rd – What are you doing to accomplish or to have success?

4th – How much will it cost you to have success? (Count up the cost, Luke 14:28)

5th – Once you obtain success, have you made preparation for how to keep and maintain success at that next level? (Succession plan) In order to understand good success not bad success, you must always identify what is the focus of your assignment from beginning to end. Your focus should always be the center or main attraction of your assignment. Wherever your focus is, that's what you will give most of your time and attention too? (WHAT HAS YOUR FOCUS NOW?)

So, if you ever lose sight or become distracted from your focus, your assignment will turn from good success to bad success (Matthew 14: 28-31). Your assignment will always attract your enemy, but your enemy is not your assignment, neither is your enemy representing your walls or dead end but your enemy represents the doors to your next assignment. Anytime your "enemy," which may be your giants, or your storms, shows up, it's an indication that you are entering into the next place of promotion or elevation for new success. But if you stay focused on your assignment, your enemies become the door to your next assignment. (A NEW LEVEL OF SUCCESS)

EXAMPLES: Goliath became the door to David's success. The Red Sea became the door to Moses' success. The three year famine became the door to Elijah's success. The seven year famine became the door to Gideon's success. The fiery furnace became the door to the three Hebrew boys' success. The Cross and the crucifixion became the door to Jesus' success.

What enemy are you facing right now, that's ready to become the next door to your success? You are no longer letting your giants and storms keep you from your next level of success, but they are a reminder to you of how close you are to the other side, called the door of success.

Peter had good success as long as he focused on the target of his assignment. The first instruction Jesus gave to Peter and the disciples in the beginning was to get to the other side. Peter was able to keep his focus on the target of his assignment until the storm came and interrupted his focus. This caused Peter's target and assignment to shift from the other side to focusing on the storm.

The second instruction Jesus gave Peter was a command Word of instruction and that was to walk on water. As long as Peter stayed focused on the target (Jesus) of that assignment he was able to do the impossible but when Peter became distracted, he lost the focus of his assignment and placed it back on the storm. Peter went from a moment of good success and turned good success into bad success all because he lost his focus.

Anytime we lose our focus we lose sight and purpose for our assignment which causes us to delay completion of the assignment that has been given to us. This delay causes us to focus more on the target of the storm than the target of the assignment. The storm was never the disciples' assignment but getting to the other side was. Too many times we become more focused on the distractions that are coming at us and it causes us to detour from what we've been assigned and instructed to do.

DOMINO SUCCESS

In order to understand good success from bad success we must identify how Domino's success works. It's called the Domino Effect Theory. The Domino Effect Theory occurs when one wrong move affects the other pieces and causes a chain or ripple reaction which causes all of the other Dominos to come falling down. So it is in life that one wrong or bad decision can affect all of the other good decisions that you have made. This one move will cause all of the success and good things that you have done to come falling down. Many good successes have turned into bad successes because we have had a Domino reaction. Domino success is always bad success because it was never designed to be a permanent way of success but only temporary.

HOUSE OF CARDS

The House of Cards success is just like the Domino Effect Success, where you're building something nice that attracts attention. You have taken cards very delicately and tried to build a house of cards, but the problem with the house of cards is that it doesn't take much to bring it down. So what you have put so much time into putting together has become an attraction and it has drawn attention, it looks good, but it has no stability because it is not structurally sound. The smallest disturbance, commotion, or wind can cause the house of cards that you call success to come falling down, because what you are trying to build success upon only looks good, draws a lot of attention to you, impresses people, but in reality you have no structure to give you stability and consistency. The smallest problem, disturbance, commotion or trouble will cause you to give up and quit because of all the work you've put in on something that has no stability.

LEGO SUCCESS

Many people build their success with Legos. Although Legos are more stable than Domino's and the House of Cards, the disadvantage is you have to continue to make it up as you go. People like Lego success because they want to make it up as they go because they don't have any goals, plans or purpose for what they're doing to be successful.

PUZZLE SUCCESS

Good success is similar to puzzle success. When you build success out it's like putting together a puzzle you will always have an expected successful end. The puzzle success may have a whole lot of pieces that you have to put together but the reality is every piece matters and if you are missing one or two pieces it cannot be completed. The best way to put together a 1,000 piece jigsaw Puzzle is to do what God did in the Beginning. Isaiah 46:10, God declared the end from the beginning. This means you don't start in the middle putting a Puzzle together. You start at the end with outside pieces and work your way back to the middle which is called the beginning. If you ever think that the lesser or inner pieces of the puzzle are less important than the bigger outer pieces of the puzzle, you will only lose value and focus of what success is. God's Word declares in Zechariah 4:10 do not despise the days of small beginnings or small things.

In order to build or have good success we must change the way we think and stop marketing or advertising the problem and begin to advertise the promise. Because the reality is when you begin to advertise or promote your problem people will always run away from your problem, but they will always run to your promise. People will always run away from you because of what you cannot do for them, but they will always run to you for what you can do for them. So, you must first understand what type of success you are living or building; Domino Success, House of Cards Success, Lego Success or Puzzle Success.

THE 5 "P" FACTORS OF SUCCESS (Mark 6:34-44)
1st – "P" FACTOR IS CALLED PASSION
2nd – "P" FACTOR IS CALLED POSITION
3rd – "P" FACTOR IS CALLED PURPOSE
4th – "P" FACTOR IS CALLED PROVISION
5th – "P" FACTOR IS CALLED PROMOTION

The 1st – "P" FACTOR is called PASSION. (Mark 6:34)

Your passion will always relate to the hurt, pain, burden and suffering that you have within you to help someone else. In order to be a successful leader, you must understand that even though people are coming to be taught the Word of God, that's not enough. Although Jesus taught the multitude the Word of God through spiritual inspiration; Jesus also knew they needed natural compensation. So, Jesus told the disciples to go find resources to feed hungry people by natural compensation.

The 2nd – "P" FACTOR is called POSITION.

Position is a location, a place, a situation, or a spot and it is a privilege to be placed in. Position is not what you believe you are deserving of, or what you want to do but a position is where you are placed by a higher authority to do what you are assigned to do. You do not choose your position, you are chosen for your position.

> **John 15:16a NKJV**
> *"16 You did not choose Me, but I chose you and appointed you that you should go and bear fruit."*

POSITION is not passed up, it's passed down!

Mark 10:37 NLT

"37 They replied, "When you sit on your glorious throne, we want to sit in PLACES OF HONOR next to you, one on your right and the other on your left.""

James and John, two of the disciples of Jesus, were looking for positions of power and authority in Jesus' ministry, but Jesus told them God has prepared those positions and places for those whom He has chosen or those whom He deems as having earned them. A position in the lower level of leadership is the starting place for having and maintaining successful leadership.

Mark 10:39-40 NLT

39 "Oh yes," they replied, "we are able!" Then Jesus told them, "You will indeed drink from my bitter cup and be baptized with my baptism of suffering. 40 But I have no right to say who will sit on my right or my left. GOD HAS PREPARED THOSE PLACES FOR THE ONES HE HAS CHOSEN."

The 3rd – "P" FACTOR is called PURPOSE.

Purpose is what you are and the motivation to do when you don't have the strength to do and or don't want to do but you are motivated to do any how! Purpose is a blueprint, a plan, and a strategy for success.

1 Samuel 17:29 NKJV

"29 And David said, "What have I done now? Is there not a cause?" (PURPOSE)

Your purpose will always justify your cause, your reason to get involve in controversy and or where there is a problem and need concern. It also will always lead you to where the giant and storm is. (THE DOORWAY TO SUCCESS)

The 4th – "P" FACTOR is called PROVISION.

Provision is providing supply and resources in abundance. It is the place where your needs are being supplied and met but you can only receive provision through vision. Provision is occurs when God is leading you to the place or position of your assignment through your purpose with an end result that will always supply your need and be a place of provision.

> **Genesis 22:8 NKJV**
> *"8 And Abraham said, "My son, God will PROVIDE for Himself the lamb for a burnt offering." So the two of them went together.*

> **Genesis 22:14 NKJV**
> *14 And Abraham called the name of the place, The-Lord-Will-PROVIDE; as it is said to this day, "In the Mount of the Lord it shall be PROVIDED."*

Abraham's passion, position, and purpose lead him to the place called Jehovah Jireh, the place of his provision where God supplied all of his needs. God, Himself, will lead you to a place of testing that will cause you to sacrifice, to suffer, to be in pain and hurt. He will lead you to a place called worship and exchange so He can promote you at the next level of your assignment. The ram in the bush was God's exchanged blessing for the sacrificed Lamb.

The 5th – "P" FACTOR is called PROMOTION.

Promotion means advancement, elevation, encouragement, help, and assistance, stimulation, renewing strength and the next place or new place of an assignment or the new place for success.

> **Psalms 75:6-7 TLB**

" 6-7 For PROMOTION and power come from nowhere on earth, but only from God. He PROMOTES one and deposes another.

Daniel 3:30 AMP
30 Then the king gave PROMOTIONS to Shadrach, Meshach, and Abednego, so that they prospered greatly there in the province of Babylon."

The three Hebrew boys showed forth their passion to suffer and hurt because of their position to worship only God no matter what the consequences were because they knew their purpose and the God they served. They knew and believed that God had a plan to deliver them from the fiery furnace and they had confidence in the God they served, that God Himself would make provision for them to escape.
Daniel 3:30 says, after they were delivered out of the fiery furnace, the king promoted them to a higher position of power and authority in the kingdom.

GOOD SUCCESS

The instructions that God gave Joshua for Good Success were (1) to be strong and confident, (2) to be of good courage, and (3) God reminded Joshua that if the people following him lose their confidence and become discouraged that he must stay courageous, and never lose confidence in the promise that God had made to him and the people that are following him. He promised Joshua that if he would learn to study and meditate on the Word from God day and night, God promised him Good Success.

Chapter 27
The Stronghold of Self-Sabotage / Self-Destruction

"No More the Victim"
(Get out of your own way!)

We can no longer afford to play the "victim" card while our lives are being sabotaged by self-destruction. Now is the time to make destiny decisions, if you don't like your life then change it. You have the right to do a total reconstruction or renovation because you are the only one with the power of attorney who can make changes in your own life.

Matthew 11:12 states that the kingdom of heaven suffers violence, but now the violent take it by force! It's time to check yourself into rehab and begin your rehabilitation process for change. You can no longer afford to sabotage your life by bringing self-affliction into it by becoming self-destructive and playing Russian roulette with your life. This kind of behavior has caused you to bring the self-harm which has brought pain, hurt, brokenness, rejection, and hatred. It's time to allow the healing to begin by changing the way you think and believe. You are no longer the victim and it's time to get out of your own way.

MARK 5: 1-8 GW
"¹They arrived in the territory of the Gerasenes on the other side of the Sea of Galilee.
² As Jesus stepped out of the boat, a man came out of the tombs and met him. The man was controlled by an evil spirit
³ and lived among the tombs. NO ONE COULD RESTRAIN HIM ANY LONGER, NOT EVEN WITH A CHAIN.

⁴ He had often been chained hand and foot. However, he snapped the chains off his hands and broke the chains from his feet. No one could control him.

⁵ Night and day he was among the tombs and on the mountainsides SCREAMING AND CUTTING HIMSELF WITH STONES. (SELF – SABOTAGE)

⁶ The man saw Jesus at a distance. So he ran to Jesus, bowed down in front of him,

⁷ and shouted, "Why are you bothering me now, Jesus, Son of the Most High God? Swear to God that you won't torture me."

⁸ He shouted this because Jesus said, "You evil spirit, come out of the man."

Self-sabotage brings self-destruction, self-destruction is caused by self-affliction. Self-affliction brings self-harm and self-harm produces self-injuries. You've become destructive in (1) your thinking, (2) your belief, (3) your conversation, (4) your behavior and (5) your actions. Everything started with a thought, your thoughts created your beliefs, your beliefs produced your conversation, your conversation reflected your behaviors, and your behaviors manifest your actions, which exposes your character and tells the world who you really are.

What is self-sabotage and self-destruction? Self-sabotage/ Self-destruction is when part of your personality is in conflict with another part of your personality and causes a person to begin having split or multiple- personalities. This stronghold of self-sabotage/ self-destruction is caused by Satanic attacks is used as a deception or a ploy of demonic forces to torment and cause self-affliction, and to bring about self-harm to a person mentally, physically, as well as to their spiritual life. A stronghold of this type causes a person to bring self-afflicted acts of destruction on their life. In spiritual terminology self-sabotage/self-destruction is caused by spiritual warfare attacks on a person's life to cause torment on an individual's welfare by making them become destructive to their own well-being.

The medical terminologies for this condition of are called a psychotic breakdown, a psychotic disorder, or a psychotic depression that manifests psychotic behaviors which cause a person to begin to live in a world of phobias (fears). They begin to see everything and everyone as the enemy and a threat to their life.

SYMPTOMS, SIGNS AND SIDE EFFECTS OF THE STRONGHOLD OF SELF – SABOTAGE/ SELF – DESTRUCTIVE BEHAVIOR

The 1st – is Eating Disorder

The 2nd – is Alcohol Abuse

The 3rd – is Drug Abuse

The 4th – is Gambling Addiction

The 5th – most direct form of Self – Destruction is physical, mental, and spiritual abuse that causes self-injury, self-affliction, or self-harm. The ultimate plan of this stronghold is to bring destruction that causes a person to become suicidal and eventually end their own life.

Self-sabotage/ Self-destruction causes a person to experience personality disorders and impulsive behaviors which are triggered by a relationship breakup or divorce, and or repeated series of sicknesses in which they begin to experience being sick more than being healthy. This disorder causes a person to experience not only physical breakdown but mental and spiritual personality disorder. It torments a person that is in its debt and causes the loss of a job, home, cars or other repossessions as well as problems with your children and can also lead to impulsive behavior. Impulsive behavior is defined as acting rashly or acting without thinking. (DON'T PANIC IN THE FACE OF TROUBLE!)

The 31 Self-Strongholds

2 SAMUEL 4:4 GW
[4] In addition, Saul's son Jonathan had a son who was crippled. When the boy was five years old, the news about the death of Saul and Jonathan came from Jezreel. His nurse picked him up and fled to Gittaim. She was in a hurry when she left, and he fell from her arms and became disabled. His name was Mephibosheth.

ADDITIONAL SIGNS TO LOOK FOR WHEN A PERSON IS STRUGGLING WITH SELF – SABOTAGE BEHAVIORS or SELF – DESTRUCTIVE MINDSETS

1st - Going out of their way to harm others.

2nd – Self-pity is a destructive behavior that convinces a person, that they have a legitimate reason to do nothing but feel sorry for themselves.

3rd – Hiding from their own emotions- by suppressing their true feelings, and they begin to live a lie.

4th – Refusing to be helped, they begin pushing the people out of their life that can genuinely help them.

5th – Spending addiction - some people hide in alcohol and or drug addiction to cope with hurt while others have a spending addiction. They go on shopping and spending sprees because they struggle with impulsive behavior caused by self-sabotage.

6th - Physical neglect becomes evident as appearance goes down because of too much or no sleep. Other symptoms include changes in attire; bathing may decrease, they may stop doing their hair and let their hygiene such as bad breath and their body odor get out of hand.

7th – Mental neglect such as avoiding or failing to confront psychological health issues because of a mental lapse caused by stress, anxiety, depression and paranoia are behaviors that delay the healing process.

8th – Sabotaging relationships will occur when a person experiences a mindset that develops impulsive behaviors; such as jealousy, possessiveness (they are controlling), emotional manipulation, and very abusive behaviors that may lead to violence.

5 KEY THINGS THAT CAUSE SELF–SABOTAGE BEHAVIORS

The 1st is called the fear of success. When people talk about the fear of success they are really talking about the fear of change. The reason a person sabotages their own success is because they are afraid of change. Psychological barriers are the beliefs and emotions you have that inhibit your actions that are caused by a fear of change, a fear of failure and a fear of becoming comfortable with failing.

The 2nd is called dwelling on too many options. Trying to do too many things at one time, having too many options can lead to decision paralysis. Decision paralysis causes a person to over analyze or over think a situation. Making a decision or taking action causes a person's thinking to become paralyzed and ineffective because they always try to control the outcome.

Some of the greatest thinkers, planners and organizers have failed because they tried to do too many things at one time and when it was time to make necessary decisions that concerned their destiny they suffered from decision paralysis. They froze up under the pressure while trying to make all the right decisions; they ended up making bad decisions. Simply because they over analyzed and began over thinking the right decision that needed to be made. (GET OUT OF YOUR OWN WAY!!!!)

The 3<u>rd is always quitting when life gets tough.</u> One of the most self-defeating, self-sabotage/self-destructive actions is not when someone else quits on you but the greatest self-defeat in life is when you quit on yourself. When another person quits on you, you can still be successful in life, but when you quit on yourself, you forfeit and disqualify yourself from succeeding in life. You give up your perpetuity for success. THE REALITY IS A LOSER NEVER WINS AND A WINNER NEVER QUITS!!!!!!!

So, stop being the victim and get out of your own way, get back up and fight some more because you may have been knocked down by life but life has not knocked you out!

The 4<u>th is allowing too many people to monopolize your time.</u> Time is your most valuable resource you have to invest. You can replace a house, car, job, relationship, or even money you have mismanaged, but you cannot replace the time you have used unwisely. Too many times we allow people to monopolize our time, by telephone, Facebook, Instagram, Twitter, or by just showing up in your day unexpectedly and wasting all your valuable time. So, until we learn how to manage our time we will always fail at managing our success. GET OUT OF YOUR OWN WAY!!!!

> **Ecclesiastes 3:1-8 GW**
> *" ¹Everything has its own Time, and there is a specific Time for every activity under heaven:*
> *² a TIME to be born and a TIME to die,*
> *a TIME to plant and a TIME to pull out what was planted,*
> *³ a TIME to kill and a TIME to heal,*
> *a TIME to tear down and a TIME to build up,*
> *⁴ a TIME to cry and a TIME to laugh,*
> *a TIME to mourn and a TIME to dance,"*

DO YOU KNOW WHAT TIME IT IS?

<u>The 5th is always avoiding the hard work and favoring the trivial things in life.</u> A person that struggles with self-sabotage/self-destruction always fails to understand anything worth having is worth working hard for. The reason individuals always come up short in having the best in life and the best life has to offer is because they are always taking short cuts and avoiding the harder things in life and favoring the trivial things.

The word trivial means unimportant, minor, insignificant, foolish, silly, shallow, superficial, or something that has little value. When people chase or run after unimportant, insignificant trivial things, that have no value, they discover year after year, season after season, what they thought was hard work turns out to be trivial and unimportant. IT'S A WASTE OF TIME! You can no longer afford to focus on the minor and trivial things so it's time to focus on the major things in life. So don't focus on the minor, focus on the major because it will always pay off!

THE 5 STEPS TO ELIMINATE SELF – SABOTAGE BEHAVIOR

<u>1. Take Ownership and Stop The Blame Game.</u> When you feel like the victim of your circumstances you spend too much time blaming everything and everyone else around you. Although it may feel good to vent and release your frustration and disappointments about the decisions you made on everyone else, it's time to take ownership and stop the blame game.

<u>2. Acknowledge the mistake you made and focus on moving forward.</u> You cannot move forward if you cannot acknowledge you made the mistake. Once you've shifted your mindset from being a victim to a person of complete confidence you will begin to change the mistakes you've made and start correcting them. Only then you will begin to witness failure turned into success. People operating in the victim mentality have a tendency to fill their schedules with things that are unimportant. They always make excuses about their wrong decisions, about what they've done wrong, and why they did what they've done,

but until they acknowledge their mistakes, own up to their mistakes; whether they were an accident, error or intentional, we cannot begin to focus on moving forward in life.

3. Downsize Your Task or Plan into Smaller Steps. Don't bite off more than you can chew. Too many times a person becomes exhausted and discouraged about their assignment and the plan that they have strategized to do. The plan sometimes reveals that it will take months or years to accomplish when in reality a person only has days to get it done. This makes a person become discouraged instead of encouraged. So, sometimes we must take the task or plan of our assignment and downsize it into smaller steps. This is called not biting off more than you can chew. Stop moving so fast and take smaller steps so you don't trip up.

4. Enlist designated drivers and motivators in your circle. This step helps with anything that can go wrong and will go wrong. We must have designated drivers in our circle and life so that when we experience a bad day, week, month, year or season, it's our designated driver that keeps us accountable and responsible so we don't crash and burn. We must have people in our life that can tell us no! There must be people in our life that regardless of what's going wrong in our life, how we are feeling about our life, regardless of how upset you may be, they can speak to you and calm you down, and stop you from saying and doing the wrong thing. It's your designated driver that knows how to become your ambassador, lawyer, and guardian, that will speak on your behalf when you are not capable to speak rationally or professionally for yourself.

Our designated driver is in our life to protect our future and guard our presence but you also must have a motivator in your circle or life. A motivator is someone that knows when you are discouraged, aggravated, frustrated, or on the verge of quitting and giving up on life. It's your motivator that motivates new strength and life within you.

Your motivator is not in your life to tolerate who you are but celebrate who you are. It's your motivator that can still see the best in you when you are experiencing the worse in you, and or when you have failed in life and have hit rock bottom. Such a person reminds you, when you feel like you're ready to die, that you will live and not die!

2 Corinthians 12:10 AMP

"10 So for the sake of Christ, I am well pleased and take pleasure in infirmities, insults, hardships, persecutions, perplexities and distresses; for when I am weak [in human strength], then am I [truly] strong (able, powerful in divine strength)."

5. Setup failure triggers. Surround yourself with people that can complement your weaknesses and failures as well as you being able to complement theirs. A failure trigger can be something or someone to have in place that when your plans go wrong, they will force you to ask yourself these questions:

- What is your weakness?

- What causes you to fail?

- What are you good at and what are you not good at?

You must understand setting up the failure trigger is like the release lever on a gun that causes the bullet or the firing pin of the weapon to disengage. They could the difference between saving your life and losing your life. We must surround ourselves with people that accommodate our failure and complement what we don't know. People that cause us to look smarter and better then we really are. In order to understand, adapt, adjust, and improve, you must anticipate the changes, instead of reacting to them. You must have the right people in your life, as well as yourself, to be proactive not reactive. Proactive people are prepared for anything. People that are reactive are unprepared for everything and they act out of fear and panic. So, GET OUT OF YOUR OWN WAY!!!

Thank You:

Although there is much more to add, we pray that you are blessed by the words of this book and by the Spirit of God that has given utterance, clarity and the anointing to say the things that were said and to teach the things that were taught. God's word has so much to offer concerning strongholds and the keys to having the mind of a conqueror. We pray that this book will cause you to study and to learn more about what He (God) has to say.

We also would like to thank you for choosing this book to read. We know that you had many choices when you found this book but we know that it was God's divine Spirit that led you to choose this book on strongholds, so we thank you.

You can learn more about Apostle Tommy R. Twitty online at www.trtministries.com, on facebook at Tommy R. Twitty or at his local church website www.wodca.org. To book Apostle Twitty as a speaker or for your next event, program, or conference please contact us at tommytwitty@yahoo.com or call 864-461-7178.

About the Author:

Apostle Tommy R Twitty

"An anointed vessel of God,

seeking the heart of God for God's people"

A visionary, teacher, prophet, author and founder of TRT Ministries and Reaching Outside the Walls Ministry (R.O.T.W.). He is a native of Chesnee, South Carolina, the Apostle of Word of Deliverance Assemblies in Gaffney, S.C. and Word Church Atlanta in Forest Park, GA. Apostle Twitty is a devoted husband and father to his lovely wife, Elect Lady Nicole Humphries Twitty and their three beautiful children, Shante', Rashawn, and Amber.

The Word of Deliverance Assemblies is a youthful, multi-cultural, soul-winning ministry with a message of love, healing and deliverance where "All People of All Races are Freely Welcomed." Apostle Twitty's vision is to "work diligently to build the Saints that the Saints might build the City. The first step in the building process is to get people to understand that "if you change the way you think you will change the way you live". With this vision in his heart, he is dedicated to "Reaching Outside The Walls" at whatever cost to seek and to save the lost.

In 1998, God gave Apostle Twitty a vision to establish R.O.T.W. and to write the vision as He had instructed and to make it plain. God told Apostle Twitty to bring both the church and the world together to become the Kingdom of God. The mission of R.O.T.W. Ministries is to go out into the cities, cross over into other states, travel around the world and to other nations to restore, deliver, and to liberate God's people that they may declare unto themselves and others that they shall live and not die in the Kingdom of God.

God revealed to Apostle Twitty what the latter days would be like if he did what he believed was God. He told him how to bring the world into the Kingdom of God. He told him how to lead the 20th century church from its current state, how to dress her, arm her, and to equip her, that she may lose her traditional form and her religious status. Apostle Twitty was told to prepare for both a kingdom position and a priesthood role alongside men and women of God with the same Vision. The vision is to bring the body of Christ together as one, that we may go outside the walls and begin the work of the kingdom by gathering those who are lost in the system and have gotten entangled in the snares of the system. The "System" has failed us but the Kingdom will enable the world and the church to come together.

As founder of TRT Ministries, Apostle Twitty has authored the book Wait For It, which is based upon Isaiah 40:31: *"But they that wait upon the Lord shall renew their strength; they shall mount up with wings as eagles; they shall run, and not be weary; and they shall walk, and not faint."* This book is based upon everyday living and is backed by God's Word. He has taught several leadership series, but is most proud of the series "Making of a Leader" and *"The Nehemiah Strategic Planning Manual and Study Guide"* Where he has taken the Word of God and the things of the spirit and made them applicable to the lives of everyday people seeking an understanding of God's plan for their life. Apostle Twitty has also published the book *"The Answer"* which is based upon the book of Nehemiah. This book provides you with answers to the questions that you continue to seek God for as it relates to building your life, ministry, career and business. Apostle Twitty has authored *"The Revelation of Jesus Christ" Characteristics of the Seven Churches*, a dynamic book for learning about the seven churches of Asia Minor and the time that we are living in. Most recently he has authored the "P.M.S. (Power, Money & Sex) Book", which deals with the excitement and woes of relationships. It teaches you how to avoid bad relationships and ungodly soul-ties when choosing the mate that you were purposed by God to be with.

God has blessed Apostle Twitty to be heard on the radio and to be seen on several television shows. He is becoming more and more involved in his role in the communities as he expands the ROTW program, **Bridging the Gap**. In spite of all that Apostle Twitty has accomplished, he always, without hesitation or reservation gives God the glory because he knows that nobody could have opened the doors that have been opened for him, but God.

www.ingramcontent.com/pod-product-compliance
Lightning Source LLC
Chambersburg PA
CBHW062038090426
42740CB00016B/2943